THE BIG DROP

THE BIG DROP

HOW TO GROW YOUR WEALTH DURING THE COMING COLLAPSE

SECOND EDITION

JAMES RICKARDS

BESTSELLING AUTHOR OF *THE DEATH OF MONEY* AND *CURRENCY WARS*

FOREWORD BY PETER COYNE

For Ann

Second Edition

ISBN: 978-1-6212918-3-1

19 18 17 16   1 2 3 4 5 6 7

Published by Laissez Faire Books, 808 St. Paul Street, Baltimore, Maryland
www.lfb.org

Cover and Layout Design: Mena Fusco
Managing Editor: Megan Boyce

CONTENTS

Foreword to the Second Edition

Apparently, they don't have a way to spell "James Rickards" in Chinese, I thought to myself...

I had just flipped through the Chinese version of *The Big Drop*—the same book you're holding in your hands. All of the characters were Chinese except for Jim's name, which was spelled using the English alphabet.

It was the eighth country to translate this work and distribute it to foreign readers. A few weeks later, we connected with someone in Japan who wanted to translate it and spread it across the island nation.

I'll be honest: I never expected this underground book to catch on like it has. The U.S., U.K., France, Australia, the Czech Republic, Chile, Argentina, Spain, Brazil, Japan and China all have their own versions of *The Big Drop*. And hundreds of thousands of subscribers around the world receive Jim's *Strategic Intelligence* newsletter monthly as a consequence.

Our ranks are branching out far and wide. So are the ideas and warnings about what's wrong in the world and what it means for you in the future. As pessimistic as I am about where the world's headed, the growing global community of subscribers like you gives me some comfort in knowing not everyone will be led to slaughter.

It was only in November 2014 that Jim Rickards and I started our publishing project with a 5,000-word monthly investment newsletter. Over time, we added supplemental features, like recommended reading, live monthly briefings with readers where Jim would speak off the cuff about issues he was starting to research and special reports that detailed special opportunities.

After eight months of hard work, I looked at all of the analysis, forecasts and advice we had produced and thought to myself, *we have a book's worth of material here…*

That was *The Big Drop's* humble origin. But it soon took on a life of its own.

The *Strategic Intelligence* initiative has evolved organically and has easily become the largest globally circulated investment newsletter in history because of its own inertia. An audience that size deserves an update. Thus, the second, revised edition you now hold.

What is this thing? Why isn't it in bookstores next to *Currency Wars, The Death of Money* or *The New Case for Gold?*

Jim likes to call this book a "live cut."

The Beatles debuted their original greats on albums like *Rubber Soul, Abbey Road, Sgt. Pepper's Lonely Hearts Club Band*, etc. That was their core work. But they also produced live recordings at the BBC and did great concerts like Shea Stadium in '65 that gave fans a different and deeper take on that existing material. That's how you should think of *The Big Drop*.

"It's a great book," readers often tell me, "but why do you have to tie it to a newsletter subscription?"

I like to respond, "Because the book should have no back cover…"

The Big Drop is the beginning of the story of our times — not a summary of it. The last page isn't actually the last page. New chapters are always emerging and never-ending. They are the monthly newsletter issues and briefings Jim toils over for you.

If you agree with the severity of the problems Jim outlines, then you'd also agree we'd be doing you a disservice by not making the book and his monthly letter a single package.

We've gone back through to update the material, add fresh content and fix things we would've liked done better on our first pass. All the hard work of breaking down the problems and listing solutions has been done for you.

All that's left is for you to read it. Then read Jim's new work and updates in his monthly issues, live briefings and weekly recommended reading. And then ask questions of it all. Do the critical thinking necessary to manage your money and life in these tumultuous times. If you don't, no one else will do it for you.

Your journey starts here. Read on...

Peter Coyne
Publisher *Rickards' Strategic Intelligence*
Publisher *The Daily Reckoning*

Foreword

Seven years after the 2008 crisis, "The Big Drop: How to Grow Your Wealth During the Coming Collapse" could strike you as a trite title for a worn out topic. Countless books have been published forecasting financial calamity.

What rescues this tome are the experiences, connections and scientific know-how of the writer.

Many have watched their net worth evaporate before their eyes. Fewer have recovered only to experience it again. Still fewer have had the stamina to learn *why* it happened and regain everything they had lost despite the odds.

But only a few of those people, if any, have also had the desire and wherewithal to help thousands of others avoid the same fate.

Jim Rickards is one of those men.

Jim's personal history plus his countless and ongoing professional encounters in intelligence work, non-profit endeavors, finance and academia are responsible for the book you hold in your hands — and for our monthly financial newsletter, *Jim Rickards' Strategic Intelligence*.

The fact that you're reading this foreword means one thing, you've joined our ranks. You couldn't ask for a better guide for your investments.

"I want to help everyday Americans" Jim told me candidly

after partnering with us at Agora Financial to launch his advisory. "There are people in positions of real power who see what I see, but won't be honest with people about it. They're perfectly prepared for other people to lose all their money."

"The next collapse — the big drop — is coming. You can see it coming because of the dynamics."

Not everyone will be prepared. But those who are will be happy they were in the aftermath. This book is a means to that end.

On February 6, 2015, we wrote about the slowly unfolding "de-dollarization" in the *Daily Reckoning*. "The dollar would die with a whimper" we suggested, "not with a bang." Soon after, I received the following note from a reader:

> My mother tells the story of her first day working as a bank teller. It was when my father was in Vietnam — circa 1968.
>
> Her manager, a guy who was otherwise reasonable, took her aside and told her the following: 'You probably won't be working here long because the dollar is going to become worthless. It will be good for nothing more than kindling for the stove.'
>
> She was also told that the money she was contributing to Social Security was a waste since the program was a pyramid scheme and would collapse in a few years.
>
> Nearly fifty years later, here we are. The dollars in my wallet are still accepted for goods and services and my mother is still receiving the social security she paid into.
>
> The sky has always been about to fall... but never seems to get around to it.
>
> People lap this stuff up and there's always, always, always someone there to make a buck on it.

At first glance, such cynicism might seem worthy of credence.

Since 1971, learned men in the minority, newsletter editors, fringe pundits, goldbugs and gadflies have predicted the end of the dollar standard. Despite them all, here we are.

But as Jim points out in Chapter 11, "The Beginning of the End for the Dollar", the reader's argument is specious at best — and downright dangerous at worst.

What the reader who wrote that note may not realize, or chooses not to recall, is that the dollar actually *did* lose over half its purchasing power in five short years from 1977 to 1981. Inflation in those five years was over 50 percent. If you had a job, maybe you got a raise or the value of your house went up. But, if you were relying on savings, insurance or a fixed income, half your value was lost forever. Maybe that bank manager knew something after all.

In fact, the international monetary system *has* collapsed three times in the past 100 years. First, in 1914 after World War I, then in 1939 after the gold exchange standard and finally, in 1971 when President Nixon ended the convertibility of dollars into gold.

The monetary system seems to collapse "about every thirty or forty years and it's been about forty years since the last one" writes Jim.

"That doesn't mean the system is going to collapse tomorrow morning like clockwork. It does suggest, however, that the useful life of the international monetary system, if you will, is about thirty or forty years. We're at the end of that period so we shouldn't be surprised if it collapses again."

The Big Drop: How to Grow Your Wealth During the Coming Collapse shows you how to protect and build your wealth ahead of and during the coming monetary collapse. Perhaps even more interesting, it may play a part — however small — in helping to sidestep disaster altogether.

No doubt, you've heard of a self-fulfilling prophecy.

Say you're hired as a truck driver from New York to

Baltimore — but you believe you are going to be the worst courier of all time. As a consequence, you're distracted and take 95 North to Maine. By thinking you'd be the worst truck driver, you became it. Your prophecy became true because of itself.

But have you heard about the opposite phenomenon? The self-*negating* prophecy?

Jim tipped us off to the concept. He, in turn, learned it from its originator, Robert K. Merton, a respected sociology professor at Columbia University who passed away in 2003.

"A self-negating prophecy is when you make a prediction" Rickards related. "You can help it not come true. By alerting people to the risk, they can behave in ways that make it not come true, which is what you want."

"By sounding a warning — that the 'Big Drop' is right under our nose — based on troubling trends that are in play today, it helps people do things that collectively will help move us in the right direction."

Therefore, as you read, you should repeat the words of the *Financial Times* review of Jim's forecast in your head: "Let's hope he's wrong." But also remember to prepare as if he's right.

Jim admits, the outlook is grim. But he also makes it clear there are unique and lucrative opportunities for the sagacious.

Everything you need to get started is right here, in your hands. Read on…

Peter Coyne
Publisher *Rickards' Strategic Intelligence*
Publisher *The Daily Reckoning*
March 2015

Introduction: In the Year 2024…

The following describes a fictional dystopia in the spirit of **Brave New World** *or* **1984**. *It is not a firm forecast or prediction in the usual analytic sense. Instead, it's intended to provide warning, and encourage readers to be alert to dangerous trends in society, some of which are already in place…*

As I awoke this morning, Sunday, October 13, 2024, from restless dreams, I found the insect-sized sensor implanted in my arm was already awake. We call it a "bug." U.S. citizens have been required to have them since 2022 to access government health care.

The bug knew from its biometric monitoring of my brain wave frequencies and rapid eye movement that I would awake momentarily. It was already at work launching systems, including the coffee maker. I could smell the coffee brewing in the kitchen. The information screens on the inside of my panopticon goggles were already flashing before my eyes.

Images of world leaders were on the screen. They were issuing proclamations about the fine health of their economies and the advent of world peace. Citizens, they explained, needed to work in accordance with the New World Order Growth Plan to maximize wealth for all. I knew this was propaganda, but I couldn't ignore it. Removing your panopticon goggles is viewed with suspicion by the neighborhood watch committees. Your "bug" controls all the channels.

I'm mostly interested in economics and finance, as I have been for decades. I've told the central authorities that I'm an economic historian, so they've given me access to archives and information denied to most citizens in the name of national economic security.

My work now is only historical, because markets were abolished after the Panic of 2018. That was not the original intent of the authorities. They meant to close markets "temporarily" to stop the panic, but once the markets were shut, there was no way to reopen them without the panic starting again.

Today, trust in markets is completely gone. All investors want is their money back. Authorities started printing money after the Panic of 2008, but that solution stopped working by 2018—probably because so much had been printed in 2017 under QE7. When the panic hit, money was viewed as worthless. So markets were simply closed.

Between 2018 and 2020, the major powers' Group of Twenty, or G-20, abolished all currencies except for the dollar, the euro and the ruasia. The dollar became the local currency in North and South America. Europe, Africa and Australia used the euro. The ruasia was the only new currency—a combination of the old Russian ruble, Chinese yuan and Japanese yen—and was adopted as the local currency in Asia.

There is also a new world money called special drawing rights, or SDRs for short. They're used only for settlements between countries, however. Everyday citizens use the dollar, euro or ruasia for daily transactions. The SDR is also used to set energy prices and as a benchmark for the value of the three local currencies. The World Central Bank, formerly the IMF, administers the SDR system under the direction of the G-20. As a result of the fixed exchange rates, there's no currency trading.

All of the gold in the world was confiscated in 2020 and placed in a nuclear bomb–proof vault dug into the Swiss Alps.

The mountain vault had been vacated by the Swiss Army and made available to the World Central Bank for this purpose. All G-20 nations contributed their national gold to the vault. All private gold was confiscated and added to the Swiss vault as well. All gold mining had been nationalized and suspended on environmental grounds.

The purpose of the Swiss vault was not to have gold backing for currencies, but rather to remove gold from the financial system entirely so it could never be used as money again. Thus, gold trading ceased because its production, use and possession were banned. By these means, the G-20 and the World Central Bank control the only forms of money.

Some lucky ones had purchased gold in 2014 and sold it when it reached $40,000 per ounce in 2019. By then, inflation was out of control and the power elites knew that all confidence in paper currencies had been lost. The only way to re-establish control of money was to confiscate gold. But those who sold near the top were able to purchase land or art, which the authorities did not confiscate.

Those who never owned gold in the first place saw their savings, retirement incomes, pensions and insurance policies turn to dust once the hyperinflation began. Now it seems so obvious. The only way to preserve wealth through the Panic of 2018 was to have gold, land and fine art. But investors not only needed to have the foresight to buy it, they also had to be nimble enough to sell the gold before the confiscation in 2020 and then buy more land and art and hang onto it. For that reason, many lost everything.

Land and personal property were not confiscated, because much of it was needed for living arrangements and agriculture. Personal property was too difficult to confiscate and of little use to the state. Fine art was lumped in with cheap art and mundane personal property and ignored.

Stock and bond trading were halted when the markets

closed. During the panic selling after the crash of 2018, stocks were wiped out. Also, the value of all bonds was wiped out in the hyperinflation of 2019. Governments closed stock and bond markets, nationalized all corporations and declared a moratorium on all debts. World leaders initially explained it as an effort to "buy time" to come up with a plan to unfreeze the markets, but over time, they realized that trust and confidence had been permanently destroyed, and there was no point in trying.

Wiped-out savers broke out in money riots soon after but were quickly suppressed by militarized police, who used drones, night vision technology, body armor and electronic surveillance.

Highway-tollbooth digital scanners were used to spot and interdict those who tried to flee by car. By 2017, the U.S. government required sensors on all cars. It was all too easy for officials to turn off the engines of those who were government targets, spot their locations and arrest them on the side of the road.

In compensation for citizens' loss of wealth to inflation and confiscation, governments distributed digital claims and liabilities called Social Shares and Social Donations. These were based on a person's previous wealth. Americans below a certain level of wealth got Social Shares, which entitled them to a guaranteed income.

Those above a certain level of wealth got Social Donations, which required them to give their wealth to the state. Over time, the result was a redistribution of wealth so that everyone had about the same net worth and the same standard of living. The French economist Thomas Piketty was the principal consultant to the G-20 and World Central Bank on this project.

To facilitate the gradual freezing of markets, confiscation of wealth and creation of Social Units, world governments coordinated the elimination of cash in 2016. The "cashless society" was sold to citizens as a convenience. No more dirty, grubby coins and bills to carry around!

Instead, you could pay with smart cards and mobile phones and could transfer funds online. Only when the elimination of cash was complete did citizens realize that digital money meant total control by government. This made it easy to adopt former treasury secretary Larry Summers' idea of negative interest rates. Governments simply deducted amounts from their citizens' bank accounts every month. Without cash, there was no way to prevent the digital deductions.

The government could also monitor all of your transactions and digitally freeze your account if you disagreed with their tax or monetary policy. In fact, a new category of hate crime of "thoughts against monetary policy" was enacted by executive order. The penalty was digital elimination of the wealth of those guilty of dissent.

The entire process unfolded in small stages so that investors and citizens barely noticed before it was too late. Gold had been the best way to preserve wealth from 2014 to 2018, but in the end, it was confiscated because the power elites knew it could not be allowed. First, they eliminated cash in 2016. Then they eliminated diverse currencies and stocks in 2018. Finally came the hyperinflation of 2019, which wiped out most wealth, followed by gold confiscation and the digital socialism of 2020.

By last year, 2023, free markets, private property and entrepreneurship were things of the past. All that remains of wealth is land, fine art and some (illegal) gold. The only other valuable assets are individual talents, provided you can deploy them outside the system of state-approved jobs.

▓ Shock Doctrine: How We Get From Here to 2024

One of the most influential books among global power elites in the past 10 years has been *Shock Doctrine: The Rise of Disaster Capitalism*, by Naomi Klein, published in 2007. The shock doctrine is an essential concept for understanding how power elites such as central bankers, finance ministers and the ultra-rich work behind the scenes to advance their agendas. It's also how today's world could quickly turn into the dystopian 2024 I describe above. This is not conspiracy-mongering or science fiction; this is fact.

The shock doctrine is simple. Political leaders use crises to ramrod policies into place no one would accept in normal times.

The shock doctrine begins with the fact that power elites have agendas that take decades or even centuries to implement. These agendas include things like world money, global taxation, control of physical gold, population control and other plans intended to increase the power and wealth of the few at your expense. Political elites are not fools. They understand that their agenda is highly unpopular. They also understand that democracy empowers everyday citizens and makes their unpopular plans hard to implement. This is where the shock doctrine comes in handy.

A shock can take many forms. It can be a financial panic, terror attack, natural disaster, assassination or other extreme event of a kind that seems to come out of the blue but is actually somewhat regular and predictable. When the shock occurs, people become fearful and look to their leaders for comfort. People begin to value order above liberty. It is at these critical moments that the elites stand ready with a "plan" that will restore order but also secretly advance their agenda.

In effect, inevitable shocks are used as a cover to implement plans you would not accept in ordinary times. Order is restored at the expense of liberty. When the shock wears off, the new order remains but liberty is lost forever. This is the shock doctrine at work. After each episode, the elites retreat and wait for the next shock, which is always just a matter of time.

A good example is the USA Patriot Act, passed by the U.S. Congress in 2001. This was the legislative response to the 9/11 terrorist attacks. There were a lot of good items in the Patriot

Act—ones that aided the global war on terror and helped to eliminate Osama bin Laden. But there is also much that has been abused in the years since.

You and I have lost our privacy and have had our private communications, e-mails, phone calls and other records collected. If you've traveled abroad lately, you may have seen the new kiosks at Customs that take a digital retinal scan of each returning traveler. This is something that used to be handled with a paper passport. That retinal scan goes into a digital data bank, perhaps to be used to pursue political enemies, as happened in the IRS scandal in 2015. Privacy and liberty are mostly gone as a result of policy responses to various shocks such as 9/11. There are many other examples.

For investors, the important question is how will the shock doctrine be used next? What is the unfinished business of the power elites? What is the next part of the hidden agenda to be revealed? And what shock will be used as cover to advance that agenda?

These questions have definite answers we will explore in this book. Regardless of those agendas and coming shocks, there are things investors can do today to avoid being manipulated by the power elites.

There are investments such as gold, land and fine art that are not digital and cannot be wiped out by computers. There are wealth-preservation strategies that are not currently susceptible to taxation. There are portfolio-diversification strategies that are robust to many types of shocks even if each particular shock cannot be predicted exactly.

These strategies should be implemented now before the next shock arrives and options become limited or unavailable. The power elites will continue to play the shock-doctrine game. But you do not have to be the victim. The key is to know how the shock doctrine works and prepare now before the next shock strikes.

CHAPTER 1

The Financial Warning You Were Never Supposed to Hear

You may be surprised to learn what I'm about to tell you. But the globe's most connected financial insiders recently signaled that the markets are on the brink of catastrophe. Many of these global elites are already taking steps to prepare for the worst. Fortunately, it's not too late for you to take concrete steps to protect your own wealth ahead of time.

There's an old saying in the stock market that when prices are about to collapse, "nobody rings a bell." In other words, it's up to you to be alert to important turning points in markets. No analyst or adviser is going to tell you exactly when the bull market is over. In fact, they probably don't know themselves; the experts will be taken just as much by surprise as everyday investors.

Yet sometimes, the global power elites do ring a bell. But they ring it for the wealthiest and most powerful individuals only. Everyday investors like you are not intended to hear it. Here's an example of how these insider warnings are sounded.

On June 29, 2014, the Bank for International Settlements (BIS) issued its annual report, which said markets had become "euphoric." That report went on to say that "time and again… seemingly strong balance sheets have turned out to mask unsuspected vulnerabilities."

The BIS, based in Switzerland, is a private meetinghouse

for the most powerful central bankers in the world. It exists under a unique legal structure that is not accountable to any government.

During the Second World War, the BIS, under the direction of an American CEO, fenced Nazi gold to help the Germans fight the Allies.

The BIS is also the leading institution for central bank gold manipulation today. No institution in the world keeps more central bank secrets than the BIS. When they warn about market bubbles, you should take heed. But they weren't the only ones.

Three months later, on September 20, 2014, the G-20 finance ministers met in Australia. The G-20 is a group of 20 economies including rich countries such as the United States and emerging markets such as Brazil, China and India.

Since the crisis of 2008, the G-20 has been the most important forum for directing global economic policy. The final report of their September 2014 meeting said, "We are mindful of the potential for a buildup of excessive risk in financial markets, particularly in an environment of low interest rates and low asset price volatility."

A few days after the G-20 meeting, a private think tank based in Switzerland called the International Center for Monetary and Banking Studies, ICMB, with strong links to major banks and government regulators, issued its so-called Geneva Report on the world economy, which it has done since 1999.

The 2014 Geneva Report said, "Contrary to widely held beliefs, six years on from the beginning of the financial crisis... the global economy is not yet on a deleveraging path. Indeed, the ratio of global total debt... over GDP... has kept increasing... and breaking new highs." The report then went on to warn about the "poisonous" impact of that debt today.

On October 11, 2014, shortly after the Geneva Report release, the International Monetary Fund issued its own warnings. The head of the IMF's most powerful policy committee said capital markets are "vulnerable to 'financial Ebolas' that are bound to happen."

The IMF's final press release said, "Downside risks arise from… increased risk-taking amidst low volatility in financial markets and heightened geopolitical tensions."

Finally, while attending the same IMF meeting in Washington, the vice chairman of the Federal Reserve, Stan Fischer, warned that world growth may be weaker than expected, which could delay the Fed's next move toward raising interest rates.

The message is impossible to ignore. The world's most powerful financial institutions and think tanks, including the BIS, the G-20, the ICMB, the IMF and the Fed, all warned about excessive leverage, asset bubbles, slow growth and systemic risk. They did this publicly, and seemingly in a coordinated fashion, since all of these warnings were issued within 100 days from late June to early October 2014.

As if on cue, the Dow Jones index peaked on September 19, 2014, and then began a 700-point nosedive that continued through October 10, 2014, at the start of the IMF meeting. The market temporarily bounced back, but the volatility and nervousness has continued through today.

As a matter of fact, in September 2015, as Janet Yellen was considering raising interest rates for the first time in nine years, she was met with a barrage of criticism from Christine Lagarde of the IMF, the World Bank, the G-20, the BIS, Larry Summers and others warning her not to do it.

They knew global growth was too weak to bear monetary tightening in the world's largest economy. Yellen blinked then and did not raise rates. But she did raise rates in December 2015. Now Lagarde's worst fears are coming true and world growth is slowing down precipitously.

The U.S. rate hike is partly to blame. The IMF is revising its forecast for world growth downward. Unfortunately, the damage is done. Yellen tightened into weakness just as Lagarde and others warned. This slowdown will only get worse.

■ Are the Global Financial Elites Trying to Tell You Something?

All of the reports and press releases noted above are written in highly technical language and were read only by a relatively small number of expert analysts. Some of these reports may have been picked up and mentioned briefly in the press, but they didn't make the front pages.

For you, such pronouncements are just more financial noise in a flood of information that washes over you every day on TV, radio, the web, in newspapers and in other publications. The power elites were not signaling you—they were signaling each other.

Have you noticed that government officials, billionaires and major CEOs rarely seem to suffer when the financial system collapses, as it does from time to time?

It's not a coincidence that it's everyday investors and middle-class savers who see their 401(k) accounts and stock portfolios take a beating during collapses. This is because the elites have inside information. They see the catastrophe coming and warn each other to get out of the way in advance.

Not every billionaire is a full-time financial expert. Some made their money in telecommunications, social media, Hollywood or other endeavors. But they do share tips and inside information at private conclaves in Davos, Sun Valley, Aspen, Jackson Hole and other hangouts of the rich and famous.

They see trouble coming and scramble out of the broad stock market and into hard assets, art, cash, land and other safe havens. When the collapse comes, they emerge from their financial bunkers to snap up valuable companies that small investors have been panicked into selling at bargain-basement prices. As soon as elite institutions like the BIS and IMF start sounding the alarm, the smart money knows where to hide.

These elite warnings serve another purpose in addition to giving fellow elites a heads-up. They insulate politicians and officials from blame after the crash. When the collapse comes, you can be sure the BIS, G-20 and IMF and the rest will point to the statements I just told you about and say, in effect, "See, we told you it was coming. Don't blame us if you didn't take action."

▨ A Guide to Today's New Power Elite

To understand what the global financial elites are trying to tell you, you need to know who they are what they do. You and I as citizens are often victimized by power-elite policy choices. We're relatively powerless to change this state of affairs. Democracy and elections are a facade through which citizens get to choose those particular elites who rule them for specified terms in office. But elections do nothing to change the fundamental dynamic of elite rule.

The Three Power Groups And Six Types Of Elites

C. Wright Mills divided his power elite into three power groups and six types of actors in his book *The Power Elite*. The three power groups were economic, military and political. The six types of actors were "CEOs," "Warlords" (senior military officers), "Corporate Rich" (major investors), "Celebrities," the "Metropolitan 400" (notable families in major cities) and the "Political Directorate" (top White House officials and senior bureaucrats).

There is overlap among these players. For example, a Warlord might also be a member of the Metropolitan 400. Similarly, a single individual might pass through several actor roles in a single lifetime, starting as a descendent of the Metropolitan 400, becoming a CEO, and then ending his career in the Political Directorate.

Membership in the power elite could be hereditary, merit-based or both. In the case of merit-based admission, certain institutions were used to perform a screening process. These institutions included prominent preparatory schools (Hotchkiss, Taft, Choate, etc.), Ivy League universities (Harvard, Yale, Penn, etc.), exclusive clubs and achievement awards.

Much has changed in the 60 years since *The Power Elite* was published—and much has not.

The United States is still run by a power elite of money, political power and social connections. In fact, income inequality and concentration of wealth in very few hands is more extreme than at any time in U.S. history since the Roaring Twenties, and before that, the Robber Baron period of the 1890s.

If *The Power Elite* were being rewritten today, it would place less emphasis on social connections (although they still count), and more emphasis on raw wealth (on display in the Forbes 400). Merit counts for more (individuals from poor economic backgrounds who achieve straight-A averages at Stanford can expect many doors will open for them).

Mills' "Corporate Rich" would include many more hedge fund and private-equity billionaires. His "Celebrities" would include sports figures and hip-hop promoters in addition to film and TV stars. The "CEOs" would be drawn from the ranks of technology and banks rather than old-line industries such as steel and autos.

Above all, the power elite would be postnational and global. Mills assumed that each country had its own power elite with similar dynamics and characteristics. Power-elite members from one country would certainly be in contact with those of another, but Mills saw each country's power elite as exercising power on a national level. Today, power is exercised on a global level. Hip-hop and Twitter are as popular in Mumbai as they are in Manhattan. Goldman Sachs' tentacles reach into Shanghai and Seattle.

Mills' most interesting observation was that the power elite wasn't a tight conspiracy with unified leadership. It was more like a club where members knew the rules and abided by them because that allowed them to enjoy the benefits of club membership and the company of other club members. Those who broke the club rules quickly found themselves on the outside looking in, with greatly diminished prospects for sweetheart deals, political appointment or career advancement.

I agree with Mills' conclusion and have witnessed it firsthand. My own career has been eclectic with regard to power-elite interactions (although I am not myself a member of the power elite). I have the "right" academic background (top grad school in international economics, Ivy League law school), have done official business in the elite venues (Federal Reserve boardroom, West Wing, CIA seventh floor, etc.), and met personally with CEOs, Fed chairs, four-star generals and the like. But I never bothered to join the club. In some ways, I'm like Mills—a close observer of the elite scene without being part of it.

Many everyday Americans insist on the conspiracy theory of the elite. The elite's power is so great and concentrated in so few hands that it must be a conspiracy. It's not. Take it from me, the closer you get to real power, the more you realize how out of touch with reality our rich and powerful really are. They have power and money, yet they are just as frequently surprised by events as you are, maybe more so. In fact, when important changes emerge our elites are often the last to know.

The reason for these blind spots is not hard to discern. Elites mostly talk to other elites. They are too important (in their own minds) to interact with everyday Americans. As a result, they are in a policy bubble. Once the conventional wisdom forms, they continually repeat it to each other and never hear contrary opinion. Elites may have money and power, but they suffer from a lack of cognitive diversity. I've seen this firsthand.

I Was At A Bilderberg Enclave...

The head of Bilderberg and 10 of his close associates asked me to give them a private briefing. Just the mention of "Bilderberg" is enough to send chills down the spine of most conspiracy theorists. It is often cited as the pinnacle of the global-elite power structure.

There is no doubt that Bilderberg committee members and conference participants are rich or powerful (or both) and qualify as true power elites. But there is more transparency than most critics give them credit for. In fact, you can learn quite a bit about Bilderberg and its meetings from its website: http://www.bilderbergmeetings.org/index.html.

This particular briefing took place in 2012 in a secure conference room in New York City's Rockefeller Center. (David Rockefeller, former CEO of the Chase Manhattan Bank and last surviving grandson of John D. Rockefeller, is a longstanding Bilderberger and is still listed on the Bilderberg website as a member of their advisory group.)

My audience, mostly European bankers and industrialists, was deeply disturbed by the ongoing Greek financial crisis and the prospect of a break-up of the Eurozone and the demise of the euro. I told the group categorically that Greece would not be kicked out of the Eurozone, no other members would quit, new members would be added and the euro would survive as a leading global currency. Every one of my forecasts turned out to be correct.

When the briefing was over, the head of Bilderberg said he was quite relieved to hear my conclusions. He thanked me, and graciously presented me with a dark-blue, hand-made glass bowl (with a vortex swirl pattern on the inside) that I still keep near my writing desk in Connecticut.

Every person in that room was far richer and more powerful than me. Yet they had bought into conventional wisdom about the euro and missed the real story until I explained it to them. It was a good lesson for me also. Being rich, powerful and well-connected does not mean you're a good forecaster or analyst. Forecasting requires special skills and a state-of-the-art analytic toolkit.

Elites may be vulnerable to event shocks and policy surprises (due to the lack of cognitive diversity in elite circles), but that does not mean they don't run the show the rest of the time. They do.

Knowing which policies the power elite favors (or disfavors), and the programs for implementing those policies, is invaluable when trying to identify investment opportunities.

Trying to invest in a way that is opposed by the power elite is like standing in front of a moving train—you'll be run over. A real train will flatten you. The metaphorical power-elite train will handicap you with taxes, regulation, investigations, negative publicity and even death if you happen to live in Russia, China or other countries where the rule of law is tenuous or nonexistent.

Conversely, investing in sync with the power elite is like having the wind at your back. You'll be favored with tax subsidies, research grants, favorable treaties and tariffs, and some assurance that you're above the law. (Just ask the bankers who escaped scot-free after looting the world in 2008.)

Here's our brief overview of the current state of the financial power elite game divided into programs, rules and players.

The Power Elite's Plan For You And The Entire World

The agenda of the global power elite is world money, world taxation, world government, a cashless society, negative interest rates and inflation through debt monetization.

The primary long-term goal of the power elite is **world money**. This will take the form of special drawing rights, SDRs, issued by the International Monetary Fund. This world money will not be available to individuals, but it will be used by countries that are IMF members.

It will be the de facto benchmark for oil prices and other essential goods and services in world trade. By this channel, unelected officials will control inflation and erase the real value of debts to alleviate government debt burdens. Control of money means control of society and social welfare.

Close behind world money is the plan for **world taxation**. Continual sources of revenue are needed by global elites to enrich themselves and pursue programs to perpetuate their control. The primary path to achieve this is climate change. This explains why the IMF, the World Bank, the BIS and other "financial" bodies continually speak of climate change. To impose global solutions (such as taxation), you need global problems (such as climate change). Since climate change knows no borders, it is the perfect vehicle to impose solutions that also know no borders.

Administration of world money and world taxation will be conducted by **world government**. Most of this architecture is already in place. The United Nations is mostly a debating club, except for the climate-change agenda. The real world government is being conducted through the IMF and the G-20 Leaders Summit. The G-20 is a de facto board of directors for world government. The IMF is a de facto central bank of the world.

The IMF also functions as the secretariat, staff and implementation arm of the G-20. The climate-change agenda is being pursued through the United Nations Framework Convention on Climate Change, negotiated at the Earth Summit in June 1992. Over time the G-20, IMF, and UNFCC will converge into a de facto world government.

The power elite is also implementing the **cashless society**. This is needed to impose hidden taxation in the form of negative interest rates. (There are two forms of hidden taxation: inflation and negative interest rates. Inflation is the preferred method, but in deflationary episodes, negative interest rates are useful.)

Cash is one way to avoid negative interest rates (with cash you preserve principal; with negative interest rates you do not). A slaughterhouse will round up cows into pens before killing them. Likewise the power elite will round up savers into digital accounts before taking their money. Cash is a free-range alternative to the slaughterhouse pen. Therefore it must be eliminated. (The other free-range alternative to digital accounts is gold.)

The power elite will confiscate wealth through **negative interest rates**. This is the end game of the cashless society discussed above. Negative interest rates are the mirror image of inflation. Inflation steals your money directly by making it worth less. Deflation makes money more valuable, so it must be stolen through other means. Negative interest rates serve this purpose.

Negative interest rates are not the power elites' preferred method of stealing your savings. Elites prefer **inflation**, but that has been difficult for central banks to achieve recently. Quantitative easing, zero interest rates, negative interest rates and currency wars have all failed to catalyze inflation since 2008.

One method that is guaranteed to cause inflation is **debt monetization**. (This is also known as "helicopter money" and "People's QE.") The technical term for it is "fiscal dominance." (Government spending dominates central bank policy and forces money printing.)

However, global elites seem to have settled on "debt monetization" as a preferred term. The process is simple. When individuals refuse to borrow and spend (as is the case today), the government will borrow and spend for them.

The spending is designed to favor elite cronies such as Elon Musk and Tesla. Increased spending means larger deficits, which are covered with more government bond issues. The bonds are purchased by central banks with newly printed money.

The central banks then stash the bonds on their balance sheets forever. The public is oblivious to the process. With enough forced spending, inflation will emerge, although the process may take several years. Central banks will be powerless to resist debt monetization.

Club Etiquette And Rules For The Power Elite

Although the power elite is not a conspiracy, it does function as a club, and like any club there are "house rules." These rules are imparted informally, and are then internalized by elites who behave accordingly. Violations of the rules result in "expulsion" from the club.

Expulsion takes the form of denial of access to platforms such as academic appointments, media exposure, sweetheart investments and government policy making positions. Those expelled from the club may be subject to ridicule (to marginalize heterodox views) or the silent treatment (similar to the "memory hole" from Orwell's novel *1984*, where traces of an individual were erased from memory).

In fact, most elites play by the rules their entire lives because the material rewards are worth it to them. There are four major ones.

Rule #1: Elites Help Elites.

The system is such that elites enrich other elites by mutual cronyism. Examples include CEOs naming other CEOs to their board of directors. CEOs enrich other CEOs by membership on "compensation committees" of those boards. Appointments to foundation boards, think tank fellowships and academic tenure are other obvious cases.

The best example of this recently is JPMorgan's multimillion-dollar loan to Timothy Geithner after Geithner had previously bailed out JPMorgan and lobbied the Justice Department not to prosecute JPMorgan executives. Geithner will now use the loan proceeds to invest in private deals sponsored by other elites. The result will be that Geithner will achieve dynastic wealth that he can use to perpetuate the elite system as he ages.

Rule #2: Elites Never Criticize Other Elites.

In this context "criticism" means exposure of the real motives and methods behind the elite game. There is ample room for disagreement, especially during election contests where mudslinging is allowed. What is not allowed is discussion of the fact that left-wing and right-wing elites are in the same club and elections are basically for show to appease citizens. This rule was laid bare when Larry Summers (an established elite) was in a private discussion with Elizabeth Warren (an up-and-coming elite) as recounted in Warren's memoir. Here's the full quote from Warren:

> Larry leaned back in his chair and offered me some advice… I had a choice. I could be an insider or I could be an outsider. Outsiders can say whatever they want. But people on the inside don't listen to them. Insiders, however, get lots of access and a chance to push their ideas. People—powerful people—listen to what they have to say. But insiders also understand one unbreakable rule: They don't criticize other insiders.

Rule #3: Silence Is Rewarded.

Elites obviously have access to enormous amounts of true inside information about policy, plans and behind-the-scenes dynamics. There is a constant temptation to draw attention to oneself by spilling the beans in some TV interview or book. This temptation must be avoided. This is why so-called "memoirs" by prominent individuals such as Ben Bernanke, Hillary Clinton and Timothy Geithner are not worth reading. They are mostly bland, self-flattering, revisionist histories of well-known events. The important discussions and motivations of the actors are left out.

Rule #4: Patience Pays.

Not criticizing your ideological opponents and keeping your mouth shut for decades can be difficult. Yet it has its rewards. Loyalty among elites is recognized by other, more senior elites and is well-rewarded with top jobs and great wealth. A good example is Peter Orszag. He is the quintessential power-elite member and a seasoned member of Bilderberg. His educational background is typical of elites: prep school at Phillips Exeter Academy, undergraduate at Princeton University, doctorate at the London School of Economics.

He performed some relatively low-paid government service to Democrats as congressional budget director and as director of the White House Office of Management and Budget. Upon leaving the Obama administration, he was named vice chairman at Citigroup at the age of 41. His brilliance and academic achievements are undeniable.

His qualifications to lead a global bank are less obvious. But those banking qualifications don't matter. What matters is that he will make millions from his position at an insolvent bank propped up by you, the taxpayer. As is the case with Geithner, Orszag's wealth will leave him well positioned to empower and groom a new generation of power elites.

Power-Elite Players

A full roster of the power elite would run into the thousands of names. Most are completely unknown to the general public. That's how the power elites like it. Meanwhile, some names do stand out because particular positions require confirmation or are inescapably newsworthy.

Here's a short list of the top tier of the power elite today:

- **Robert Rubin.** He is the most powerful financial figure in the world today because of his current and prior positions and the large number of protégés he has groomed to hold powerful positions. Rubin was formerly the CEO of Goldman Sachs, chairman of Citigroup, U.S. secretary of the Treasury and head of the White House National Economic Council. He is currently the chairman of the Council on Foreign Relations. The CFR is the world's leading bastion of power-elite communication and influence.

- **Christine Lagarde.** She is the managing director of the International Monetary Fund, former finance minister of France, and former chairman of the world's largest international law firm, Baker & McKenzie.

- **James A. Johnson.** He has the lowest public profile of any top-tier member of the power elite. He is a former CEO of Fannie Mae, the government-backed mortgage giant, which for decades has been used as a way to enrich political cronies. He is currently vice chairman of a private bank. Other positions have included director of Goldman Sachs, banker at Lehman Brothers and faculty member at Princeton. He is also a member of the Council on Foreign Relations, Trilateral Commission and Bilderberg (a kind of power-elite Trifecta).

- **James Wolfensohn.** He was president of the World Bank from 1995 to 2005, and is a member of the Council on Foreign Relations. He was also chairman of the international advisory board of Citigroup.

- **Robert Zoellich.** Like Wolfensohn, Zoellich was president of the World Bank. He was also U.S. deputy secretary of state, U.S. trade representative and White House deputy chief of staff. Zoellich is a member of the Republican Party, in contrast to figures such as Rubin and Johnson with strong ties to the Democratic Party. This is a good illustration that the power elites are well-organized to exercise the continuity of elite power regardless of which political party is in power at any point in time.

- **Michael Froman.** Froman is one of the most powerful of a new generation of Rubin protégés to rise to levels of great influence. He held a rare joint appointment to the National Security Council and the National Economic Council in the White House. He is currently the U.S. trade representative. Earlier in his career he served as chief of staff to U.S. Treasury Secretary Robert Rubin. After leaving the Clinton White House in 2001, he followed Rubin to Citigroup. This is typical of the elite reward system. Froman made over $7 million in 2008 and 2009 as Citigroup collapsed into insolvency and was rescued with your money. Froman then returned to the White House, where he was Obama's chief advisor at the G-20 Leaders Summits from 2009 to 2013.

- **David Lipton.** Lipton is another Rubin protégé who has risen to great influence in the power elite. He is currently first managing director at the IMF. Since the IMF is always headed by a non-American, the seat of first managing director, the number-two job at the IMF, is reserved for Americans. In effect, Lipton is America's "eyes and ears" at the IMF and is in charge of the U.S. veto of important IMF initiatives. Prior to joining the IMF, Lipton worked at the White House side by side with Froman. Between the Clinton and Obama administrations, Lipton also worked at Citigroup with Rubin and Froman.

- **Timothy Geithner.** Geithner is the third of the group of Rubin protégés (along with Froman and Lipton) among the power elite. He was president of the Federal Reserve Bank of New York, and U.S. Treasury secretary. He is a graduate of the School of Advanced International Studies (also my alma mater). His earlier career included work with Kissinger Associates, the IMF and the Treasury Department. Geithner is also a member of the Council on Foreign Relations.

The main object of the power elite is to enhance their wealth and power at your expense. The best defense is to keep a close watch on how the players interact to advance their program. Meanwhile, at the very least you should have a portfolio of gold, fine art, raw land, cash, bonds, select stocks and some alternatives in strategies like global macro hedge funds and private equity. Not all of those strategies will pay off, but some will do well enough to outperform others and preserve wealth.

▦ Welcome to the New Depression

The United States is living through an economic depression that began in 2007. It's part of a larger global depression, the first since the 1930s. This New Depression will continue indefinitely unless policy changes are made in the years ahead.

The present path and future course of this depression have profound implications for you as an investor. If you don't grasp this once-in-a-lifetime dynamic, you are at risk of seeing all of your wealth wiped out.

Calling the current economic malaise a depression comes as a surprise to most investors I speak to. They have been told that the economy is in a recovery that started in 2009.

Mainstream economists and TV talking heads never refer to a depression.

Economists don't like the word "depression" because it does not have an exact mathematical definition. For economists, anything that cannot be quantified does not exist. This view is one of the many failings of modern economics.

But no one under the age of 90 has ever experienced a depression until now. Most investors like you have no working knowledge of what a depression is or how it affects asset values. And economists and policy makers are engaged in a conspiracy of silence on the subject. It's no wonder investors are confused.

The starting place for understanding depression is to get the definition right. You may think of depression as a continuous decline in GDP. The standard definition of a recession is two or more consecutive quarters of declining GDP and rising unemployment. Since a depression is understood to be something worse then a recession, investors think it must mean an extra-long period of decline. But that is not the definition of depression.

The best definition ever offered came from John Maynard Keynes in his 1936 classic, *The General Theory of Employment, Interest and Money*. Keynes said a depression is "a chronic condition of subnormal activity for a considerable period without any marked tendency towards recovery or towards complete collapse."

Keynes did not refer to declining GDP; he talked about "subnormal" activity. In other words, it's entirely possible to have growth in a depression. The problem is that the growth is below trend. It is weak growth that does not do the job of providing enough jobs or staying ahead of the national debt. That is exactly what the United States is experiencing today.

The long-term growth trend for U.S. GDP is about 3 percent. Higher growth is possible for short periods of time. It could be caused by new technology that improves worker productivity. Or it could be due to new entrants into the workforce. From 1994 to 2000, the heart of the Clinton boom, growth in the U.S. economy averaged over 4 percent per year.

For a three-year stretch from 1983 to 1985 during the heart of the Reagan boom, growth in the U.S. economy averaged over 5.5 percent per year. These two periods were unusually strong, but they show what the U.S. economy can do with the right policies. By contrast, growth in the United States from 2007 through 2013 averaged 1 percent per year. Growth in the first half of 2014 was worse, averaging just 0.95 percent.

That is the meaning of depression. It is not negative growth, but it is below-trend growth. The past seven years of 1 percent growth when the historical growth is 3 percent is a depression exactly as Keynes defined it. That is not a pace that will sustain an economic recovery.

Other observers point to declining unemployment and rising stock prices as evidence that we are not in a depression. They miss the fact that unemployment can fall and stocks can go up during a depression. The Great Depression lasted from 1929 to 1940. It consisted of two technical recessions from 1929 to 1932 and again from 1937 to 1938.

The periods 1933–36 and 1939–40 were technically economic expansions. Unemployment fell and stock prices rose. But the depression continued because the United States did not return to its potential growth rate until 1941. Stock and real estate prices did not fully return to their 1929 highs until 1954, a quarter century after the depression started.

The point is that GDP growth, rising stock prices and falling unemployment can all occur during depressions, as they do today. What makes it a depression is ongoing below-trend growth that never gets back to its potential. That is exactly what the U.S. economy is experiencing. The New Depression is here.

Investors are also confused about depression dynamics because they are continually told the United States is in a "recovery." Year after year, forecasters at the Federal Reserve, at the International Monetary Fund and on Wall Street crank out forecasts of robust growth. And year after year they are disappointed. The recovery never seems to get traction. First there are some signs of growth, then the economy quickly slips back into low-growth or no-growth mode.

The reason is simple. Typically, a recovery is driven by the Federal Reserve expanding credit and rising wages. When inflation gets too high or labor markets get too tight, the Fed raises rates. That results in tightening credit and increasing unemployment.

This normal expansion-contraction dynamic has happened

repeatedly since the Second World War. It's usually engineered by the Federal Reserve to avoid inflation during expansions and alleviate unemployment during contractions.

The result is a predictable wave of expansion and contraction driven by monetary conditions. Investors and the Fed have been expecting another strong expansion since 2009, but it's barely materialized.

Growth today isn't strong, because the problem in the economy is not monetary—it is structural. That's the real difference between a recession and a depression. Recessions are cyclical and monetary in nature. Depressions are persistent and structural in nature. Structural problems cannot be solved with cyclical solutions. This is why the Fed has not ended the depression. The Fed has no power to make structural changes.

What do I mean by structural changes? Shifts in fiscal and regulatory policies. The list is long but would include things like lower taxes, repeal of Obamacare, approval of the Keystone Pipeline, expanded oil and gas production, fewer government regulations and an improved business climate in areas such as labor laws, litigation reform and the environment.

Power to make structural changes lies with the Congress and the White House. Those two branches of government are barely on speaking terms. Until structural changes are made by law, the depression will continue and the Fed is powerless to change that.

The difference between 3 percent growth and 1 percent growth may seem small in a single year, but it's enormous over time. From the same starting place, an economy that grows 3 percent per year for 35 years will be twice as rich as one that grows 1 percent per year. After 70 years, about an average lifetime, the 3 percent economy will be four times as rich as the 1 percent economy.

These differences not only affect your wealth but also the ability of the economy to service its debts. The 3 percent economy can manage annual deficits of 2 percent of GDP. The 1 percent economy will eventually go broke with the same deficits. The difference between 3 percent growth and 1 percent growth is lost wealth that can never be recovered. It is the difference between the United States' success and failure as a nation.

Depressions pose other grave dangers to your wealth. In a depression, there is always the danger that disinflation—or falling inflation—tips into outright deflation. Deflation increases the real value of debt and forces many companies and ultimately the banks themselves into bankruptcy.

On the other hand, the Fed may try so hard to fight the deflation that it ends up causing inflation that destroys the real value of your savings, insurance, annuities, retirement checks and any other form of fixed income. So far, the Fed has managed to walk a fine line between deflation and inflation, but the situation is highly unstable and is likely to tip one way or the other quickly and soon.

The depression in the United States will continue indefinitely until structural changes are made. The 25-year depression in Japan that began in 1990 is a perfect example of this. The United States is now like Japan, and the rest of the world is heading in the same direction. Investors like you are in constant danger; both deflation and inflation are real threats.

The good news is that structural changes do not happen overnight. They require action by the White House and Congress, and such action is the product of debate and compromise that we can see coming.

If no action is on the horizon, the depression will continue and you can seek shelter from inflation *and* deflation.

A balanced portfolio of cash, gold, land, fine art, government bonds, alternative investments and stocks in the energy, transportation, agriculture and natural resource sectors should do the job. If, however, action is on the horizon, investors can prepare for the expected boom by positioning in technology, venture capital, financials and other pro-growth cyclical sectors.

You cannot know which outcome will prevail. But with the right understanding of these depression dynamics and watching your monthly *Strategic Intelligence* issues and updates closely, you can know the signs of change and see what's coming. In fact, as a *Strategic Intelligence* reader you'll be among the first to know.

▓ Everything That Made 2008 a Nightmare Is Worse Today

In 2008 all we heard about was "too big to fail." Today, however, the banks that were too big to fail in 2008 are bigger. The five largest banks have a higher percentage of the total assets in the banking system. They have much larger derivatives books and a higher concentration of assets that would seem to be moving in the wrong direction.

We all know the San Andreas Fault in California can cause massive earthquakes. We don't know how big. They can be quite big, as we saw in San Francisco in 1906. But nobody thinks it's a good idea to go out and make the San Andreas Fault bigger. We're not sending the Army Corps of Engineers out there to make the fault line bigger. In financial services, however, that's what we're doing. We're making the fault line bigger by allowing a greater concentration of assets.

Why is that? Well, there are two reasons.

Number one: policy makers don't use correct models. They don't understand that they're creating more risk with their policies. They probably think that they're making the system a little bit safer. In fact, they're creating more risk. They're a little bit blind in that sense.

The other reason is that if you want to slaughter a group of pigs, it's good to get all those pigs into one pen, so to speak. Forcing all the banking assets into a small number of banks makes it easier for the government to steal people's money in three ways. Number one, obviously, is inflation. If you've got all this money in the bank, even with one-quarter of 1 percent or half of 1 percent—the Fed says it wants 2 percent—it's enough to steal your money in small increments.

Beyond that, if there's another financial meltdown they'll be able to lock down the system and freeze bank deposits more easily. If there were more banks it would be harder to corral all of them. It would be easier for people to move from bank to bank.

Conversely, if there are a few megabanks, you only need a couple phone calls to lock down the whole system. You could reprogram the ATMs to tell people they could only have $300 a day. Even today, if you try taking $2,000 out of an ATM, you can't do it.

All the government has to do is dial the withdrawal limit to $300 for gas and groceries. It figures that's all people need and won't let you get the rest of your money. The government won't steal it in so many words, but it won't let you have it. That's easier to do if there is a very small number of banks.

So people need to be alert to these kinds of programs that are in place. Regulators, government and large banks work together to steal people's money either indirectly through inflation or directly through asset freezes.

Recently, the FCC passed a rule that locks down money market funds. A lot of people think their money market fund is as good as cash. They think they can call their broker and have cash in the bank the next day.

Well, this new rule says the FCC can freeze money market funds or impose an exit fee so you get 95 cents on the dollar instead of 100 cents. There probably was a little flier in fine print alongside your statement not too long ago about it. Most people probably opened the statement and threw the flier in the trash.

These are not things I'm making up. They're not scare

stories about things that might happen in the future. They've already happened. The concentration of bank assets has happened. The freeze-ability of money market funds has happened. These things are already in place. They're just waiting to be used in the next panic.

■ The Dollar Is Dying With a Whimper, Not a Bang

The same force that made the dollar the world's reserve currency is working to dethrone it.

July 22, 1944, marked the official conclusion of the Bretton Woods Conference in New Hampshire. There, 730 delegates from 44 nations met at the Mount Washington Hotel in the final days of the Second World War to devise a new international monetary system.

The delegates there were acutely aware that the failures of the international monetary system after the First World War had contributed to the outbreak of the Second World War. They were determined to create a more stable system that would avoid beggar-thy-neighbor currency wars, trade wars and other dysfunctions that could lead to shooting wars.

It was at Bretton Woods that the dollar was officially designated the world's leading reserve currency—a position that it still holds today. Under the Bretton Woods system, all major currencies were pegged to the dollar at a fixed exchange rate. The dollar itself was pegged to gold at the rate of $35.00 per ounce. Indirectly, the other currencies had a fixed gold value because of their peg to the dollar.

Other currencies could devalue against the dollar, and therefore against gold, if they received permission from the International Monetary Fund. However, the dollar could not devalue, at least in theory. It was the keystone of the entire system—intended to be permanently anchored to gold.

From 1950 to 1970, the Bretton Woods system worked

fairly well. Trading partners of the United States who earned dollars could cash those dollars in to the U.S. Treasury and be paid in gold at the fixed rate.

In 1950, the United States had about 20,000 tons of gold. By 1970, that amount had been reduced to about 9,000 tons. The 11,000-ton decline went to U.S. trading partners, primarily Germany, France and Italy, who earned dollars and cashed them in for gold.

The U.K. pound sterling had previously held the role as dominant reserve currency starting in 1816, following the end of the Napoleonic Wars and the official adoption of the gold standard by the U.K. Many observers assume the 1944 Bretton Woods conference was the moment the U.S. dollar replaced sterling as the world's leading reserve currency. In fact, that replacement of sterling by the dollar as the world's leading reserve currency was a process that took 30 years, from 1914 to 1944.

The real turning point was the period July–November 1914, when a financial panic caused by the start of the First World War led to the closures of the London and New York stock exchanges and a mad scramble around the world to obtain gold to meet financial obligations. At first, the United States was acutely short of gold. The New York Stock Exchange was closed so that Europeans could not sell U.S. stocks and convert the dollar sales proceeds into gold.

But within a few months, massive U.S. exports of cotton and other agricultural produce to the U.K. produced huge trade surpluses. Gold began to flow the other way, from Europe back to the United States. Wall Street banks began to underwrite massive war loans for the U.K. and France. By the end of the First World War, the United States had emerged as a major creditor nation and a major gold power. The dollar's percentage of total global reserves began to soar.

Scholar Barry Eichengreen has documented how the dollar and sterling seesawed over the 20 years following the First

World War, with one taking the lead from the other as the leading reserve currency and in turn giving back the lead. In fact, the period from 1919 to 1939 was really one in which the world had two major reserve currencies—dollars and sterling—operating side by side.

Finally, in 1939, England suspended gold shipments in order to fight the Second World War, and the role of sterling as a reliable store of value was greatly diminished, apart from the U.K.'s special trading zone of Australia, Canada and other Commonwealth nations. The 1944 Bretton Woods conference was merely the recognition of a process of dollar-reserve dominance that had started in 1914.

▨ Today, the Dollar Is Slipping

The significance of the process by which the dollar replaced sterling over a 30-year period has huge implications for you today. Slippage in the dollar's role as the leading global reserve currency is not necessarily something that would happen overnight, but is more likely to be a slow, steady process.

Signs of this are already visible. In 2000, dollar assets were about 70 percent of global reserves. Today, the comparable figure is about 64 percent. If this trend continues, one could easily see the dollar fall below 50 percent in the not-too-distant future.

It is equally obvious that a major creditor nation is emerging to challenge the United States today just as the United States emerged to challenge the U.K. in 1914. That power is China. The United States had massive gold inflows from 1914 to 1944. China has massive gold inflows today.

For the first time in six years, China reported its gold holdings in June 2015. China reported then that it had 1,658 metric tons of gold in its reserves. In 2009, China reported it had 1,054 metric tons. However, between 2009 and 2015,

China acquired thousands of metric tons without reporting these acquisitions to the IMF or World Gold Council.

Based on available data on imports and the output of Chinese mines, it is possible to estimate that actual Chinese-government and private gold holdings exceed 8,500 metric tons, as shown in the chart below.

Assuming half of this is government-owned, with the other half in private hands, then the actual Chinese-government gold position exceeds 4,250 metric tons, an increase of over 300 percent. Of course, these figures are only estimates, because China operates through secret channels and does not officially report its gold holdings except at rare intervals.

Estimated Total Chinese Gold Reserves

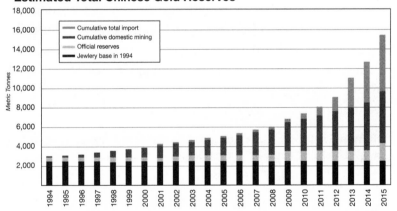

China's gold acquisition is not the result of a formal gold standard, but is happening by stealth acquisitions on the market. It's using intelligence and military assets, covert operations and market manipulation. But the result is the same. Gold is flowing to China today, just as gold flowed to the United States before Bretton Woods.

■ The Anti-Dollar Alliance

China is not alone in its efforts to achieve creditor status and to acquire gold. Russia has doubled its gold reserves in the past five years and has little external debt. Iran has also imported massive amounts of gold, mostly through Turkey and Dubai, although no one knows the exact amount because Iranian gold imports are a state secret.

Other countries, including the other BRICS members, Brazil, India and South Africa, have joined Russia and China to build institutions that could replace the balance-of-payments lending of the International Monetary Fund and the development lending of the World Bank. All of these countries are clear about their desire to break free of U.S. dollar dominance.

Sterling faced a single rival in 1914, the U.S. dollar. Today, the dollar faces a host of rivals—China, Russia, India, Brazil, South Africa, Iran and many others. In addition, there is the world supermoney, the Special Drawing Right, which I expect will also be used to diminish the role of the dollar. The United States is playing into the hands of these rivals by running trade deficits, budget deficits and a huge external debt. What are the implications for your portfolio? Once again, history is highly instructive.

Inflation Exploded After Sterling Lost Its Lead Reserve Role

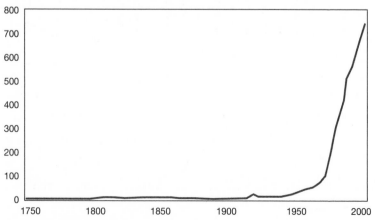

Source: Inflation: The Value of the Pound, 1750–2005, Research Paper 06/09, Feb. 13, 2006, U.K. House of Commons

During the glory years of sterling as a global reserve currency, the exchange value of sterling was remarkably stable. In 2006, the U.K. House of Commons produced a 255-year price index for sterling that covered the period 1750–2005.

The index had a value of 5.1 in 1751. There were fluctuations due to the Napoleonic Wars and the First World War, but even as late as 1934, the index was at only 15.8, meaning that prices had only tripled in 185 years.

But once the sterling lost its lead-reserve-currency role to the dollar, inflation exploded. The index hit 757.3 by 2005. In other words, during the 255 years of the index, prices increased by 200 percent in the first 185 years while the sterling was the lead reserve currency but 5,000 percent in the 70 years that followed.

Price stability seems to be the norm for money with reserve-currency status, but once that status is lost, inflation is dominant.

The decline of the dollar as a reserve currency started in 2000 with the advent of the euro and accelerated in 2010 with the beginning of a new currency war. That decline is now being amplified by China's emergence as a major creditor and gold power—not to mention the actions of a new anti-dollar alliance consisting of the BRICS, Iran and others. If history is a guide, inflation in U.S. dollar prices will come next.

In his 1925 poem "The Hollow Men," T. S. Eliot writes: "This is the way the world ends/ Not with a bang but a whimper." Those waiting for a sudden, spontaneous collapse of the dollar may be missing out on the dollar's less dramatic, but equally important, slow, steady decline. The dollar collapse has already begun. The time to acquire insurance is now.

On the Knife-Edge of Runaway Inflation and Destructive Deflation

Today's investment climate is the most challenging one we

have faced—at least since the late 1970s, perhaps since the 1930s. This is because inflation and deflation are both possibilities in the near term. Most investors can prepare for one or the other, but preparing for both at the same time is far more difficult. The reason for this challenging environment is not difficult to discern.

Analysts and talking heads have been wondering for five years why the recovery is not stronger. They keep predicting that stronger growth is right around the corner. Their forecasts have failed year after year, and their confusion grows. Perhaps even you, who have seen scores of normal business and credit cycles come and go for decades, are confused.

If this "cycle" seems strange to you, there's a good reason. The current economic slump is not cyclical; it's structural. This is a new depression that will last indefinitely until structural changes are made to the economy. Examples of structural changes are reduction or elimination of capital-gains taxes, corporate income taxes and the most onerous forms of regulation.

Building the Keystone Pipeline, reforming entitlement spending and repealing Obamacare are other examples. These have nothing to do with money printing by the Fed. This is why money printing has not fixed the economy. Since structural changes are not on the horizon, expect the depression to continue.

What's the first thing that comes to your mind when you think of a depression? If you're like most investors I've spoken to, you might recall grainy, black-and-white photos from the 1930s of unemployed workers in soup lines, or declining prices. Yet if you look around today, you'll see no soup lines, read that unemployment is only 4.9 percent and observe that prices are generally stable. How can there be a depression? Well, let's take these one by one.

The soup lines are here. They're in your local supermarket. Government issues food stamps in debit card form to those in need, who just pay at the checkout line.

Despite popular beliefs, unemployment too is at 1930s levels. If the Bureau of Labor Statistics measured the rate using the Depression-era method, it would be much higher than 4.9 percent. Also, millions today are claiming disability benefits when unemployment benefits run out—that's just another form of unemployment when the disabilities are not real or not serious, as is often the case.

What about prices? Here the story is different from the 1930s. Prices declined sharply from 1929 to 1933, about 25 percent, but they have been relatively stable from 2009 to 2016, rising only about 10 percent over the seven-year period.

The Federal Reserve's money printing is responsible. The Fed had an overly tight monetary policy in the early 1930s but has employed unprecedented monetary ease since 2009. Ben Bernanke, who was in charge in 2009, was reacting to what he viewed as the erroneous Fed policy of the 1930s. In a 2002 speech on the occasion of Milton Friedman's 90th birthday, Bernanke said to Friedman, "Regarding the Great Depression. You're right, we did it. We're very sorry. But thanks to you, we won't do it again."

But this did not mean that Bernanke had single-handedly discovered the cure for depression. Fighting deflation by itself does not solve the structural problems of the economy that lead to depressed growth. Instead, Bernanke, and now Yellen, has created an unstable dynamic tension.

Depressions are naturally deflationary. In a depression, debtors sell assets to raise cash and pay their debts. That pushes down asset prices. Falling asset prices, in turn, put other investors in distress, causing further asset sales. So it goes on in a downward price spiral.

Printing money is naturally inflationary. With more money chasing a given quantity of goods and services, the prices of those goods and services tend to rise.

The relative price stability you're experiencing now is an artifact of deflation and inflation *acting at the same time.* Far from price stability, what you're seeing is an extremely unstable situation. Think of the forces of deflation and inflation as two teams battling in a tug-of-war.

Eventually, one side wins, but the battle can go on for a long time before one team wears out the other side. If central banks stop causing inflation, deflation will quickly overwhelm the economy. If central banks don't give up and keep printing money to stop deflation, they will eventually get more inflation than they expect.

Both outcomes are very dangerous for you as an investor. The economy is poised on the knife-edge of destructive deflation *and* runaway inflation. Prices could quickly and unexpectedly fall one way or the other.

This doesn't mean you should throw up your hands and say, "I don't know." Plenty of analysts will tell you why you should fear inflation. And prominent policy makers such as Christine Lagarde of the IMF and Mario Draghi of the ECB have warned of deflation. Yet analysis has to be more than a matter of guesswork or stating a bias. The correct analysis is that *both* deflation and inflation are possible. Anyone who warns just of inflation or deflation is missing half the puzzle.

If you knew deflation was coming, you'd have an easy time constructing a profitable portfolio. You would have some cash and invest primarily in bonds. The value of cash goes up during deflation as prices decline, and bonds rally as interest rates decline. You might want to own some raw land in that case also.

During a deflationary period, the nominal value of the land might go down, but the costs to develop the land go down faster. The key would be to develop it cheaply in time for the next up cycle.

If, on the other hand, you knew inflation was coming, it would also be easy to construct a robust portfolio. All you would need to do is buy commodities like gold and oil, and stocks of companies with hard assets in sectors such as transportation, energy, natural resources and agriculture. You could also purchase fine art, which has excellent wealth-preservation properties in an inflationary environment.

What should you do when the outcome is on the knife-edge and could tip either way, toward deflation or inflation?

The answer is to prepare for both, watch carefully and stay nimble. Your initial portfolio should have gold, fine art, raw land, cash, bonds, select stocks and some alternatives in strategies like global macro hedge funds and venture capital. Not all of those strategies will pay off, but some will do well enough to outperform others and preserve wealth.

As a *Strategic Intelligence* subscriber, once the trend toward inflation or deflation becomes clearer, I'll alert you to sell assets positioned for the opposite outcome. That way, you can redeploy that month to prepare for the dominant outcome. For example, if inflation begins to spin out of control, I may tell you to convert cash and bonds into gold and land. If deflation gets the upper hand, I will advise you to liquidate some of your stocks in favor of more cash and bonds, and so on.

In future *Strategic Intelligence* issues, I'll maintain close watch on the tug-of-war between inflation and deflation for you. I'll give you early warnings about which way to pivot. For now, however, the outcome is uncertain and you need to place some bets on both inflation and deflation happening. But be ready to cut losses on losers and double down on winners when the time comes.

CHAPTER 2

Five Crisis Scenarios

▤ Enemy Hedge Fund Scenario

A country like China or Russia could conduct a financial attack on the United States using the trillions of dollars of reserves it has in its sovereign wealth fund.

China is a good example. It has about $3 trillion in reserves. By reserves, I just mean its savings account. If you make $50,000 a year and you spend $40,000 on rent or car payments or whatever and you've got $10,000 left over, you can put what's left in the bank or you can use it to buy stocks and bonds. That $10,000 is your savings, or your portfolio, if you will.

Individual countries are no different. Countries earn money by having a trade surplus or getting direct foreign investment, and they have to decide how to invest it. That's what's called their reserve position.

A lot of it goes into liquid assets, but the sovereign wealth funds are set up to invest in less liquid instruments, including normal stocks and bonds. They could, however, also be used to fund a hedge fund with layers of Cayman Island trusts, Maltese banks, cybercenter intermediaries and, perhaps, some corrupt lawyers or bankers—though you could also have unwitting, unknowing lawyers and bankers, those who think they're working for a legitimate hedge fund and don't know who's really behind it. That's what's called "layering"—it's the use of trust and other vehicles to disguise the true ownership.

This fund could come into the market and buy and sell on a continual basis, not really trying to make money. That's because its purpose would not be to make money like a normal hedge fund. Instead, it would actually have a malevolent, geopolitical, financial-warfare intent.

It could build up its credit lines, build up its credibility, get facilities with major banks and then, one day, just flood the market with sell orders in a particular stock. It could sell the big stocks too—Apple, Google and the like.

It could use options to amplify its attack—and it wouldn't do it on a sunny day. It would most likely pick a day when the market was already down, maybe 3 or 4 percent already. That would be a big day—say, down by as much as 600 points. By piling on, this enemy hedge fund could create a panic and then disappear the next day, taking its money and going back to Beijing or wherever it came from.

A hedge fund entity could be set up, funded and left to be operated normally for years or even longer until one day, it attacks U.S. financial markets. That's one scenario that could play out, and the United States certainly needs to be alert to it.

▨ Inflation Takes Hold

The important thing to understand about inflation is that the Fed wants it. That's very hard for people to understand because most people remember the late 1970s or early 1980s, when we had out-of-control inflation.

From 1977 to 1981, cumulative inflation over that five-year period was *50 percent*. That means, if you were a saver, had an annuity, an insurance policy, a retirement income or any kind of fixed income at all, you lost half of your purchasing power in five years.

People go back to the creation of the Fed in 1913 and explain that the dollar has lost 95 percent of its purchasing power since 1913—100 years. That's true, but the late '70s was a case where it lost 50 percent of its purchasing power, not in 100 years, but in 5 years. That could happen again.

The Fed spent 30 years getting the inflation genie back in the bottle. It started with Paul Volcker and continued through the 1980s, 1990s and early 2000s. The Fed succeeded, eventually getting inflation under control.

Now, however, the Fed is trying to open the bottle and let the genie out once again. It has its reasons. First, the United States can't pay its debt, so inflation is a way to reduce the value of that debt. It still owes the same amount of money—around $18 trillion—but in real terms, it's worth a lot less.

The United States can't pay $18 trillion, but maybe it could pay $8 trillion; so, the Fed can reduce its bill by cutting the value of the dollar in half.

The Fed also wants to get the economy going again. To do so, it's using what's called "financial repression." You force the banks to buy bonds and use other regulatory means to keep interest rates low. Meanwhile, you try to stoke inflation. Whenever inflation is higher than interest rates, you have what's called a negative real rate.

That's like free money. In fact, it's better than free money. The bank actually pays you to be a borrower in the sense that you get to pay the bank back in cheaper dollars.

The Fed is trying to engineer a situation like that to get people borrowing, lending and spending again. It thinks that will get the economic machine going. But what it doesn't understand is that once it does that, it'll have to change expectations.

Right now, inflation expectations are extremely low. Investors fear the opposite of inflation right now—deflation. It's very hard to change those expectations, but once you do, they can go out of control.

The Fed thinks it can dial inflation up to 3 or 4 percent and then dial it back down to 2. It's going to find out that instead, inflation goes from 2 to 3 to 4 to 9, and all of a sudden, you're back to the very destructive borderline hyperinflation we saw in the late 1970s.

It's playing with fire.

■ Deflation Takes Hold

No one knows what deflation looks and feels like today. We worried for decades about inflation, and today, the Fed's trying to get more inflation. Deflation, however, is a real danger.

The reason it's a danger is that we are not in a normal cyclical recovery. We're in a new depression. This is a global depression that began in 2007 and will run on indefinitely. The Fed's trying to treat the depression with monetary remedies, but it won't work. The reason it won't work is that depressions are structural.

Monetary solutions and liquidity solutions are cyclical. They help you out of the business cycle. If credit becomes too tight, the Fed loosens. If things get a little hot, the Fed tightens.

That's the normal kind of sine wave business expansion and contraction we've seen since the Second World War. But today is different. It's more like the Great Depression.

Depressions are structural. You cannot get out of them without structural changes in fiscal policy or regulatory policy.

In a depression, people want to deleverage. They sell assets and get cash to pay off debts to reduce their balance sheet.

What happens when they sell assets? It lowers the price. That puts the next investor in distress. He now has to sell assets to deleverage his balance sheet, and the process feeds on itself. That is very, very difficult for the Fed to control.

It actually creates a state of mind where cash is more valuable. In a deflation, cash actually goes up in real terms. In fact, cash can be one of your best assets in a deflationary environment.

The natural state of the world today is deflationary because we're in a depression. The government, however, can't tolerate deflation. It has to cause inflation. That's why the Fed's money printing is going on.

The best way to understand this is to picture two tectonic plates, like at the San Andreas Fault. There's the Pacific plate and the North American plate. They're pressing on each other.

One plate is inflation and the other is deflation. The opposite forces of money printing and depression dynamics are the forces pushing them together.

They're pressing and pressing. Like at a fault line, not much happens at first. At some point, however, it's going to break.

It could break either way. It could break into inflation, which we talked about, but it could also break into deflation.

The assets that will perform very well in a deflationary environment are things like cash and, believe it or not, gold.

Over the long run, I think inflation is more likely because the government wants it. That said, deflation is the state of the world today, and you cannot rule it out.

■ Geopolitical Crisis

The fourth scenario I'd like to highlight is a geopolitical shock. People yawn and say, "Gee, haven't we had enough of those lately?"

It could, however, be something like an assassination or a more momentous event than what we've seen so far. Or one of today's current geopolitical struggles could spin out of control.

When Russia invaded Crimea—that's something that could have triggered a crisis. When the Islamic State declared a caliphate—that's another. When Libya completely fell apart, and it stopped pumping oil—that's another.

I frequently make the point that any snowflake can cause an avalanche. But not every snowflake does.

A lot of snowflakes fall harmlessly, except that they make

the ultimate avalanche worse because they're building up the snow pack. Then, when one of them hits the wrong way, it starts an avalanche, which cascades out of control.

Sometimes people have this idea that all geopolitical events are little things. They mistakenly believe they should be waiting for a massive event that will trigger the next crisis with a bang. That's actually not good science.

The way to think about the trigger for the next crisis is that it might not look that different from the little things. All that is necessary to trigger the crisis is for an event to react with the system the wrong way. If an event happens on a bad day or when markets were leaning a certain way—that could be the straw that breaks the camel's back.

The straw that breaks the camel's back is not different than all the other straw. It's just that there was a tipping point. Likewise, one snowflake starts an avalanche—and one small event can trigger a crisis.

The one thing that causes the Big Drop might not be that different than the events we've seen already—except that the system is getting more and more unstable, and it might not take that much to make it collapse.

▓ Market Collapse

The fifth scenario is a market collapse. This would happen very suddenly and unexpectedly. The forces of inflation and deflation that I wrote about take a while to play out, but this collapse could happen very suddenly and catch investors completely unaware. We've come within hours or days of total global financial gridlock and total market collapse in the last two decades.

Everyone knows about the 2008 crisis. People have a sense of that. But few people know that market collapse also happened in 1998, as a result of the Russia default and the collapse of hedge fund Long-Term Capital Management.

I was involved in LTCM. I actually negotiated its bailout. I was in the room. I saw the $4 billion moved into its bank accounts to prop up the balance sheet. The money came from Wall Street.

A lot of give-and-take almost didn't happen, and we were literally hours away from markets collapsing. We muddled through that, but officials learned all the wrong lessons.

Instead of banning derivatives, backing away from overleverage and putting a lid on banks, public policy did the opposite. Congress repealed Glass Steagall, which allowed banks to act like hedge funds, and it repealed Schwab's regulation, which meant that you could now trade derivatives on anything.

The Securities and Exchange Commission, in 2006, repealed broker-dealer leverage or increased it from 15:1 to 30:1. The Basel III capital requirements also allowed greater bank leverage. Basically, the officials looked at LTCM's failure and said, "The game's on. You can do whatever you want, with as much leverage as you want and with as much opaqueness as you want."

Is it any surprise that in 2008 we had another collapse? At that time, Bear Stearns went down, then Fannie Mae, and then Freddie Mac, followed by Lehman Brothers and AIG. One by one the dominos fell.

We were days away from total collapse. Morgan Stanley would have been next; Goldman Sachs would've been right behind it, then Citibank, Bank of America and JPMorgan. All the dominos were falling.

What the government did was drop a steel curtain between two of the dominos. It stopped the process after Lehman Brothers and AIG. That's why Morgan Stanley didn't fall—but it was days away from collapse. The point is, how much more stress can the system take? The system almost collapsed in 1998, and it almost collapsed in 2008. It's three strikes, you're out.

The next collapse—the Big Drop—is coming.

You can see it coming because of the dynamics. The difference is that next time, the crisis will be bigger than the Fed.

The Fed was able to bail out LTCM, Morgan Stanley and Goldman Sachs. But when the Big Drop comes, it's going to be too much for the Fed to handle. The Fed's used up all its dry powder; it's taken its balance sheet to $4 trillion.

What is it going to do—take its balance sheet to $8 trillion?

How can it take its balance sheet that high to re-liquefy against the next collapse without destroying confidence in the dollar?

The answer's simple: it can't.

That's why, after the Big Drop, the system won't get another chance.

■ "It Can't Happen Here"

People tell me all of the time that these sorts of scenarios can't happen here.

I have to remind them that it *has* happened here. I point out that the international monetary system has collapsed three times in the past 100 years—in 1914, 1939 and 1971.

The global financial system has come very close to complete collapse twice in the past two decades—in 1998 and again in 2008.

The stock market also dropped 22 percent in a single day on October 19, 1987. That is the equivalent in today's terms of the Dow Jones dropping *4,000 points.*

Not 40, not 400, but *4,000 points.* The Mexican peso crisis in 1994, the dot-com bubble and the Nasdaq collapse provide more examples—the last of these sending the stock market from 5,000 points to 2,000 points in a very short period of time.

Yet these things keep happening.

It's true we get bailouts and money printing from the Fed, but we're at the point where the risk is bigger than ever. We've had our warnings, and we've had our lessons—we haven't learned them, and we're making the same mistakes. When the Big Drop comes, it's going to be bigger than the Fed.

CHAPTER 3
The Threat of Inflation

■ Money Illusion

A money illusion sounds like something a prestidigitator performs by pulling $100 bills from a hat shown to be empty moments before. In fact, money illusion is a longstanding concept in economics that has enormous significance for you if you're a saver, investor or entrepreneur.

Money illusion is a trick, but it is not one performed on stage. It is a ruse performed by central banks that can distort the economy and destroy your wealth.

The money illusion is a tendency of individuals to confuse real and nominal prices. It boils down to the fact that people ignore inflation when deciding if they are better off. Examples are everywhere.

Assume you are a building engineer working for a property-management company making $100,000 per year. You get a 2 percent raise, so now you are making $102,000 per year. Most people would say they are better off after the raise. But if inflation is 3 percent, the $102,000 salary is worth only $98,940 in purchasing power relative to where you started.

You got a $2,000 raise in nominal terms, but you suffered a $1,060 pay cut in real terms. The difference between your perception and reality is money illusion.

The impact of money illusion is not limited to wages and prices. It can apply to any cash flow, including dividends and interest. It can apply to the asset prices of stocks and bonds. Any nominal increase has to be adjusted for inflation to see past the money illusion.

The concept of money illusion as a subject of economic study and policy is not new. Irving Fisher, one of the most famous economists of the 20th century, wrote a book called *The Money Illusion* in 1928. The idea of money illusion can be traced back to Richard Cantillon's *Essay on Economic Theory* of 1730, although Cantillon did not use that exact phrase.

Modern economists argue that money illusion does not exist. Instead, they say, you make decisions based upon "rational expectations." That means that once you perceive inflation or expect it in the future, you will discount the value of your money and invest or spend it according to its expected intrinsic value.

Like much of modern economics, this view works better in the classroom than in the real world. Experiments by behaviorists show that people think a 2 percent cut in wages with no change in the price level is "unfair." Meanwhile, they think a 2 percent raise with 4 percent inflation is "fair."

In fact, the two outcomes are economically identical in terms of purchasing power. The fact, however, that people prefer a raise over a pay cut while ignoring inflation is the essence of money illusion.

The importance of money illusion goes far beyond academics and social science experiments. Central bankers use money illusion to transfer wealth from you—a saver and investor—to debtors. They do this when the economy isn't growing because there's too much debt. Central bankers try to use inflation to reduce the real value of the debt to give debtors some relief in the hope that they might spend more and help the economy get moving again.

Of course, this form of relief comes at the expense of savers and investors like you who see the value of your assets decline. Again, a simple example makes the point.

Assume a debtor bought a $250,000 home in 2007 with a $50,000 down payment and a $200,000 mortgage with a low teaser rate. Today, the home is worth $190,000, a 24 percent decline in value, but the mortgage is still $200,000 because the teaser rate did not provide for amortization.

This homeowner is "underwater"—the value of his home is worth less than the mortgage he's paying—and he slashes his spending in response. In this scenario, assume there is another individual, a saver, with no mortgage and $100,000 in the bank who receives no interest under the Fed's zero-interest-rate policy.

Suppose a politician came along who proposed that the government confiscate $15,000 from the saver to be handed to the debtor to pay down his mortgage. Now the saver has only $85,000 in the bank, but the debtor has a $190,000 house with a $185,000 mortgage, bringing the debtor's home above water and giving him a brighter outlook.

The saver is worse off and the debtor is better off, each because of the $15,000 transfer payment. Americans would consider this kind of confiscation to be grossly unfair, and the politician would be run out of town on a rail.

Now assume the same scenario, except this time, the Federal Reserve engineers 3 percent inflation for five years, for a total of 15 percent inflation. The saver still has $100,000 in the bank, but it is worth only $85,000 in purchasing power due to inflation.

The borrower would still owe $200,000 on the mortgage, but the debt burden would be only $170,000 in real terms after inflation. Better yet, the house value might rise by $28,000 if it keeps pace with inflation, making the house worth $218,000 and giving the debtor positive home equity again.

Setting aside the home's appreciation, the two cases are economically the same. In the first case, the wealth transfer is achieved by confiscation, and in the second case, the wealth transfer is achieved by inflation. The saver is worse off and the debtor is better off in both cases. But confiscation is politically unacceptable, while inflation of 3 percent per year is barely noticed. In effect, inflation is a hidden tax used to transfer wealth from savers to debtors without causing the political headaches of a real tax increase.

Why do central banks such as the Fed pursue money-illusion policies? The answer involves another academic theory— one that doesn't work in the real world. The Fed believes that underwater debtors are from a lower income tier than savers and investors. This means the debtors are supposed to have what's called higher marginal propensity to consume, or MPC.

The MPC measures how much you spend out of each dollar of wealth you gain. If you gain $1,000 and decide to spend $50, your MPC would be 5 percent. If you spend nothing after getting an additional $1,000, your MPC would be 0 percent.

Academic theory says that poorer debtors have a higher MPC than wealthier savers. This means that if inflation transfers wealth from savers to debtors, total spending will go up because the debtors will spend more of the money than the savers would have. This is said to benefit debtors and savers, because debtors gain from the increased wealth, while savers gain from more overall spending in the form of jobs, business revenues and stock prices. This makes inflation a win-win.

This theory sounds neat and tidy, but it has serious flaws. By lumping all savers together, the theory fails to distinguish between truly wealthy savers and middle-class savers. It may be true that if you're a very wealthy saver, you have a low MPC. If you are spending a certain amount on vacations and fine wine and the Fed steals some of your savings through inflation, you will probably spend just as much on vacations and fine wine.

But if you're part of the middle class and are struggling with an unemployed spouse, children's tuition, elderly parents' health care and higher property taxes, your savings and investments are a lifeline you cannot afford to lose. If your savings are eroded by inflation, the pain is real you might cut your spending. There is no free lunch.

■ Insidious Cantillon Effects

Cantillon in the 1730s suggested an even more insidious flaw in central banks' actions. He said that inflation does not move uniformly through an economy. It moves with lags, something Milton Friedman said in the 1970s. Inflation, according to Cantillon, moves in concentric circles from a small core of people to an ever-widening group of affected individuals.

Think of the way ripples spread out when you drop a pebble in a pond. Cantillon said that the rich and powerful are in the inner circle and see the inflation first. This gives them time to prepare. Those in the middle class are in the outer circles and see the inflation last. They are the victims of lost purchasing power.

This Cantillon effect may explain why wealthy investors such as Warren Buffett are buying hard assets like railroads, oil and natural gas that will retain value when inflation hits. Official measures of inflation are low today, but those in the inner circle already see it coming, just as Cantillon suggested.

If you're in the wider circles, however, you may stay in conventional stock and bond portfolios too long and will see the value of your assets diluted by inflation. You may not realize it until it's too late, either. The money illusion deceives everyday investors.

Money illusion has four stages. In stage 1, the groundwork for inflation is laid by central banks but is not yet apparent to most investors. This is the "feel good" stage where people are counting their nominal gains but don't see through the illusion.

Stage 2 is when inflation becomes more obvious. Investors still value their nominal gains and assume inflation is temporary and the central banks "have it under control." Stage 3 is when inflation begins to run away and central banks lose control. Now the illusion wears off. Savings and other fixed-income cash flows such as insurance, annuities and retirement checks rapidly lose value. If you own hard assets prior to stage 3, you'll be spared. But if you don't, it will be too late because the prices of hard assets will gap up *before* the money illusion wears off.

Finally, stage 4 can take one of two paths. The first path is hyperinflation, such as in the Weimar Germany or Zimbabwe. In that case, all paper money and cash flows are destroyed and a new currency arises from the ashes of the old. The alternative is shock therapy of the kind Paul Volcker imposed in 1980. In that case, interest rates are hiked as high as 20 percent to kill inflation—but nearly kill the economy in the process.

Right now, we are in late stage 1, getting closer to stage 2. Inflation is here in small doses, and people barely notice. Savings are being slowly confiscated by inflation, but investors are still comforted by asset bubbles in stocks and real estate. Be nimble and begin to buy some inflation insurance in the form of hard assets before the stage 3 superspike puts the price of those assets out of reach.

Hyperinflation: It Can (Still) Happen Here

Eight years and $4 trillion of Federal Reserve money printing after the 2008 crash—you may think to yourself—if hyperinflation were ever going to happen in the United States, it would've already.

In fact, when I write "hyperinflation," you might only think of two images. First, you might think of a reckless third-world country like Zimbabwe or Argentina printing money to cover government expenses and worker salaries to the point where trillions of local "dollars" or pesos are needed to buy a loaf of bread.

The second image is of the same phenomenon in an advanced country such as Germany, but long ago. Perhaps you think of grainy, black-and-white photos from the 1920s. The last thing you'd probably think of is a hyperinflation in a 21st-century developed economy such as the United States. We tell ourselves that hyperinflation might happen in faraway or long-ago places but can't happen here.

Yet it can happen here. In fact, the United States flirted with hyperinflation in the late 1970s, and before that in the late 1910s. Other episodes arose after the Civil War and the American Revolution. Hyperinflation acts like a deadly virus with no cure. It may be contained for long periods of time, but once it breaks out into a general population, there may be no stopping it without enormous losses.

To explain why, it's essential to know what hyperinflation is, how it begins and how it feeds on itself. In a complex system such as the U.S. economy, small initial blunders can have catastrophic consequences once feedback loops and behavioral changes take over.

There is no universally agreed-upon definition of hyperinflation. But one widely used benchmark says hyperinflation exists when prices increase 50 percent or more in a single month. So if gasoline is $3.00 per gallon in January, $4.50 per gallon in February and $6.75 per gallon in March, and if prices of food and other essentials are going up at the same pace, that would be considered hyperinflationary.

It also tends to accelerate once it begins, so the monthly 50 percent increase soon becomes 100 percent, then 1,000 percent, and so on, until the real value of the currency is utterly destroyed. Beyond that point, the currency ceases to function as currency and becomes almost litter, good only for wallpaper or starting fires.

Many investors assume that money printing by governments to cover deficits is the root cause of hyperinflation. Money printing does contribute to hyperinflation, but it is not a complete explanation. The other essential ingredient is velocity, or the turnover of money. If central banks print money and that money is left in banks and not used by consumers, then actual inflation can be low.

This is the situation in the United States today. The Federal Reserve has expanded the base money supply by over $3 trillion since 2008. But very little actual inflation has resulted. This is because the velocity of money has been dropping at the same time. Banks are not lending much, and so consumers are not spending much of the new money; it's just sitting in the banks.

Money printing first turns into inflation, and then hyperinflation, when consumers and businesses lose confidence in price stability and see more inflation on the horizon. At that point, people dump money in exchange for current consumption or hard assets, and velocity increases.

As inflation spikes, expectations of more inflation grow, and the process accelerates and feeds on itself. In extreme cases, consumers spend their entire paycheck on groceries, gasoline and gold the minute they receive it. They know holding their money in the bank will result in their hard-earned pay being wiped out. The important point is that hyperinflation is not just a monetary phenomenon—it is first and foremost a psychological or behavioral phenomenon.

As you'll see below, hyperinflation does not affect everyone in a society equally. There are distinct sets of winners and losers. The winners are those with gold, foreign currency, land and other hard assets including factories, natural resources and transportation equipment. The losers are those with fixed income claims such as savings, pensions, insurance policies and annuities. Debtors win in hyperinflation because they pay off debt with debased currency. Creditors lose because their claims are devalued.

Hyperinflation doesn't emerge instantaneously. It begins slowly with normal inflation and then accelerates violently at an increasing rate until it becomes hyperinflation. This is critical for investors to understand because *much of the damage to your wealth actually occurs at the inflationary stage, not the hyperinflationary stage.* The hyperinflation of Weimar Germany is a good case in point.

For Your Eyes Only—An Exclusive Hyperinflation Debriefing

Many intelligent analysts have been pounding the table about hyperinflation since 2008. Perhaps you've followed their advice and are wondering why the scenario hasn't materialized yet. That's why I sat down in Agora Financial's studio to record a six-part video debriefing. You'll learn such things as

- the reason you haven't experienced hyperinflation yet;
- why inflation can appear faster than you may think possible;
- why companies like LendingTree and Social Finance are some of the hottest around;
- the reason why the Fed may soon resort to "helicopter money" to get inflation; and
- the misconception about excess banking reserves.

Altogether, it's nearly half an hour's worth of additional insights for your eyes only. It'll help you sleep soundly at night knowing full well what's on the horizon. Simply visit **www.agorafinancial.info/hyperinflation** to watch all six parts.

In January 1919, the exchange rate of German reichsmarks to U.S. dollars was 8.2 to 1. By January 1922, three years later, the exchange rate was 207.82 to 1. The reichsmark had lost 96 percent of its value in three years. By the standard definition, this is not hyperinflation, because it took place over 36 months and was never 50 percent in any single month.

By the end of 1922, hyperinflation had struck Germany, with the reichsmark going from 3,180 to the dollar in October to 7,183 to the dollar in November. In that case, the reichsmark did lose half its value in a single month, thus meeting the definition of hyperinflation.

One year later, in November 1923, the exchange rate was 4.2 *trillion* reichsmarks to one dollar. History tends to focus on 1923, when the currency was debased 58 billion percent. But that extreme hyperinflation of 1923 was just a matter of destroying the remaining 4 percent of people's wealth at an accelerating rate. The real damage was done from 1919 to 1922, *before* the hyperinflation, when the first 96 percent was lost.

If you think this can't happen here or now, think again. Something like this started in the late 1970s. The U.S. dollar suffered 50 percent inflation in the five years from 1977 to 1981. We were at the takeoff stage to hyperinflation, exactly where Germany was in 1920 on a relative basis. Most wealth in savings and fixed income claims had been lost already. Hyperinflation in America was prevented then by the combined actions of Paul Volcker and Ronald Reagan, but it was a close call.

Today the Federal Reserve assumes if inflation moves up to 3 percent or more in the United States, it can gently dial it back to its preferred 2 percent target. But moving inflation to 3 percent requires a huge change in the behavior and expectations of everyday Americans. That change is not easy to cause, but once it happens, it is not easy to reverse, either.

If inflation does hit 3 percent, it is more likely to go to 6 percent or higher, rather than back down to 2 percent, because the process will feed on itself and be difficult to stop. Sadly, there are no Volckers or Reagans on the horizon today. There are only weak political leaders and misguided central bankers.

Inflation will accelerate, as it did in the United States in 1980 and in Germany in 1920. Whether hyperinflation comes next remains to be seen, but it can happen more easily than most people expect. By then, the damage is already done. Your savings and pensions will mostly be gone.

The assets you need now to preserve wealth in the future are simple and timeless. Gold, silver, land and select tangibles in the right amounts will serve you well. Mutual funds designed specifically to protect against inflation should also be considered.

■ Excess Reserves Held at Banks

The reason the Fed is paying interest on excess reserves today is to give banks the money to pay higher insurance premiums to the FDIC. Remember, the Dodd-Frank bill raised the insurance premiums on the banks that they have to pay for their deposit insurance. That would have hurt bank earnings. So the Fed said, "Fine, we'll just pay you on your excess reserves; take the money and pay your premiums."

This is just another game—another shadow play providing a backdoor way of financing the FDIC premiums with printed money so the banks don't actually have to bear the cost.

Beyond that, some theorize that if the Fed stops paying the interest, all of a sudden, the banks will say, "Well, we've got to make some money. We'll go out and lend all this money."

The dynamic is different than these theorists suppose. The real problem is that to have inflation, you need two things: money supply and velocity.

Velocity is simply the turnover of money. Say I go out tonight, buy a drink at the bar, then tip the bartender; then the bartender takes a taxicab home; and the taxicab driver puts some gas in his car. Then that money has a velocity of three. You've got the bartender, the taxicab and the gas station. But if I stay home and watch TV or buy gold and leave it in a vault, that money has a velocity of zero.

The nominal GDP, the nominal gross value of all the goods and services in the U.S. economy, is simply the money supply times velocity. You need both to cause inflation.

You need money supply times velocity to be greater than potential GDP. Then, the excess shows up in the form of inflation. Today the Fed has taken the money supply to the moon, yet velocity is collapsing. That's the problem.

More money printing or less payment of interest on excess reserves won't cause inflation. What would cause inflation is the change in velocity, which is behavioral. It's the change in psychology. That's what you have to look for. It's what the Fed actually calls "inflationary expectations."

And so I like to say, if you want inflation, it's like a ham-and-cheese sandwich. You need both the ham and the cheese. Money printing is the ham and velocity is the cheese.

The thing to watch for is a change in inflationary expectations or a change in behavior. That can happen very quickly, and that's why inflation is so dangerous. It might not show up at all, and then, suddenly, it will come very quickly because it's very difficult to change behavior. But, once you do, it's very difficult to change it back again. That's why inflation runs out of control.

▪ $4 Trillion and Counting

Over the past seven years the Federal Reserve has ballooned its balance sheet above $4 trillion. People say, "Well, that's got to cause inflation." But it doesn't automatically mean inflation.

What it means is that you *could* have inflation. The potential is there. Certainly, if the Fed hadn't printed that much money, the potential for inflation would be much lower.

But the money by itself is not enough. You need money plus the change of behavior. You need something that's going to catalyze a change of behavior. Think of the money supply as a big pile of dry wood or maybe a big drum of gasoline. The behavioral change is the match—it's the thing you throw in that lights the fire, or, in this case, the hyperinflation.

We should absolutely be concerned about the money. The problem is that because there has been no inflation thus far, the Fed is going to keep printing.

We haven't seen that much inflation yet. That's a fact. Paul Krugman sees that and says, "See. I told you. You can print all the money you want and you don't get inflation. So go print some more."

My answer: That's not quite correct. You can print all the money you want and not get inflation. But that's only if the behavior doesn't change. Again, once the behavior does change, two things happen. First, the inflation can come very quickly, much more quickly than people expect.

Second, once you change behavior, it's very hard to change it back again.

Right now, the Fed says, "We want 2 percent inflation." Some of the FOMC members will tell you privately they wouldn't mind seeing 3 percent inflation. To get it, they're going to keep printing and printing and printing until they get the 3 percent inflation.

But there are two problems. Most obvious is that the Fed's printing all of that money. It might actually destroy confidence in the dollar before they get us to 3 percent inflation.

This is where Britain, Russia, China and other foreign countries begin buying gold. These are governments backing away from the dollar because they don't like what they see.

The second problem is that the Fed might get to 3 percent inflation but then cruise past it to 9 percent inflation. Again, once you turn that battleship around you can't turn it back very easily.

The Fed thinks it's playing with a thermostat. If your house is too cold, you dial it up. If your house is too warm, you dial it down. The Fed wants to dial it up. It wants a little more inflation, and it thinks if things get a little too hot it can dial it down again.

What the Fed's going to discover, probably the hard way, is that the process isn't reversible. When it gets inflation to 3 percent, which won't be easy, inflation might go right on up to 9 percent.

That's when investors will lose a lot of money.

▪ Helicopter Money and Peer-to-Peer Lending

Printing money by itself does not cause inflation. It's a necessary condition, but it's not a sufficient condition. You do need the money to cause that kind of inflation, but you need something else. You need this change in behavior or velocity.

A lot of people say, "Well, all that money sloshing around is going to lead to a lot of lending." That's not how it works.

Banks don't need reserves to lend. They'll make the loan and then go get the reserves. The fact that the Federal Reserve is throwing reserves at the banks does not mean that people want to borrow, and it does not mean banks want to lend.

In fact, people don't want to borrow and the banks don't want to lend. This is why we're seeing that some of the hottest companies around are LendingTree and Social Finance. These are peer-to-peer lenders.

People use internet platforms to disintermediate the banks. They take the banks out of the equation and say, "Hey, there are people over here with money and people over there who want to borrow money. We'll match the two online." Essentially, it's like an Uber for money lending.

You wouldn't have the opportunity for peer-to-peer lending if the banks were doing their job. Right now, they're not doing their job. The short answer to why is that reserves are never constrained on lending. The banks can lend all they want. Then they'll go get the reserves if they need them. That's why all of the reserves are piling up right now.

This could lead to what's called "helicopter money."

What is helicopter money? A lot of people say, "Oh, helicopter money. That's when Ben Bernanke or, now, Janet Yellen gets behind the controls of a helicopter and flies up and pushes money out of a helicopter, and the money floats down. Everybody picks it up and spends it."

That's the image. Probably a lot of us are seeing cartoons of a Fed chair doing exactly that, shoving money out of helicopters. It's a cute metaphor, but that's not actually what they do, of course. No one thinks that the chair of the Fed is going to fly a helicopter and push money out.

That's the name and that's the image, but what is it actually? How does it work technically? What does it mean for you as an investor? To get past the clichés and past the cartoons you should understand helicopter money at a very serious technical level about what it is and what it means for you.

Helicopter money is a solution to a problem. Before the solution, you need to understand the problem because no solution makes sense in awestruck. What are policy makers actually confronting?

There's a big problem in the world today. It's probably the biggest problem in the world. It's not that the stock market is going down. It's not that economic growth isn't quite what it should be. The problem in the world is too much debt and not enough nominal growth to pay the debt. The world is heading for a massive, unprecedented, systemic debt crisis—a debt crisis we're heading to relentlessly.

It's not here yet. It pops up in certain countries getting distressed or certain corporations getting distressed. But we're not quite to the stage where the entire world is breaking down. This is the big macro problem that elites worry about. It's too much debt and not enough growth.

Now, I use the words "nominal growth." Nominal growth is real growth plus inflation. It's that simple. If you have real growth of 2 percent and inflation of 2 percent, just add them together: 2 + 2 is 4, and your nominal growth is 4 percent.

Why focus on nominal growth instead of real growth? The reason nominal growth is important is because debt is nominal. In other words, if I owe you a dollar, then I owe you a dollar. Maybe the dollar will be worth 90 cents because we have some inflation, or maybe it'll be worth $1.10 because we have some deflation. The real value of that dollar can fluctuate. We all know that, but contractually if I borrow a dollar, I owe you a dollar. That's nominal. To pay nominal debt, you need nominal growth. Now, real growth is great. Everyone's in favor of real growth. What the elites are saying is, "Well, real growth seems stuck around 2 percent." It actually may be going lower than that right now. Debt is growing about 3 percent or higher. A 2 percent growth rate is not enough to pay off a 3 percent increase in debt. If you have 2 percent real growth with 3 percent debt growth, the debt is growing faster than your economy, and eventually you're going to go bankrupt.

To understand that, imagine you owe $50,000 on a MasterCard. You have a big line of credit. You owe $50,000, and your debt's going up $1,000 a month because you're spending more than you're paying off. Is that a problem or not? Well, if you make $1 million a year, it's not a problem. You just write a $50,000 check. Done. If you make $20,000 a year, it's a huge problem. You're probably going bankrupt.

You can't answer whether debt is a problem without putting it in the context of income. If you have enough income to pay the debt, then the debt's not a problem. If you don't, it's a big problem.

We all know what's going on with the debt. Deficits are going up. There's not a major country that's running a surplus. The U.K., Germany, France, Italy, obviously Greece, all the other parts of Europe, the United States, China and Japan are all running deficits. Every one of them is running deficits. Not one of those countries is running a surplus. That's okay if you have enough growth, but they don't. This is the big macro problem. Debt is going up faster than growth.

What the elites need is nominal growth. Real growth is running about 2 percent. Debt's going up about 3 percent, or a little higher in some cases. Nominal growth is real growth plus inflation, so what's the missing ingredient? What are we really missing?

The answer is inflation, because if you had enough inflation added to the real growth, then your nominal growth would be big enough. In other words, you want to write an equation that says 2 + 2 = 4. Right now, the equation says 2 + 1 = 3, because inflation is 1 percent and real growth is 2 percent. Well, it doesn't equal 4, so we need to make that 2 + 2. That's why the Fed always talks about a 2 percent inflation target.

I don't know think the 2 percent inflation target is okay. When I hear the word "inflation," I think theft. In other words, inflation is how governments steal money from you. Most people think theft is through taxation. That's one way the government does it. But the main way it steals is through inflation. You're making money. You're working hard. You're investing. You're earning some dividends. You're earning some interest. Your earnings are all in money, but the money loses value because of inflation. That's why governments steal your money—because they are the debtors, and they owe money. When money loses value, its debt goes down. I don't know why people think it's okay for the Feds to target 2 percent inflation, but they do. Maybe this sounds low enough—not too horrible—and people don't really understand quite what's going on.

That's the setup. But where's the inflation? The Fed has been trying to get inflation for seven years, and it hasn't been able to do it. Depending on the measure you want to use, there's maybe 1 to 1.5 percent inflation, but it says it wants 2. It really wants 2.5 to 3, but whatever the target is, it's not getting the inflation it needs.

Why not? There are a couple of problems. One is structural, meaning that governments are standing in the way of growth with high taxes, excessive debt and over-regulation. There's a long list of things. Japan needs more immigration, but the government's not allowing it. The country needs better outcomes for women. In the United States, we need fewer regulations and lower taxes. We're not making that happen. Europe needs greater labor mobility. It's not encouraging that—a little bit, but not much. You can go around the world and come up with a long list of structural impediments to growth.

The other problem, and it's a huge one, is demographic. People are not having kids. Populations are aging and in some places declining. China's population has flatlined. Japan's is going down. Russia's is going down. The only reason the population in the United States is going up is immigration—not births, at least not U.S. births.

Economists debate whether the structural problems just mentioned, some demographic and some policy-driven, are permanent. The old world of 3 to 4 percent growth is gone, some say, and we're in a new world of 2 percent growth. We should just get over it. I don't agree with these economists. We're entirely capable of 3 to 3.5 percent growth. If we're not going to get it through population growth, we can get it through productivity growth. The way to improve productivity is with some of the policy changes I mentioned. Whether the slowdown in growth is permanent or temporary, and whether it's structural or something that can be fixed, everyone agrees that there's not enough growth—that there's a problem.

Where is the inflation supposed to come from? A lot of people assume that to get inflation, you just print money. That's what Milton Friedman said, and that's what the Austrians said. It doesn't work that way. Printing money by itself does not cause inflation. You need people to do something with the money. They need to borrow it and spend it or invest it. You need banks to lend it or invest it. That money can't just sit there.

Printing money is half of what you need to get inflation. The other half is lending and spending: increasing leverage, creating credit, borrowing and so on. But it's not happening because corporations or other decision-makers are still frightened and still licking their wounds from the meltdown of 2008. When people get money, they aren't going out and spending it. They're saving it or paying down debt, so we're still going through a debt-deleveraging cycle.

We see the best evidence of that if we go back to the fall of 2014. That's when oil prices climbed. The oil-price decline really started in the summer of 2014. It accelerated in the fall of 2014—November 2014, in particular. It chugged along with some volatility through most of 2015, and in late 2015 it had another spike down—from around $45 to near $30. Economists at that time said, "This is great news because with the lower price of oil, the price of gasoline at the tank is going down. People use, say, 50 gallons a week in their SUVs, and gas is down $1.00 a gallon. That's $50 in their pocket a week, $2,500 a year. They'll go spend it. Retail sales will go up. Happy days are here again."

That turned out to be completely wrong. The price did go down at the pump. People did get more money in their pockets. But they didn't spend it. As I said, they paid off debt or stuck the money in the bank. The transmission mechanism running between putting money in people's pockets and people going out and spending it is broken.

The breakdown is psychological. That's not something the Fed can do anything about. It can print all the money it wants, but it can't actually make people spend it if they're not in the mood. That's why QE1, QE2 and QE3 have all failed. That's why the Fed's expansion of its balance sheet from $800 billion in 2008 to $4.4 trillion today has not done the trick—all the Fed did was give the money out to the banks, but the banks didn't do anything with it, and people didn't spend it, so we never got the inflation machine going.

That was one policy failure. The other way to get inflation is through currency wars, by cheapening your currency. You cheapen your currency, and that makes the price of imports go up. Right? Everyone thinks it makes exports cheaper for foreign buyers and helps exports. It might. It does that a little bit.

But the real reason policy makers cheapen their currency is not just to increase exports—it's to import inflation.

The United States runs a trade deficit. We buy more from other countries than we sell them. If you cheapen the dollar, the cost of everything we buy goes up. But the dollar's been getting stronger since 2011, and so the price of stuff we buy is actually going down. If you take a Swiss vacation, or buy a German car, French wine, Chinese manufactured goods, Indian textiles or iPhones, you'll find that prices generally have been going down because the dollar's been getting stronger. Devaluation hasn't worked. Other countries have tried it too.

Japan tried it by cheapening the yen in 2013, Europe tried it by cheapening the euro in 2015, and the United States tried it by cheapening the dollar in 2011. China tried it in 2009, and it's trying it again today. Everybody's trying it. The problem with currency wars is that they're a zero-sum game. If one currency goes down, by definition another currency goes up. Currencies are just cross rates: so many euros to the dollar, so many yuan to the dollar, or so many dollars to the yen. One country can get a little, temporary bump by cheapening its currency, but the bump doesn't last because others strike back—they cheapen their currencies, and you're back where you started except you've created economic inefficiency along the way. Currency wars don't work in the long run. They don't work for the world as a whole because at best all you're doing is stealing growth from your trading partners. They don't even work for the de-valuing country because any benefit is only temporary.

Money creation has not worked. Currency wars have not worked. We're starting to run out of ways to create inflation. The elites want inflation because that's the only way out of a debt problem.

Is there any guaranteed way to get inflation? Can we just look at one thing and say, "You know what? This will do it. This will get us the inflation"? Yes, and that thing is helicopter money. Helicopter money is coming because it's necessary for the reasons I've described. Everything else has failed. It's the only thing left, so the elites are going to turn to it.

What's the difference between quantitative easing and helicopter money?

The way quantitative easing works is that the central banks—I'll use the Fed as an example—print money. What do we mean by "print money"? The Fed doesn't, of course, actually print money. The money is digital. Yes, the Bureau of Engraving prints some $100 bills and $20 bills, and they're floating around. But that's not most of the money supply. Most of the money supply is digital. "Printing money" is just a metaphor for "creating money."

How do central banks actually create money? The Federal Reserve Bank is a bank operating through 12 regional banks, the main one being the Federal Reserve Bank of New York. Fed officials pick up the phone, call a dealer like Goldman Sachs, Morgan Stanley or Bank of America, and buy Treasury debt— 10-year notes, 5-year notes, 2-year notes or whatever else. They don't get the debt for free.

When the Fed pays for the debt, the money comes from nowhere. It just pushes a button and Goldman Sachs delivers it a 10-year note, and the Fed credits Goldman Sachs' account. So now there's money in the Goldman Sachs account. That money comes out of thin air. That's how the Fed creates money.

The opposite is true for destroying money. When the Fed wants to reduce the money supply, it sells bonds to Goldman Sachs; Goldman Sachs pays the Fed, and the money disappears.

That's how the Fed creates money or destroys money by buying and selling bonds, and that's how QE works. So we've just increased the basic money supply at zero. What does Goldman Sachs do with the money? It gives it back to the Fed because the Fed's a bank.

You can open a bank account at the Fed—or rather,

Goldman Sachs can. Goldman Sachs gives the money back to the Fed as a deposit, the same way you would take money and stick it in the bank. Every bank is required to have a certain level of reserves at the Fed. You can deposit more reserves than the Fed's required amount—they're called excess reserves. So the Fed buys the bonds from Goldman with the money that comes from thin air. Goldman takes the money and deposits it at the Fed in the form of excess reserves. The Fed pays Goldman interest, which is just a way to pass money on to Goldman. That's quantitative easing. It does increase the money supply. But what good does it do? Is that money being spent? Is anybody borrowing? Is Goldman Sachs giving it to you? It's not.

I'm talking about Goldman Sachs, but it could be Citibank or Bank of America. They also are not giving you the money. If all the banks are taking the money from the Fed and giving it back to the Fed and not lending it, and no one's borrowing, and no one's spending, how is that increasing inflation or velocity? The answer is it's not. In theory, the money's there. Any bank with excess reserves at the Fed could take those excess reserves and use them as a base for lending lots of money. It could, but it doesn't. So the whole thing is not working. The transmission mechanism is broken. That's quantitative easing.

For helicopter money, you have to combine the forces of central banks and the fiscal authority. The fiscal authority is Congress or a parliament or any legislature that can pass laws and spend money. This takes us all the way back to the Great Depression and John Maynard Keynes. Keynes' great insight in the late 1920s and early 1930s was to say, "We need to spend money to get the economy moving." I spend money. What am I spending it on? If I go to a gas station, someone's got to run the gas station. If I buy a piece of furniture, someone's got to build the furniture. If I buy some clothing, someone's got to make that clothing. If I go to a restaurant, someone's got to cook the meal and serve it. And so on and so on.

If I start spending money, then I'm creating work for somebody else. Or maybe someone spends money and creates work for me. However it is, that's how you get the economy moving. What Keynes said was that if people won't spend the money, the government can. Make the government spend the money, and that way we'll get the economy moving again. That was Keynesianism 101. How does the government spend money? Governments are really good at spending money. They have increased the deficit in the past; all they have to do is increase it more. Now, wait a second. Originally, I said the problem was that government deficits are too high and the debt is growing faster than inflation and the economy. Now I'm saying, "The answer is to spend more."

It sounds a little crazy, but believe me, this is what economists think. They say, "Oh, you think too much debt is a problem—that there's not enough growth? Then we need to get more growth. How do we get the growth? Let's spend more. Let's make the deficits bigger." This is how the elites think about it. Force the spending. Instead of relying on individual consumers to go on a spending spree, the government's going to do it for them. Of course, it'll spend the money on what it likes. In the case of the Democrats, that's probably community organizers and teachers' unions. In the case of the Republicans, it's probably defense contractors. Everybody's got their wish list. In December 2015, when Paul Ryan pushed a budget-reconciliation bill through Congress, and the Senate passed it, and the White House signed it, it was like a big love-in in Washington.

After six years of fighting and not talking to each other, they all agreed to bust the budget caps. They went on a spending spree. What's not to like about politicians spending money in an election year? So, the deficit went up. The deficit is covered by borrowing money. That's what the Treasury does. The Fed printed the money and bought the bonds the Treasury issued for the loan. We're back to money printing.

In QE, the Fed printed the money by buying existing bonds and gave it to the banks, and the banks just kept it. Nothing else happened. But with helicopter money, Congress spends the money, covers the deficit by borrowing and the Fed prints the money to cover the borrowing. The Fed monetizes the debt. Helicopter money is debt monetization. In the case of QE, there was no extra spending. In the case of debt monetization, there is extra spending because the fiscal authority, Congress, went out and spent a bunch of money. That's where we are. We need more inflation to get nominal growth to pay off nominal debt. We're not getting real growth because of all the structural impediments and the dominant trends in demographics, technology and elsewhere. So we need nominal growth. You get that through inflation. QE1, QE2 and QE3 were failures, but there's one thing that always works—helicopter money. Helicopter money is about Congress incurring bigger deficits and borrowing, and central banks monetizing the debt.

That's the game plan. This is coming. It will work. Not right away, not in six months and maybe even not before late this year, but this will work. If you do it long enough and strong enough, you will actually get the inflation you want. However, short-term forecasts show more of the same. We're stuck in a deflation trap right now. You see it in the price of commodities. You see it in the global slowdown. The world is definitely heading toward a recession. The United States is almost certainly heading toward a recession. Of course, the official bureau that declares recessions— the National Bureau of Economic Research, in Cambridge, Massachusetts—doesn't actually declare them until they're over. Probably they'll say in early 2017, "The recession started in January 2016."

We need inflation. At time of writing, deflation is winning. But sooner rather than later, inflation will start to win. And what I try to do in *Strategic Intelligence* is help you understand the tug-of-war dynamic, keep you informed and give you port-folio suggestions so you can win either way.

How High Could Inflation Get?

In the last 50 years, inflation in the United States went as high as 13 percent. But let's say it didn't get that high. Instead, let's say it got to 9 percent.

Nine percent inflation will cut the value of the dollar in half in about eight years. Eight years is not a long time. If you've got three children and they're heading off to college, the time from when the first one goes till when the last one finishes is probably eight or nine years.

What does that do to your retirement income, your insurance policies, your annuities and your savings?

It cuts them in half. It potentially cuts your retirement in half. That's something to be concerned about.

Now, inflation might not stop at 9 percent. Or it could go to 10 or 12 percent. As I mentioned, we saw 13 percent inflation in 1980, so it's not impossible. That's in the lifetime of many Americans. They probably remember that.

Of course, hyperinflation in a modern industrialized nation is something much more extreme. Everyone talks about Zimbabwe in recent years or nationalist China in 1949.

But Germany was not Zimbabwe. Germany was the third-largest economy in the world in 1929, and a major industrial power and exporter, yet it had hyperinflation. It was the result of bad policy and psychology taking over. Hyperinflation usually starts out with bad policy, but once people realize what's going on, they'll do the rest. They dump the money as fast as they can.

You know what happened during the Weimer hyperinflation? People were getting paid twice a day—not once a month or twice a month or once a week.

They would break for lunch and the wives would come out

to meet the husbands at the factory gate. The husbands would get paid in stacks of notes, which had been brought over from the bank in a car or a wheelbarrow.

Then the wives would run right out and buy a ham, a bottle of wine, a stick of butter or whatever they needed for that day. Then they'd do the same thing again at the end of the day when the husband got another stack of notes.

Of course, by 5:00 p.m. the price had probably doubled since lunchtime. However, if you got the ham you didn't care if the price had doubled, quadrupled or gone up a billion times. Think about the ham as a hard asset. I think of a bar of gold the same way.

Once you dump the dollars or whatever currency and get the hard asset, you're protected. You don't really care. You might care, but the fact that the money is going to zero as it hyperinflates doesn't hurt you anymore because you've got the hard asset. In the case of a family trying to get through the day, that ham might have been dinner. Then perhaps they would go out later that night and buy a loaf of bread for the next morning. That's how bad it was.

People treat money like it's radioactive during a hyperinflation. You get some money in a paycheck, but you don't want it. You want to dump it as fast as you can. And when you give it to the guy who sells me the ham, he dumps it immediately too. He pays the wholesaler. In a hyperinflation, money's like a hot potato. You want to get rid of it.

The velocity pushes infinity, which means the currency approaches zero. That's the psychology behind it. So it's not all about money printing. It's about changing the psychology. Now, you need the money to get hyperinflation. You can run out of money. That's happened from time to time, but it's the combination of the two that matters. It's the printing of money by the central bank and the change in the psychology of the people that can cause hyperinflation.

Today, we have the money printing—more than $4 trillion. The psychology hasn't changed, but psychology and confidence are fragile things.

They can change quickly. And when they do, it's very hard to change them back. You need to be prepared for that.

We don't have much inflation today. That's a fact. And there's no sense arguing we do. The data says otherwise. But it could return suddenly, and that's the reason to have some hard assets. Don't go all in or 50 percent, but have a slice of your portfolio in hard assets. That's your insurance policy.

Getting the Timing Right

A lot of analysts, since 2008, have been saying, "The next crisis is right around the corner. We're going to have hyperinflation. Buy gold. Get ready now."

Many people have bought into that narrative and have been disappointed. They say, "Wait a second. We don't really see much inflation. In fact, deflation appears to be more of a danger in recent times. Oil's down. Gold's down. Commodities are down." At some point, the narrative loses its credibility.

Here's what I say to confused investors: Inflation, much higher inflation, is a danger. But so is deflation.

So, again, my advice for investors is to be prepared for both. The investor who's doing this is Warren Buffett.

Warren Buffett's not only buying hard assets, he also has $55 billion in cash. The hard assets are his inflation insurance. The cash is his deflation insurance.

It's a lesson not to put all of your bets on one side of the table. My advice is to have some inflation protection. Have some wealth in hard assets, whether gold, energy stocks, silver, land or fine art. But don't go all in—make that a slice. If the hyperinflation, or even just extreme inflation, comes faster than we expect, that's going to preserve your net worth.

On the other side, however, have some deflation protection. That could include bonds, fixed income and cash.

When I recommend cash to investors, a lot of them reply, "I hate cash. It has no yield. It just sits there. It's not sexy or interesting."

They don't understand what cash does. The first thing cash does is it takes the volatility out of the rest of your portfolio. If stocks, gold and commodities have been volatile, having cash reduces their impact. It's a little bit technical, but that's what it does. It helps you sleep a little bit better at night.

Cash is also a great deflation hedge. Remember, during deflation the value of cash goes up. It doesn't deliver a high yield, but in real terms, it's becoming more valuable every day.

The third thing cash offers you is the ability to pivot. You might not be in cash forever, but you should consider having some now.

That way, you're ready for anything. If deflation takes off, you're glad you have bonds.

If inflation takes off, you're glad you got the gold and other hard assets.

And, if there's confusion, you're glad you have the cash because it reduces your volatility and lets you pick up bargains.

If the market crashes and you have equities in one part of your portfolio, you might lose on that. But then, you'll have cash and can go buy bargains. That's the way the smartest investors do it. They're ready for anything.

▓ Hugo Stinnes: The Inflation King

Hugo Stinnes is practically unknown today, but this was not always the case. In the early 1920s, he was the wealthiest man in Germany, at a time when the country was the world's third-largest economy.

He was a prominent industrialist and investor with diverse

holdings in Germany and abroad. Chancellors and cabinet ministers of the newly formed Weimar Republic routinely sought his advice on economic and political problems.

In many ways, Stinnes played a role in Germany similar to the role Warren Buffett plays in the United States today. He was an ultrawealthy investor whose opinion was eagerly sought on important political matters, who exercised powerful behind-the-scenes influence and who seemed to make all the right moves when it came to playing markets.

If you're a student of economic history, you know that from 1922 to 1923 Germany suffered the worst hyperinflation experienced by a major industrial economy in modern times. As I explained above, the exchange rate between the German paper currency, the reichsmark, and the dollar went from 208 to 1 in early 1921 to 4.2 *trillion* to 1 in late 1923. At that point, the reichsmark became worthless and was swept down sewers as litter.

Yet Stinnes was not wiped out during this hyperinflation. Why was that?

Stinnes was born in 1870 into a prosperous German family that had interests in coal mining. He worked in mines to obtain a practical working knowledge of the industry and took courses in Berlin at the Academy of Mining. Later, he inherited his family's business and expanded it by buying his own mines.

Then he diversified into shipping, buying cargo lines. His own vessels were used to transport his coal within Germany along the Rhine River and from his mines abroad. His vessels also carried lumber and grains. His diversification included ownership of a leading newspaper, which he used to exert political influence. Prior to the Weimar hyperinflation, Stinnes borrowed vast sums of money in reichsmarks.

When the hyperinflation hit, Stinnes was perfectly positioned. The coal, steel and shipping retained their value. It didn't matter what happened to the German currency—a hard asset is still a hard asset and does not go away even if the currency goes to zero.

Stinnes' international holdings also served him well because they produced profits in hard currencies, not worthless reichsmarks. Some of these profits were kept offshore in the form of gold held in Swiss vaults. That way he could escape both hyperinflation and German taxation. Finally, he repaid his debts in worthless reichsmarks, making them disappear.

Not only was Stinnes not harmed by the Weimar hyperinflation, but his empire prospered and he made more money than ever. He expanded his holdings and bought out bankrupt competitors. Stinnes made so much money during the Weimar hyperinflation that his German nickname was *Inflationskönig*, which means Inflation King. When the dust settled and Germany returned to a new gold-backed currency, Stinnes was one of the richest men in the world, while the German middle classes were destroyed.

Interestingly, you see Warren Buffett using the same techniques today. It appears that Buffett has studied Stinnes carefully and is preparing for the same calamity that Stinnes saw—hyperinflation.

Buffett purchased major transportation assets in the form of the Burlington Northern Santa Fe Railroad in November 2009. This railroad consists of hard assets in the form of rights of way, adjacent mining rights, rails and rolling stock. The railroad makes money moving hard assets such as ore and grains.

Buffett next purchased huge oil and natural gas assets in Canada in the form of Suncor (SU:NYSE). Buffett can now move his Suncor oil on his Burlington Northern railroad in exactly the same way that Stinnes moved his coal on his own ships in 1923. Buffett is also a major holder in Exxon Mobil, the largest energy company in the world.

For decades, Buffett owned one of the most powerful newspapers in the United States: *The Washington Post.* He sold that stake in 2014 to Jeff Bezos of Amazon, but still retains communications assets. He's also purchased large offshore assets in China and elsewhere that produce nondollar profits that can be retained offshore tax-free.

A huge part of Buffett's portfolio is in financial stocks—particularly in banks and insurance companies—that are highly leveraged borrowers. Like Stinnes in the 1920s, Buffett can profit when the liabilities of these financial giants are wiped out by inflation, while they nimbly redeploy assets to hedge their own exposures.

In short, Buffett is borrowing from the Stinnes playbook. He's using leverage to diversify into hard assets in energy and transportation and into foreign currencies. He's using his communications assets and prestige to stay informed on behind-the-scenes developments on the political landscape. Buffett is now positioned in much the same way that Stinnes was positioned in 1922.

If hyperinflation were to slam the United States today, Buffett's results would be the same as Stinnes'. His hard assets would explode in value, his debts would be eliminated and he would be in a position to buy out bankrupt competitors. Of course, the middle classes in the United States would be wiped out, as they were in Germany.

My advice to you when it comes to billionaires like Buffett is to watch what they do, not what they say. Stinnes saw the German hyperinflation coming and positioned himself accordingly. Buffett is following the Stinnes playbook. Perhaps Buffett sees the same hyperinflation in our future. It's not too late for you to take some of the same precautions as Stinnes and Buffett.

Should You Be Borrowing Money?

A common question I get from readers is, "Should I be borrowing money, given the threat of hyperinflation?"

My answer is that if you have a legitimate reason to borrow, such as to finance a house or something like that, and you can afford it without being overleveraged, that's fine.

But I would not advise you to go out and borrow a lot of money right now to lever up. That strategy only works if we do, in fact, experience inflation. The trouble is that the inflation might not come right away. We might be faced with deflation. That's why I recommend having a balance of hard assets and cash.

When I say cash, I'm not talking about money market funds or bank CDs. Instead, I mean the highest-quality instruments you can get. If you're a U.S. investor, that would be U.S. Treasury bills or one-year notes.

Then get hard assets to protect you from inflation. The cash protects you in deflation and reduces volatility. It's hard to know which one we're in for, so you should prepare for both.

CHAPTER 4
The Threat of Deflation

▨ A Central Banker's Worst Nightmare

From a mathematical perspective, inflation and deflation are two sides of the same coin. Inflation is a period of generally rising prices. Deflation is a period of generally falling prices. Both are deviations from true price stability, and both distort the decisions of consumers and investors.

In inflation, consumers may accelerate purchases before the price goes up. In deflation, consumers may delay purchases in the expectation that prices are going down and things will be cheaper if they wait.

To investors, inflation and deflation are bad in equal, if opposite, measure. But, from a central banker's perspective, inflation and deflation are not equally bad. Inflation is something that central bankers consider to be a manageable problem and something that is occasionally desirable. Deflation is something central bankers consider unmanageable and potentially devastating. Understanding why central banks fear deflation more than inflation is the key to understanding central bank monetary policy today.

Central bankers believe they can control inflation by tightening monetary policy. Generally, monetary policy is tightened by raising interest rates. Since rates can be raised to infinity, there is not a limit on this tool. Therefore, no matter how strong inflation is, central banks can always tame it with more rate increases.

The classic case is Paul Volcker in 1980, who raised interest rates to 20 percent to crush inflation that had reached 13 percent. Central bankers feel that if the inflation genie escapes from the bottle, they can always coax it back in.

Central bankers also believe that inflation can be good for an economy. This is because of something called the marginal propensity to consume, or MPC, which I've mentioned above. The MPC is a measure of how much an individual will spend out of an added dollar of income. The idea is that if you give a poor person a dollar they will spend all of it because they struggle to pay for food, housing and health care. If you give a rich person a dollar, they will spend very little of it because their needs are already taken care of, so they are more likely to save or invest that dollar. Based on this, poorer people have a higher MPC.

Inflation can be understood as a wealth transfer from the rich to the poor. For the rich person, his savings are worth less, and his spending is about the same because he has a low MPC. By contrast, the poor person has no savings and may have debts that are reduced in real value during inflation. Poor people may also get wage increases in inflation, which they spend because of their higher MPC.

Therefore, inflation tends to increase total consumption because the wealth transfer from rich to poor increases the spending of the poor but does not decrease spending by the rich, who still buy whatever they want. The result is higher total spending, or aggregate demand, which helps the economy grow.

Deflation is not so benign and hurts the government in many ways. It increases the real value of the national debt, making it harder to finance. Deficits continue to pile up even in deflation, but GDP growth may slow down when measured in nominal dollars. The result is that the debt-to-GDP ratio can skyrocket in periods of deflation. Something like this has been happening in Japan for decades. When the debt-to-GDP ratio gets too high, a sovereign-debt crisis and collapse of confidence in the currency can result.

Deflation also destroys government tax collections. If a worker makes $100,000 per year and gets a $10,000 raise when prices are constant, that worker has a 10 percent increase in her standard of living. The problem is that the government takes $3,000 of the increase in taxes, so the worker only gets $7,000 of the raise after taxes.

But if the worker gets no raise, and prices drop 10 percent, she still has a 10 percent increase in her standard of living because everything she buys costs less. But now she keeps the entire gain because the government has no way to tax the benefits of deflation. In both cases, the worker has a $10,000 increase in her standard of living, but in inflation the government takes $3,000, while in deflation the government gets none of the gain.

For all of these reasons, governments favor inflation. It can increase consumption, decrease the value of government debt and increase tax collections. Governments fear deflation because it causes people to save, not spend; it increases the burden of government debt; and it hurts tax collections.

But what is good for government is often bad for investors. In deflation, investors can actually benefit from lower costs, lower taxes and an increase in the real value of savings. As a rule, inflation is good for government and bad for savers, while deflation is bad for government and good for savers.

There are many flaws in the way the government and economists think about inflation and deflation. The idea of MPC as a guide to economic growth is highly flawed. Even if poor people have a higher propensity to consume than rich people, there is more to economic growth than consumption. The real driver of long-term growth is not consumption, but investment. While inflation may help drive consumption, it destroys capital formation and hurts investment. A policy of favoring inflation over deflation may prompt consumption growth in the short run, but it retards investment-led growth in the long run. Inflation is a case of a farmer eating his own seed-corn in the winter and having nothing left to plant in the spring. Later he will starve.

It is also not true that inflation is easy to control. Up to a certain point, inflation can be contained by interest rate increases, but the costs may be high, and the damage may already be done. Beyond that threshold, inflation can turn into hyperinflation. At that point, no amount of interest rate increases can stop the headlong dash to dump money and acquire hard assets such as gold, land and natural resources. Hyperinflation is almost never brought under control. The typical outcome is to wipe out the existing currency system and start over after savings and retirement promises have been destroyed.

In a better world, central bankers would aim for true price stability that does not involve inflation or deflation. But given the flawed economic beliefs and government priorities described above, that is not the case. Central banks favor inflation over deflation because it increases tax collections, reduces the burden of government debt and gooses consumption. If savers and investors are the losers, that's just too bad.

The implications of this asymmetry are profound. In a period where deflationary forces are strong, such as the one we are now experiencing, central banks have to use every trick at their disposal to stop deflation and cause inflation. If one trick does not work, they must try another.

Since 2008 central banks have used interest rate cuts, quantitative easing, forward guidance, currency wars, nominal GDP targets, and Operation Twist to cause inflation. None of it has worked; deflation is still a strong tendency in the global economy. This is unlikely to change. The deflationary forces are not going away soon. Investors should expect more monetary experiments in the years ahead. A fourth round of quantitative easing, so-called "QE4," perhaps in 2017, cannot be ruled out. If deflation is strong enough, central banks may even encourage an increase in the price of gold by 2017 to raise inflationary expectations.

Eventually the central banks will win and they will get the inflation they want. But it may take time, and the inflation may turn into hyperinflation in ways the central banks do not expect or understand. This tug-of-war between inflation and deflation creates the most challenging investment climate in 80 years.

The best investment strategies involve a balanced portfolio of hard assets and cash so investors can be ready for both. These strategies are the focus of our research and will be highlighted in *Strategic Intelligence* in the months ahead.

Deflation's Winning the Tug-of-War

Deflation is one of the most confusing issues for investors today.

To illustrate the point at a speech I gave once, I asked a simple question: "Will anyone in the audience who is 90 years old please raise their hand?"

As I expected, no one did.

My point was simple and relevant to your investments today: You'd have to be at least 90 years old to have any recollection of deflation in the United States. There hasn't been a sustained deflation here since the stretch from 1927 to 1933. Even if you were alive then, you were probably about five years old.

The main fear for the last few decades or more has been inflation, as the Fed continually prints money. And as we discussed, that threat is very real, so you have to prepare. But the battle between inflation and deflation is not a short-term one.

After months or even years, either force can prevail, which

is why it's imperative you be prepared for either outcome. Then, you watch for signposts along the way that will help you decide which force is more likely. Our portfolio is ready for either outcome, but we've promised to monitor which force is winning in the meantime.

As of early 2016, I believe deflation is winning in the short run, while inflation will prevail in the long run.

Both inflation and deflation are challenging to investors who have to guess future returns based on changes in price indexes in addition to navigating the normal business risks of an investment. In short, both inflation and deflation make your economic decisions more difficult by adding a wildcard to the deck.

Inflation favors the debtor because the real value of his debts goes down as money becomes worth less. Deflation favors the creditor because the real value of amounts owed to him goes up as money becomes worth more.

But if you take the time to understand the phenomenon, you can profit handsomely from it while others are scratching their head.

"You Can't Always Get What You Want"

It's natural that we have deflation today because we're in a depression. But there are powers at work to make sure nature doesn't take its course.

Mick Jagger famously sang, "You can't always get what you want." This is exactly the situation facing central banks today. They want inflation and can't get it. This is highly unusual. If a central bank, such as the Federal Reserve, wants inflation, it can typically lower interest rates and print money, and the inflation is sure to follow (with a slight lag).

But the Fed has been pursuing these policies for the past seven years, and inflation is nowhere in sight. The reason is that the Fed's efforts have been blunted by a strong deflationary force, the strongest in 80 years. This deflationary force will not abate soon.

The Fed has announced an inflation target of 2 percent, although in December 2012, it said a short-term goal of 2.5 percent for expected inflation was reasonable. Privately, I was told by Charles Evans, president of the Federal Reserve Bank of Chicago, that he wouldn't mind seeing 3.5 percent inflation for a short period of time.

Evans is now an alternate voting member of the Federal Open Market Committee, the group that sets Fed policy, so his views count. But whether they target 2, 2.5 or 3.5 percent, the fact is that inflation as measured by the Fed has been about 1 percent—well below the Fed's targets. The Fed has tried rate cuts, quantitative easing, forward guidance, currency wars and Operation Twist over the past five years, and none of it has worked. Mick Jagger was right.

The reasons the Fed wants inflation are straightforward. There is a stated reason and an unstated reason. The stated reason is that the Fed occasionally needs to cut rates to stimulate the economy. If rates are at zero, there's nothing to cut.

If you have 2 percent inflation, you can have normalized interest rates of 2.5 percent or higher. This gives the Fed something to cut when needed. This rationale is like someone saying they will steal your money so they can lend it back to you later, but the Fed hopes that 2 percent is low enough that investors won't notice the theft.

The unstated reason is that inflation reduces the real value of the U.S. debt. Right now, the United States has about $19 trillion of Treasury debt outstanding and the highest debt-to-GDP ratio since the end of the Second World War. With the economy near stalling, the United States is moving closer to a sovereign-debt crisis every day.

If the Fed can achieve, say, 3 percent inflation for about 20 years, the real value of the debt is cut in half, to about $9 trillion in today's dollars. The trick is to keep interest rates low while inflation does its dirty work. The Fed can do this through financial repression, bank regulation and quantitative easing. Of course, inflation of this slow, steady kind is a form of unseen theft of investors, but that's their problem. The Fed's job is to make the debt melt away, and inflation is the key.

As I said, since 2008, central banks have used interest rate cuts, quantitative easing, forward guidance, currency wars, nominal GDP targets, and Operation Twist to cause inflation. None of it has worked.

But don't think that will discourage them. You should expect more monetary experiments in the years ahead.

The world is not cooperating with the Fed's master plan. We are in a global depression, and the natural consequence of depression is deleveraging and deflation. Businesses in distress sell assets at fire sale prices.

This drives the price down and puts other businesses in distress, which then also sell assets to survive and so on. This is the famous debt-deflation theory of depression written about by economist Irving Fisher in the 1930s. That dynamic has now returned with a vengeance.

■ The Difference Between "Good" and "Bad" Deflation

We also live in a world of rapidly advancing technology, which is also deflationary because of improvements in efficiency. Larry Page, the cofounder of Google, gave an interview to *The Financial Times* in which he said, "Even if there's going to be a disruption on people's jobs, in the short term, that's likely to be made up by the decreasing cost of things we need, which I think is really important and not being talked about.... I think the things you want to live a comfortable life could get much, much, much cheaper."

The Google CEO told *The Financial Times* that the average price of a home in Silicon Valley today is $1 million, but he sees no reason why it couldn't be $50,000 in the future. That would be a 95 percent price decline, a form of hyperdeflation.

These insights of Irving Fisher and Larry Page highlight the fact that deflation comes in two forms: what writer James Grant has called "good deflation" and "bad deflation."

Good deflation is the type Larry Page envisions. It comes from technology, efficiency, investment and innovation. If we are getting more efficient through technology, things should cost less.

We see this in personal computers, which have dropped in price from $4,000 to $800 in recent years. This is also the kind of deflation that prevailed from 1870 to 1914, when innovations in railroads, radio, steamships, harvesters and many other fields led to strong consistent growth with low or declining prices. Today, we see good deflation coming not only from information technology, but also from fracking and other aspects of the energy revolution.

Bad deflation is the kind Irving Fisher wrote about in 1933. It prevailed from 1927 to 1933, when prices dropped over 30 percent. It is associated with asset sales, liquidations, bankruptcy, unemployment and declining output. Once this kind of deflation takes hold, consumers will stop spending because they expect lower prices in the future and prefer to wait. Cash becomes more valuable in deflation, so consumers don't mind sitting on cash. Bad deflation feeds on itself and is very difficult for central banks to reverse.

Today, investors and policy makers are faced with two challenges as a result. The first is that we are experiencing good deflation and bad deflation *at the same time*. The good deflation is coming from technology, and the bad deflation is coming from deleveraging. This double-whammy makes the deflation train almost impossible to stop. The second challenge is that the central banks *must cause inflation*. Without inflation, sovereign debts are impossible to service and the world will cascade into outright defaults.

This is extremely dangerous ground for your investments. On the one hand, you must be alert to deflation because it's the natural state of the world. On the other hand, you have to be prepared for inflation because central banks are out to cause it at any cost. We've already shown you how—and will continue to in the coming months.

The answer is to have a diversified portfolio with a selection of assets that will do well in all states of the world. We've written elsewhere about inflation hedges that include gold, land, fine art and hard-asset plays such as transportation, energy and natural resource stocks. For a deflation hedge, you should have cash or cash equivalents including high-quality money market funds. But there are potential problems with money market funds too.

▧ Money Market Reform Regulation

As I noted above, few people know about a regulation the SEC finalized in early August 2014. It allows money market funds to suspend redemptions under panic circumstances. That's always been true of hedge funds, but it was never before true of money market funds.

Money market funds are supposed to be as good as gold. You're supposed to be able to get your money back tomorrow if you want. This change means that during a crisis, you may call up your bank and say, "I'd like to redeem my money market fund."

And they'll say, "Hey, you and 10 million other people. We're suspending redemptions under a new SEC regulation. Didn't you see the brochure we slipped into an envelope a year ago?" You should be aware of the dangers to your money even in places conventionally thought of as safe.

CHAPTER 5
The Greatest Unwind in Economic History

The greatest unwind in modern economic history has begun in China, and the turmoil is only getting worse. For many investors, the fallout has been and will continue to be painful. But if you were and are properly positioned, I believe you can profit.

To do so, it's important to understand the dynamics in play. Bubbles have three consistent characteristics: they are easy to spot; they persist longer than most investors expect (that's why they're bubbles in the first place); and they end badly, with massive losses for investors who are still in at the top.

These three traits are related in terms of investor psychology and behavior. Even when investors see a bubble, they often cannot resist riding the wave, because they assume they'll be smart enough to get out at the right time. The fact that bubbles last longer than most analysts expect tends to validate this investor assumption. People waiting on the sidelines for bubbles to pop are routinely ridiculed by those reaping large gains as the bubble expands.

But in the end, the bubble profiteers tend to stay too long at the party and suffer massive losses, as bubble markets can easily lose 30 percent or more in a matter of months, sometimes weeks, as assets are dumped and investors head for the exits. Today, the greatest bubbles in modern economic history are in China.

China is at risk of seeing multiple markets in real estate, stocks, corporate loans and commodities all crash at once. Chinese growth statistics have been overstated for years. This is not because the officials lie, but because 45 percent of Chinese GDP is investment and much of that is wasted on white elephant infrastructure that will either never be used or produce scant gains in productivity.

Adjusted for waste, real Chinese GDP growth was more like 4.5 percent than the 6.9 percent claimed for 2015. Chinese growth is also slowing for other reasons having to do with demographics and declining marginal returns to factor inputs. Growth will no longer be sufficient to service the mountain of debt on which the growth was built.

The Chinese people have extremely high savings rates but limited choices as to how to invest their savings. China does not let its citizens buy foreign stocks, at least not in any big way, and one of the reasons you're seeing bubbles in Chinese stocks and saw the collapse of the Shanghai Stock Exchange Index late in the summer of 2014 is those investors are not allowed to buy foreign stocks. They're herded into Chinese real estate and Chinese stocks. That's why you see these bubbles in China.

Local banks pay almost nothing on savings accounts. This has forced Chinese savers into real estate, local stocks and so-called "wealth-management products." This has resulted in property and stock bubbles, which are just beginning to come down to Earth.

The WMPs seem safer because they are sold by banks and offer steady yields of 5 percent or more. But underneath, the WMP market is a giant Ponzi scheme. The WMPs may be sold by banks, but they are not guaranteed by the banks. The proceeds are diverted to wasted real estate projects and dubious loans to inefficient state-owned enterprises.

Chinese investors who try to cash in their WMPs receive proceeds not from profits on the loans but from new sales to new investors in an ever-expanding pool. This is the essence of a Ponzi scheme.

Almost all of the economic data coming from China lately shows that the greatest unwind in modern economic history has started. Rail and sea cargo shipments are declining, producer prices are crashing and loan growth has hit the wall.

Chinese officials see this house of cards collapsing but are still determined to prop it up as long as they can. Like central banks everywhere, the People's Bank of China is using easy money to reflate asset bubbles.

In November 2014, China cut interest rates for the first time in two years and was in the process of cutting them again in December 2015. On February 4, 2015, China cut its reserve requirements for banks, a technical move that allows banks to make more loans with the same amount of capital. Both of these moves are intended to ease credit conditions.

As I predicted in early 2015, China also joined the global currency wars raging in Europe and Japan. China devalued the yuan twice in August 2015 to try to help Chinese exports relative to competition from Japan, Korea and Taiwan. From 2012 to 2015, China was quiet in the currency wars while its Asian trading partners and competitors engaged in repeated devaluations. In August 2015, China had had enough and shot back.

China threw in the towel on pegging. They had pegged the dollar at about 6.2 yuan to 1 for the last couple of years. That was not a legal, hard, Bretton Woods–style peg, but the policy of the People's Bank of China. They did a shock devaluation, bounced it up to almost 6.3 to 1. It happened overnight, on August 10, 2015, and then it went down again to about 6.35 to 1.

I think we should expect further devaluation from China. Now the China devaluation trade is starting to look like the new Big Short. That's a reference to *The Big Short. The Big Short* is a book by Michael Lewis, and now it's a movie. If you haven't seen it, it's worth a look. It'll make you cry when you realize how corrupt the system is, but I don't want to give any spoilers.

But now people in China with local currency, with yuan, are looking at the Fed tightening, and they're looking at China easing. They're saying the fixed exchange rate between the two is not sustainable, so they're trying to get their money out. China is looking at enormous capital outflows. When I say "enormous," I'm talking over $600 billion in 2015. They're down a full trillion dollars from 2014 to 2015. One trillion dollars of hard currency has left China, but it's still going on. They lost another $100 billion in January 2016. At $100 billion a month, how long do they have to go until they're broke? The answer is that if you're doing it in a straight line, it's two years. But it's never a straight line because it actually feeds on itself. Every month that goes by another $100 billion goes out the door. Somebody says, "Wait a second. I don't want to be the last guy out. I'm going to get my money out too." So it actually accelerates. I would estimate that they'll be completely broke before the end of 2017. But this is China. They're not going to let that happen.

They can't raise rates because they'll sink their economy. They can't close the capital account because they've got to play nice with the IMF. Pegging the yuan would cause them to go broke, and that's not going to happen. Then what's left? There's only one thing left: they've got to devalue the currency.

Money may still be walking out the door, but it'll be less money than it was before because the local currency won't get them as many dollars. If someone says to the People's Bank, "Hey, give me some dollars," they're not going to get as many dollars. The capital outflow will slow down.

They might even do a shock devaluation, 10 percent in one day. And then they'll say, "Now we're going to peg at the new level." But, of course, massive, massive amounts of wealth have been wiped out overnight. That's the kind of thing that could cause the U.S. stock market to go down very, very rapidly, 5 percent or more in one day. That would start to look more like a panic, so let's not rule that out.

But if you're a U.S. investor and use dollars as a reference currency, China offers three ways to win. China has weak national fundamentals. Certain companies have weak sector fundamentals, especially those in financial services with large loan and investment portfolios. And the Chinese currency will weaken.

This means that a short position in the Chinese financial sector, including the purchase of put options, can produce profits from a slowing economy, cheapening currency and higher credit losses.

▓ A Bigger Bubble Than the United States

China, believe it or not, has a bigger credit bubble than the United States does. The United States has lots and lots of problems, and I could go on at length about them, but China is actually worse off. That may be because it hasn't experienced as many credit bubbles as we have.

China is coming out of 400 years of decline and decadence and 100 years of chaos starting with the Taiping Rebellion, all the way through the Boxer Rebellion and then the Manchu (Qing) Dynasty, the warlord period, the Japanese invasion, the Communist period and the Cultural Revolution. For 100 years, China has had something bad coming around the corner.

Their whole experience with panics and crises in markets is all very new. At least in the United States, if a crisis happens, there aren't too many people around who can say they haven't seen something like it before. Americans have seen crises many times before—especially recently.

China seems to be naïve about how bad their credit bubble can get. They're also certainly over-relying on the ability of party officials to keep a lid on it.

I remember when I was visiting the Chinese countryside, south of Nanjing, not too long ago. I witnessed the so-called ghost cities. I was with some Communist Party and provincial officials who were behind all of the construction. There was construction literally as far as the eye could see. The buildings were magnificent, but all empty.

I remember turning to the officials and saying, "This is all debt-financed and all empty. You have no revenue. So, how are you going to pay the debt?"

One of them replied, "Oh, we can't. But Beijing's going to bail us out." That's what he said. To them, a default wasn't a possibility.

What they don't understand is that Beijing has its own problems. When you look at its wealth-management products, shadow banking, real estate finance and crony capitalism, you realize the true problems China faces.

It's also suffering from flight capital—oligarchs taking all they can, like pigs at the trough, and then funneling it out to Vancouver, Australia and Park Avenue. All of this is happening on a massive scale. It has started to collapse.

China has not been anticipating this bust, and even if it had been, it doesn't know how to deal with it. The Chinese government is very slow at making decisions. U.S. policy makers are no better at seeing crises coming ahead of time. Once they show up at our doorstep, however, they are able to react quickly.

Query whether they had the right reaction, but Paulson, Geithner and Bernanke were up night and day for days on end, and patched the system together.

I've been through that. That's certainly what we did when LTCM collapsed. We were on the verge of destroying global markets, and we patched something together in five days. That involved 14 equity banks, 19 credit banks and untold trillions of dollars. Fast response time is a good American characteristic.

We have this can-do attitude: work around the clock and get the job done. In China, policy makers are just very slow. When a crisis really hits them hard, they may have the capacity to deal with it, but they don't have much experience and they're going to take their time.

That means that things will get a lot worse and maybe get away from them before they can put a lid on the crisis. That's when global contagion comes into play. China's great unwind has started, and I am watching it very closely.

CHAPTER 6
The Perfect Storm

As I predicted in the first edition of this book, the perfect financial storm was brewing in late 2014. Now, all of the components have entered into play. However, there is still time to not only sidestep the danger, but profit handsomely from it.

If you've ever read the book *The Perfect Storm* by Sebastian Junger or seen the film version starring George Clooney, you know that the perfect storm was not one storm but three: two Canadian fronts and the remnants of a hurricane from the south that all converged off the coast of New England. At the point of convergence, each storm amplified the effects of the other until, as portrayed in the film, a rogue wave 100 feet high sank the vessel *Andrea Gail*, resulting in the death of the crew.

Something similar is happening in financial markets today. Three head winds, any one of which would be challenging, have converged to create financial havoc. Some investments are safely in port and will survive the storm. Other investments are far out to sea and will suffer the effects of all three head winds. Those stocks at the point of convergence may be as helpless as the Andrea Gail when the storm intensifies. Investors buying long-dated put options on those stocks may have the most to gain.

The first storm is the continued currency wars. They have been ongoing since 2010, but the start of 2016 marks a more intense phase where beggar-thy-neighbor retaliation is happening daily. Any U.S. company with significant foreign earnings will see the value of those earnings reduced when translated into U.S. dollars as long as these competitive devaluations continue.

The second storm is the slowdown in energy production. Here the battle is being waged between Saudi Arabia and the frackers in North America. Saudi Arabia wants to maintain high production in the face of a global oil glut to force the frackers to stop drilling and even shut down some existing capacity. The cost of lifting oil from the ground in Saudi Arabia is less than $10 per barrel, whereas the cost of oil from fracking in North America averages over $70 per barrel. This is a war the frackers cannot win. The impact is already showing up in layoffs, cancelled orders for pipe and declining rig counts. The threat of bankruptcy is also real for many companies engaged in fracking. This damage will get worse.

The third storm is the slowdown in global growth generally. Japan and parts of Europe are technically in recessions. China is slowing rapidly. The U.S. growth engine seems to be slowing also, with GDP falling from 5 percent in the third quarter of 2014 to 2.6 percent in the fourth quarter of 2014, and with signs indicating even weaker growth ahead.

The question for you as an investor is, who is the *Andrea Gail* in this perfect-storm scenario? Is there a single company that has exposure to the oil patch and overseas earnings streams and that is geared for growth at a time when growth is slowing? Which companies are most exposed to all three converging fronts in this financial perfect storm?

Once you know that, positioning yourself to profit is a matter of getting the timing right and then buying the right put options.

Right now, my favorite hypothesis is that the world is facing a $2 trillion tsunami of bad debt coming from oil drilling, emerging markets and corporate junk bonds. This debt will not go bad until late 2016 and thereafter.

Even money-losing operations can keep up debt service for a while by using working capital and cash flow—at least until the cash runs out. Banks that hold some of the debt can also cover up the losses for a while with accounting games such as fiddling with what are called their loan-loss reserves. If I'm right, bank stocks may take a hit by late 2016 as these losses come home to roost.

Bad debts will be the cause of a decline in financial stocks. What effects am I looking out for to test the validity of my hypothesis? There are many.

For energy junk debt, we can look at rig counts in the oil patch and layoffs among energy-exploration companies. For emerging-market debt, we can look at the strong dollar and dwindling hard-currency reserves in countries like Russia, Turkey, Mexico and Brazil.

In short, we can work backward from these visible causes to test the validity of the original hypothesis. Right now, the idea that financial stocks will suffer due to write-offs looks like a good one.

▓ Bayes' Theorem

In my counterterrorism work for the CIA, we were constantly confronted with problems that could not be solved with the information available. That's the nature of intelligence work — you never have enough information.

After all, if you had all the information, you wouldn't need an intelligence service; a smart college kid could do the job. The reason you have intelligence analysts is to fill in the blanks and try to make sense of the puzzle even when a number of the pieces are missing.

The CIA is divided into two main branches — the clandestine service and the analytical branch. The clandestine service is the "collector." They recruit spies and gather information from hard-to-get places. The analytical branch takes the information provided by the collectors and tries to connect the dots and draw actionable conclusions to deliver to policymakers up to and including the president.

The same is true in financial analysis. You may have a lot of information, but you always need more. Some of the most important information is buried inside company management or the Federal Reserve boardroom and not easy to get to. As an investor, you can't afford to just throw up your hands. Guessing is usually a bad idea. You need an analytical method just as we do at the CIA.

One of the most powerful tools we use in the intelligence community goes by technical sounding names like "causal inference" or "inverse probability." These are methods based on a mathematical equation known as "Bayes' theorem."

Basically, you form a hypothesis based on experience, common sense and whatever data are available. Then you test the hypothesis not by what has happened before, but by what comes *after*.

Instead of reasoning from cause to effect, you reverse the process. You watch the effects to determine the cause. This will validate or invalidate the "cause" you have hypothesized.

Sometimes the effects contradict the hypothesis, in which case you modify or abandon it and adopt another. Often, the effects confirm the hypothesis, in which case you know you're on the right track and keep going.

Right now, my favorite hypothesis is that the world is facing a $2 trillion tsunami of bad debt coming from oil drilling, emerging markets and corporate junk bonds. This debt will not go bad until late 2016 and thereafter.

Even money-losing operations can keep up debt service for a while by using working capital and cash flow — at least until the cash runs out. Banks that hold some of the debt can also cover up the losses for a while with accounting games such as fiddling with what are called their loan loss reserves. If I'm right, bank stocks may take a hit by late 2016 as these losses come home to roost.

Using the language of Bayes' theorem, bad debts will be the "cause" of a decline in financial stocks. What "effects" am I looking out for to test the validity of my hypothesis? There are many.

For energy junk debt, we can look at rig counts in the oil patch and layoffs among energy exploration companies. For emerging-market debt, we can look at the strong dollar and dwindling hard currency reserves in countries like Russia, Turkey, Mexico and Brazil.

In short, we can work backward from these visible causes to test the validity of the original hypothesis. Right now, the idea that financial stocks will suffer due to write-offs by this time next year looks like a good one.

A Statistical Method That Five U.S. Presidents Have Relied On

As I mentioned above, one of the most powerful tools we use in the intelligence community goes by technical-sounding names like "causal inference" or "inverse probability." These are methods based on a mathematical equation known as Bayes' theorem.

I have also used Bayes' theorem to develop what I call the Kissinger Cross to profit from current geopolitical situations. The indicator is simple to use. When you see a Kissinger Cross flash for the first time on a specific investment, you buy. When you see a second Kissinger Cross flash on that same investment, you sell. If you'd like to see what it takes to start using my Kissinger Cross indicator, please call 1-866-361-7662 or visit **www.agorafinancial.info/KISSINGER**.

▪ Junk Bond Meltdown

Over the coming months, I believe we could see an economic meltdown at least six times the size of the 2007 subprime mortgage meltdown.

Circumstances lead me to believe it could play out like the meltdown I experienced in 1998 after Long-Term Capital Management failed.

This time, however, there will be several crucial differences that will leave investors and regulators unprepared.

To understand what market outcome is likely, we start with something we know and extrapolate from it.

In the national defense community, military commanders are known for fighting the last war. They study their prior failures in preparation for the next conflict. The problem is that each war inevitably involves new tactics for which they're completely unprepared.

The most famous case is the backward-looking Maginot Line in the 1930s.

In response to Germany's rapid advances in the First World War, France built a line of concrete and steel fortifications and obstacles on their border to buy time to mobilize if Germany tried to invade again.

Hitler made the Maginot Line irrelevant by outflanking it and invading France through neutral Belgium. The French were unprepared. A few weeks later, German forces occupied Paris.

The same mistake is made in financial circles. Financial regulators are no different than military commanders. They fight the last war. The last two global meltdowns, in 1998 and 2008, are cases in point.

In 1998, a financial panic almost destroyed global capital markets. It started in Thailand in June 1997 and then spread to Indonesia and Korea. By the summer of 1998, Russia had defaulted on its debt, and its currency collapsed. The resulting liquidity crisis caused massive losses at hedge fund Long-Term Capital Management.

I know about the losses because I was there. As LTCM's lead counsel, I was at every executive committee meeting during the height of the crisis that August and September. We were losing hundreds of millions of dollars per day. Total losses over the two-month span were almost $4 billion. But that wasn't the most dangerous part.

Our losses were trivial compared to the *$1 trillion* of derivatives trades we had on our books with the biggest Wall Street banks. If LTCM failed, those trillion dollars of trades would not have paid off and the Wall Street banks would have fallen like dominos. Global markets would have completely collapsed.

I negotiated a bailout with the leaders of the 14 biggest banks including Goldman Sachs, JPMorgan and Citibank. Eventually, we got $4 billion of new capital from Wall Street, the Federal Reserve cut interest rates and the situation stabilized. But it was a close call, something no one ever wanted to repeat.

It was a valuable lesson for me, because soon after, regulators set out to make hedge fund lending safer. They ordered banks to monitor their hedge fund exposures more closely, improve their legal documentation and require more collateral to secure the performance on open trades.

Regulators believed this would prevent the next crisis. When the Panic of 2008 hit, however, they were surprised that problems were not in hedge funds but in something new—subprime mortgages. The mortgage-market collapse quickly spun out of control and once again brought global capital markets to the brink of collapse.

After the 2008 debacle, regulators *again* set out to fight the last war. This is the setup for the crisis I'm forecasting. They made mortgage lending much safer by requiring larger down payments, better documentation, proof of income, proof of employment and higher credit scores before a home loan could be made. But once again, regulators today are fixing the last problem and totally ignoring the next one.

The next financial collapse, already on our radar screen, will not come from hedge funds or home mortgages. It will come from junk bonds, especially energy-related and emerging-market corporate debt.

The Financial Times estimated that the total amount of energy-related corporate debt issued from 2009 to 2014 for exploration and development is over *$5 trillion*. Meanwhile, the Bank for International Settlements estimated that the total amount of emerging-market dollar-denominated corporate debt is over *$9 trillion.*

Energy-sector debt has been called into question because of the collapse of oil prices. And emerging-market debt has been called into question because of a global growth slowdown, global deflation and the strong dollar.

The result is a $14 trillion pile of corporate debt that cannot possibly be repaid or rolled over under current economic conditions. Not all of this debt will default, but a lot of it will. Most of the energy-related debt was issued in the expectation that oil would remain in the $80 to $130 per barrel range.

Most of the emerging-market debt was issued with the expectation that the dollar would remain at its weak 2011 levels. Instead, at time of writing, oil is down and the dollar is up, which capsizes these expectations. The moves have been swift and dramatic.

If default rates are only 10 percent—a conservative assumption—this corporate-debt fiasco will be *six times larger than the subprime losses in 2007.* The world is looking at a debt catastrophe much larger than LTCM in 1998 and the mortgage market in 2008. Regulators are completely unprepared for this because they have been busy fighting the last war.

The good news for investors is that this fiasco will not happen overnight. It will take a year or two to play out. The panic of September 1998 started a year earlier, in Thailand in June 1997. The panic of September 2008 also started a year earlier, in August 2007, when CNBC commentator Jim Cramer screamed, "They know nothing!" on live television in reference to the Federal Reserve.

This junk-debt fiasco started in the summer of 2014 but will not reach its peak until 2016 or later. Even companies and countries with dim prospects often have enough cash on hand to make payments for a while before they actually default. In the meantime, you can profit.

The bond defaults have not happened yet, but the signs are already visible in the form of lower oil prices and the strong dollar. In intelligence analysis, we don't wait for disasters to happen. We look at today's information, what are called "indications and warnings," and use inferential techniques such as inverse probability to see the future.

The strong dollar is deflationary. If it persists, it means oil prices will likely remain low. This means much of the energy-sector debt cannot be paid off and will default. The defaults have not happened yet, but you can see them coming. There is still an opportunity for you to profit from the coming collapse in junk bonds, but the time to act is now.

▪ The Coming Bust

The drop in the price of oil from approximately $100 a barrel to the $40–$60 range roughly constitutes a 40 percent decline or more. That's extreme. Such a large drop has only happened in that short a period of time three times in the past 70 years.

Oil and other commodities are volatile, but don't think for one minute that this is a normal fluctuation. It's not. This would be like the equivalent, if you were talking about Dow points, of an 8,000-point drop. We're talking about extreme territory.

The question, of course, is, what are the implications of that?

Our job is to figure out what they are and figure out what that means for investors. This was a bit of a shock, and no one expected it, other than maybe a handful of people who were plotting it behind the scenes.

In the first edition of *The Big Drop*, I predicted the possibility of a floor around $60 per barrel.

In September 2015, oil was in the $50-$60 range and had

even gone below that level. I expect that movement in the $50–$60 range is still the essential tendency through the end of 2016.

A lot of investors tend to extrapolate from whatever is going on. Behavioral psychologists have a name for this. It's called "recency bias."

We tend to be overly influenced by whatever happened recently, and forget about the bigger picture. When the price of oil goes from $100 to $60, which as I said is extreme, people say: "Now it's going to go to $50, then it's going to go to $40 and then, soon after, to $30."

You can't rule anything out, but it does look as if oil is going to oscillate around the $50–$60 range. That's still a big deal and has caused and will continue to cause damage to junk bonds and a lot of other markets.

Why do I say $50–$60? It's not because I think I'm smarter than a lot of other analysts. And I don't have a crystal ball. But I did have the opportunity to speak to various people in the industry.

There are no guarantees, of course. I want to be clear about that. I suppose the price could go below $50–$60, but in 2015 it did settle around $50–$60.

I want to explain the reasons why, because I don't like to write things that have a categorical tone without providing the backup. This didn't just come out of the blue.

As I said in early 2015, Saudi Arabia is the marginal supplier. The Saudis can dial up the supply or dial it down. They're well-aware of what's going on in the rest of the world. They see the fracking and U.S. oil output.

They also see that the United States is now the world's largest energy producer and is close to becoming a net oil exporter. Yet even if we give the United States credit for being stronger than some of the other economies, there's no question about the global slowdown. Therefore, Saudi Arabia sees demand slowing down. It's something you learned the first day in economics: supply is up because of fracking technology, and the demand is down because of a slowing economy.

When supply is up and demand is down, you get lower prices. That's Econ 101. But the question is: how much lower and what do the Saudis want to do about it?

If they can't make fracking go away, they at least want to bankrupt a lot of the fracking companies and make them slam on the brakes. To do that, Saudi Arabia wants to get the price low enough to hurt the frackers. That's because frackers have higher costs.

The power of Saudi Arabia comes from the fact that the Saudis have the lowest marginal cost of producing oil. It only costs them a couple of bucks to lift the oil out of the ground. That oil was discovered, explored and drilled when their entire infrastructure was put in place decades ago.

Because their marginal cost of production is just a few dollars, they can still make money—even at $40 and $30 per barrel. The question is, what is the number that hurts the frackers but doesn't hurt Saudi Arabia? Because obviously, the lower the oil price, the more money that's taken out of Saudi Arabia's profit.

In theory, there's a number that's low enough to hurt the frackers but high enough that Saudi Arabia still maximizes its revenues.

It's what's called an optimization or a linear-programming problem. That number, again from very good sourcing, is about $60 a barrel. It's not a number I made up or pulled out of a hat.

Think of $60 per barrel as the sweet spot where we have all the bad stuff in terms of fracking—corporate bonds and junk bond defaults—but not so low that the Arabs hurt themselves more than necessary.

Oil below $60 is more than low enough to do an enormous amount of damage in financial markets. Losses are all over the place. We don't know necessarily where they are right now.

But I guarantee there are major losers out there and they're going to start to merge and crop up in unexpected places.

The first place losses will appear is junk bonds. There are about $5.4 trillion—that's trillion—of costs incurred in the last seven years for exploration drilling and infrastructure in the alternative energy sector. When I say "alternative," I mean fracking.

A lot of it's in the Bakken in North Dakota, but also in Texas and Pennsylvania. That's a lot of money. It's been largely financed with corporate and bank debt. These companies issued some equity, but it's mostly debt.

Here's how it works. Suppose I'm an oil-exploration company. Let's say I borrowed a couple hundred million dollars to drill for oil using fracking technology. The bank—the lender, bond investor or whoever—says: "Well, Jim, you just borrowed $200 million. How are you going to pay me back?"

And I'd say: "Well, I'm going to sell my oil at $80 a barrel." To which the bank says: "How do I know that's true?"

So I go to Morgan Stanley, JPMorgan or Citibank and I buy what's called a "swap contract." It's a kind of derivative.

Citibank or whoever basically agrees to pay me the difference between $80 and the actual price of oil. If oil goes to $50 and I have a swap contract with Citibank that guarantees me $80, Citibank has to pay me the $30 difference. That way, I've locked in the $80 price.

That's not a free lunch. Oil producers give away the upside. If crude prices go to $150 they might have to pay the lenders the difference. But oil companies try to protect their downside.

Oil companies are protected because when oil goes to $50 they can call up the bank and say: "Hey, bank, send me the other $30 a barrel because we have a deal." And the bank will have to send it to them.

Through the derivative contract the loss now moves over to the bank. It's not the oil company that suffers the loss. This is the case with the global financial system today—you never know where the risks end up.

So the first iteration is that some of the oil companies—not all of them—have shifted their risk over to the banks by doing these derivative contracts.

You might be saying to yourself: "Aha, so the banks are going to have all the losses."

Not necessarily. The banks are just middlemen. They might have written that guarantee to an oil company and have to pay the $30 difference in my example. But the bank may have also gone out and sold the contract to somebody else. Then it's somebody else's responsibility to pay the oil company.

Who could that somebody else be? It could be an ETF. And that ETF could be in your portfolio. This is where it gets scary because the risk just keeps getting moved around and broken up into little pieces.

Citibank, for example, might write $5 billion of these derivatives contracts to a whole bunch of oil producers. But then it may take that $5 billion and break it into thousands of smaller $1 million or $10 million chunks and spread that risk around in a bunch of junk bond funds, ETFs or other, smaller banks.

When many oil producers went for loans, the industry's models showed oil prices between $80 and $150. Eighty dollars is the low end for maybe the most efficient projects, and $150 is of course the high end. But no oil company went out and borrowed money on the assumption that they could make money at $50 a barrel.

So suddenly, there's a bunch of debt out there that producers will not be able to pay back with the money they make at $50 a barrel. That means those debts will need to be written off.

How much? That's a little bit more speculative.

I think maybe 50 percent of it has to be written-off. But let's be conservative and assume only 20 percent will be written-off. That's a trillion dollars of losses that have not been absorbed or priced into the market.

Go back to 2007. The total amount of subprime and Alt-A loans was about a trillion. The losses in that sector ticked well above 20 percent. There, you had a $1 trillion market with $200 billion of losses.

Here we're talking about a $5 trillion market with $1 trillion of losses from unpaid debt—not counting derivatives. This fiasco is bigger than the subprime crisis that took down the economy in 2007.

I'm not saying we're going to have another panic of that magnitude tomorrow; I'm just trying to make the point that the losses are already out there. Even at $60 per barrel the losses are significantly larger than the subprime meltdown of 2007. We're looking at a disaster.

On top of those bad loans, there are derivatives. Right now, some of the producers are kind of shrugging, saying: "We went out and borrowed all this money on the assumption of $80, $90, $100 oil. But we also sold our oil production forward for a couple of years at $90. So we're fine."

That's not true in every case, but it is true in a lot of the cases. The problem with derivatives, however, is that you don't know where the risk ends up. I don't know where it is, the Federal Reserve doesn't know where it is and neither do the bank regulators. The banks might know their piece of it, but they don't know the whole picture. That means we have to keep digging and digging.

Going back to my first point, the losses out there are larger, potentially, than the subprime crisis. The losses could actually be bigger than the sector's borrowings because you can create derivatives out of thin air. And as I say, they could be in your portfolio.

There's still time to call your investment advisors or broker to see whether you have any of this risk buried in your portfolio. You might not, but even if you don't it may be time to take a little more of a defensive posture. That could be a little more cash or other hedges. That way when things start to collapse around you—even if you're not taking a direct hit—you're not collateral damage.

I was talking to an investor recently about shifting some investments, and he said: "Well, you know, my broker took care of me. I've got some cash, some money market funds, some stocks and this bond fund."

And I said: "Do you know what's in your bond fund?"

He answered: "No, the broker recommended it." And I answered: "Well, let's get out the documents."

We dug inside. It was a municipal bond fund. We found bonds from Puerto Rico, we found the bonds from City of Detroit—absolute garbage. This is the kind of danger you're in.

Some of these fracking companies are going to go bankrupt. That means you may have equity losses on some of the companies if they didn't hedge.

Then, many frackers issued debt that is going to default. It doesn't necessarily mean the company will go into bankruptcy, although it might; it might have to restructure. That debt, however, whether it's bank debt or junk bond debt, is going to default.

Some other companies are going to be fine because they bought the derivatives. But then, where did those derivatives go?

Think back to the housing bust. We now know that a lot of the derivatives ended up at AIG.

AIG was a 100-year-old traditional insurance company that knew that it was betting that house prices would not go down. Goldman Sachs and a lot of other institutions were taking that bet too.

When house prices did go down, everyone turned to AIG and said: "Hey, pay me."

It's just like if you win at roulette in the casino: you expect the house to pay you. But AIG of course couldn't pay and had to be bailed out by the U.S. government to the tune of over $100 billion. That's the kind of thing we're looking at now. These bets are all over the place because nobody thought oil was going to go to $60.

The losses are going to start to roll in, but they'll come in slowly. I'm not suggesting that tomorrow morning we're going to wake up and find the financial system collapsed. This is the beginning of a disaster.

■ Here's How to Protect Yourself

The most specific way investors will lose is, first, on the equity side of their portfolios. To protect yourself, check to see if you have any second-tier or midtier drilling and exploration companies in your portfolio.

Exxon Mobil is not going go bankrupt. It might cut back its capital expenditures, or maybe its earnings will go down a little bit. But a company the size of Exxon Mobil is not going away, and it's not going to go bankrupt. In fact, the largest companies sometimes benefit from situations like this because it flushes out the competition and gives them more flexibility and they can buy up some of these assets on the cheap.

The fracking sector is more vulnerable than the traditional oil sector because fracking technology is a little more expensive. So much of the sector is new and was financed with debt. There are a lot of small to midsized companies. They are the ones you should look out for because you could lose on the equity if they go bankrupt.

You also have to look at the bond part of your portfolio and look to see if you have any debt from these companies. There are investors who are sick of getting no interest from the bank, no interest from Treasury bonds or other safe investments. I like gold, but gold doesn't pay any dividends or interest. You have to have a view that it's a wealth-preservation mechanism. Gold, cash, and Treasury bills pay you nothing.

That means people are chasing yield. Perhaps an investor says to himself, "Hey, I'm retired, I worked hard all my life, I've got this amount of savings, and I'm counting on 5, 6 or 7 percent out of my portfolio to enjoy a comfortable retirement."

Good luck getting that out of Treasury bills.

But what a broker will come along and say is: "I've got a fund right here; it's a bond fund and it's paying 5 or 6 percent." And the investor says: "Well, I'll take some of that."

But often, investors don't look at what's inside.

When times are good and everyone's rocking and rolling, the economy's growing, new oil is being discovered and the price of oil seems strong, those funds do pay 5 or 6 percent. I'm not saying you can't make that.

But when all of a sudden losses come rolling in, you may find that your 5 percent dividend doesn't compensate you for 20 percent portfolio losses when these things start going belly up.

Look at the equity names in your portfolio, but also look in the bond part of the portfolio to see if inside any of these funds are notes or bonds issued by some of these companies.

They're not too hard to find. Simply screen for small or midsized oil exploration and production companies, especially those in the fracking industry. Again, North Dakota, Pennsylvania and Texas are among the main centers.

The Oil Price: The Good, the Bad and the Ugly

Everyday Americans have good reason to celebrate and fear the recent collapse in oil prices. This is the fastest, steepest decline in oil prices since the mid-1980s. Results are already showing up at the gas pump. The price of regular gasoline has collapsed from almost $4.00 a gallon to $1.99 a gallon in some places.

For a driver who uses 50 gallons per week, that's an extra $100 per week in your pocket: enough to buy a new dress or take your family out to a nice dinner. If that new low price sticks, the savings keep coming, and it adds up to a $5,000 per year raise. Best of all, the government can't tax that $5,000. If you got a pay raise, the government would tax it, but if the cost of things you buy is lower, it can't tax the savings. What's not to like? That's the good news.

Economists assume this extra money in your pocket will immediately be spent. That extra spending might put some money in someone else's pocket. For example, if you spend your $100 weekly savings from gasoline by going out to dinner, you might tip the waiter $15, at which point the waiter has an extra $15 (maybe more if your neighbors are doing the same thing), and he can spend more, and so on.

This is the famous "multiplier effect" at work, where an extra amount of spending leads to more spending by the recipients so that the total economic growth, what economists call aggregate demand, is higher than the initial spending. More good news. At least that's what you'll hear on television.

When you look beneath the surface, however, you'll see some things that are not so good, are maybe even bad, for your portfolio.

For example, just because someone has an extra $100 in his pocket does not mean he'll run out and spend it in knee-jerk fashion like Pavlov's dog. Many people may use the money to pay down debt including credit cards, student loans, auto loans, home-equity loans and other forms of credit.

That can be a prudent thing to do, but it adds nothing to GDP. It's just a form of deleveraging. Both sides of your personal balance sheet, cash and debt, are reduced. There's nothing wrong with that, but there is no increase in aggregate demand and no mystic multiplier.

Also, when you spend $2 per gallon less at the pump, that

means someone else—the oil company—is getting $2 less. Your gain is their loss. None of us needs to shed a tear for Big Oil, but the practical effects of greatly reduced oil prices and energy-company revenues show up in damaging ways. The low price of oil causes new projects to be delayed and existing high-cost fields to be shut in. That means layoffs and reduced capital expenditure for pipes, equipment and transportation. Jobs in the oil field are high-paying jobs. Jobs waiting in a restaurant are not. If we gain restaurant jobs and lose oil-field jobs, it's not clear the economy is better off.

That's the bad news.

From there, things start to get ugly. The price of oil is low both because demand has slowed down along with slower global growth and because supply is up due to fracking. But all of that fracking output costs money to develop, and a lot of that money was raised in the form of junk bonds. When those junk bonds were issued, the projects behind them assumed oil would be priced in a range from $80 to $130 per barrel.

With oil in the $45–$55 per barrel range, those projects are no longer profitable and that debt will begin to default in late 2016. Who holds that debt? Some of it might be in your 401(k) buried inside a "high yield" fund sold to you by your broker. That's something you might want to take a look at. Whether it's owned by you, your neighbor or the bank across the street, the point is someone owns it and those holders are looking at a tidal wave of write-offs coming their way.

Finally, we should consider the impact of rapidly falling oil prices on the Federal Reserve and U.S. monetary policy. The Fed has a stated policy of achieving 2 percent inflation. Right now, inflation is below that target and falling fast. Recent price indexes have shown outright deflation, the opposite of what the Fed wants.

When the Fed looks at price data, it focuses on "core" inflation, which excludes the impact of food and energy prices. The basis for this is that food and energy prices are highly volatile and tend to track core inflation over long periods of time. You can ignore the spikes and dips of energy prices because they tend to be monthly noise, which evens out over the course of a year.

There is actually good empirical evidence to support this approach, which is why the Fed uses it.

It appears that the energy price drop has not just been noise. It's already lasted for about two years. What if it continues to last for years because it's driven by geopolitical and macroeconomic forces that are not going away anytime soon?

The standard Fed approach missed the significance of the move and underestimated the impact of the price drop and the deflation that comes with it. In the first edition of *The Big Drop*, I said, "in that case, the Fed might raise interest rates in 2015—as it has indicated it will—just as persistent price drops are creating deflationary expectations and driving the economy into a recession."

The Fed did raise interest rates in December 2015. An interest rate increase on the verge of a recession is the worst possible medicine. But the Fed's flawed models may be setting us up for just such an outcome.

In the long run, lower oil prices are good for consumers and good for real growth. But in the short run, they are bad for producers, disastrous for junk bond holders and possibly misleading for Fed policy. The next year could continue to be a rough ride as the layoffs pile up and the bad debts roll in. It could get even worse because the Fed misread the tea leaves and raised rates as they threatened to.

You should scour your portfolios and sell any bond funds that are stuffed with junk debt. Then, use the proceeds to build cash positions and buy high-quality U.S. Treasury notes. The cash will preserve wealth, and the notes will produce gains in the deflationary times ahead. When visibility about Fed policy improves, the cash can be deployed to buy distressed assets on the cheap. We'll have more to say about what those bargains might be in the months ahead.

▓ Spill-Over Effects and Contagion

In 1933, during the depths of the Great Depression, famed economist Irving Fisher wrote a work that became a classic of economics and is still widely read and cited today. The book was titled *The Debt-Deflation Theory of Great Depressions.*

Fisher was the most famous U.S. economist of the first half of the 20th century and made many contributions to economics, including work on monetary policy and equilibrium analysis that led to later contributions by contemporary economists including Milton Friedman and Ben Bernanke. Yet Fisher's work on debt and deflation is his best-known and most important effort.

His thesis was straightforward. Depressions are the inevitable aftermath of credit booms and extreme overindebtedness. During the expansion phase of a cycle, easy credit allows debtors to bid up asset prices.

The higher asset prices then serve as collateral for further debt, which is used to invest in other assets, causing those prices to rise also. At some stage, valuations become stretched. Creditors refuse to extend more credit and demand repayment or require more collateral from the debtors.

At this point, the entire process goes rapidly into reverse. Now debtors have to sell assets to repay creditors. This forced selling causes asset prices to drop. The lower asset prices reduce the collateral values on other loans, which cause those loans to be called by the creditors also.

Now the forced liquidation of assets becomes widespread, businesses fail, layoffs increase, unemployed workers cannot afford to spend, more businesses fail as a result and so on until the entire economy is thrown into recession or, even worse, depression.

This process played out in the period 1929–33, and again from 2007 to 2009. The latest episode is usually known as the Great Recession, but is more accurately called the New Depression. It is still with us in the form of below-trend growth, threats of deflation and low labor force participation. This new episode has led to a revival of interest in Fisher's theory.

Investors today can see Fisher's thesis at work in the field of shale-oil production. From 2009 to 2016, several trillion dollars of debt was issued to support shale-oil exploration and drilling using a method called hydraulic fracturing, or fracking.

Most of this debt was issued on the assumption that oil prices would remain above $70 per barrel. With oil now trading in a range of $50–$60 per barrel, much of this debt is unpayable, and defaults can be expected throughout 2016 and 2017 if oil prices do not recover. This has caused new exploration and new credit in the shale industry to dry up.

The next stage, exactly as Fisher predicted, has started. It consists of the bankruptcy of the smaller producers and the forced liquidation of assets. This causes existing wells to be pumped even faster to generate what revenues they can to maintain cash flows in the face of falling prices. This pumping, a kind of asset liquidation, puts more downward pressure on prices, making the situation even worse.

Unfortunately, the process has far to run. Eventually, a new equilibrium of supply and demand will be achieved, but for now, the debt-deflation story has just started. There are many ways to "liquidate" in the oil patch.

These include laying off workers, cancelling new orders for pipe and drilling rigs and shutting in existing shale reserves until prices recover. This liquidation stage affects not only the drillers, but also oil-field suppliers, labor, landowners who lease their properties for drilling, equipment-leasing companies and municipalities that will see declining tax revenues.

Fisher also pointed out that once deflation begins in one economic sector, it spreads rapidly to others. When debtors are in distress, they don't sell what they want—they sell what they can. A debtor involved in one sector of the economy who needs to raise cash will sell assets from an unrelated sector to meet his obligations.

Today, this behavior that Fisher identified in the 1930s is called a "spillover effect" or "contagion." Distress can rapidly spread from the oil patch to commercial real estate and beyond.

Some of this debt-deflation spiral has already shown up in the stock prices of affected companies. More stocks like them may be heading for a fall as the Fisher debt-deflation cycle runs its course.

■ The System Is Now Even More Unstable

Our job is to figure out how unstable the global financial system is or how big the unstable snowpack is. We knew something about the risks derivatives, bank balance sheets, sovereign debt and currency imbalances posed.

Now the oil-price drop has revealed that the snowpack is even bigger than we thought—$5.4 trillion of oil debt suddenly seems to be in jeopardy.

Will that be the snowflake that causes the financial avalanche? At the risk of sounding like a broken record, I advise readers to focus on instability.

How big is the snowpack?

How much damage is it going to cause when the avalanche comes tumbling down?

Those are the relevant questions. Now we have both at once—a bigger, more unstable mountainside and more snow falling harder from the sky. That means we have more snowflakes to take account of.

■ One Oil Snowflake to Watch

One snowflake that I've been looking at more closely is Algeria.

We've heard so much about the Islamic State in Libya and Syria, Iran, Iraq, Afghanistan and Turkey. Those are all important issues and none of them is going away. But keep an eye on Algeria.

Algeria is a major energy producer. It has a very powerful Al-Qaeda-type Islamic extremist movement that has recently declared allegiance to the Islamic State. They're the same bad guys, but they've hitched their wagon to the leadership of the Islamic State. They're gaining strength, and it may just be a matter of time before they topple the Algerian government.

At that point, the Islamic State would stretch from Iran almost to Morocco. It would begin to look more and more like the real caliphate. When I say the real one, I mean that the Islamic State has declared a caliphate and thinks what it has is a real caliphate.

If you go back in history and look at the caliphates that have existed, the biggest ones went from Spain to Indonesia and everywhere in between. There were smaller ones in North Africa and the Middle East too.

What's interesting is that when the Islamic State gets control of these oil fields, it won't shut them down. It'll keep pumping because it needs the money. That's something that a lot of investors misunderstand. They see geopolitical turmoil in the oil patch and they think it's going to cut production and send the price of oil higher. Actually, history shows the opposite is true.

The Islamic State will produce oil like crazy because it wants the money, and it's not bound by OPEC casts. That's going to make OPEC's job a little more difficult. We saw this in 1986 during the Iran-Iraq war.

Iran and Iraq are two of the largest oil producers in the world. When they got into a war—when Saddam Hussein and Ayatollah Khomeini were still around—a lot of people thought the price of oil was going to go to the moon because of supply disruptions. The opposite happened.

Both countries pumped like crazy, and the oil price went down to $12 a barrel. And to think, so far, we've been talking about distress at $50-$60 per barrel.

You could have the worst of both worlds if the Islamic State takes over Algeria because there would be no oil-production disruption. Then you may see embargos and seizing of tankers. It could get very messy.

With these geopolitical and domestic energy trends, the biggest question is what the most powerful central bank will do in 2016.

The Federal Reserve hinted, teased and implied that it was going to raise rates in 2015, and it did. The market believed that to be true, based on strong data in the U.S. economy prior to the rate hike. You should expect to see a massive emerging-markets crisis and debt defaults for the reasons we mentioned.

You should also expect to see massive deflation. The United States may even go into a recession. That's what'll happen because the Fed stayed the course.

You can look at the dynamics, use complexity theory, observe the interactions between players and see the problems before they happen. The one thing I think you can count on, though, is a lot of volatility and a lot of danger.

CHAPTER 7

Inside The Federal Reserve

▓ Now, More than Ever Before, You Should Know the Players

The Federal Reserve is the central bank of America.

Why doesn't it call itself the Central Bank of America? Because it knows Americans hate central banks. We've rejected two central banks in the past, in the 18th and 19th centuries. So it got the funny name "Federal Reserve." That way people wouldn't understand what it is.

Today, investors use the name "Fed" as shorthand for the Federal Reserve System. Shorthand is convenient, but sometimes it hides as much as it reveals. A one-size-fits-all description of an institution is easy, but highly misleading. In fact, the Federal Reserve is a complicated, multifaceted structure with diverse parts and personalities that few investors follow.

Usually, this doesn't matter, because the Fed speaks with one voice and is of one mind. Most people are familiar with Janet Yellen in her role as chair of the Federal Reserve and know that Ben Bernanke and Alan Greenspan were her predecessors. Familiarity with the views of the chair is enough most of the time. But this is not one of those times.

Today, it is critical for you to know the players while Fed-watching. Understanding Fed structure and the predilections of the players is the key to understanding interest rate policy over the next year and beyond. And your success or failure as an investor will depend on that understanding.

One reader recently e-mailed me, saying, "Who owns the Federal Reserve? I've heard that it is owned by the Rothschilds and Rockefellers plus a few other banks."

The Fed is actually a system of 12 regional reserve banks that are privately owned by the commercial banks in each district. The most powerful of these is the Federal Reserve Bank of New York. It actually carries out the money market operations needed to implement interest rate policy.

The New York Fed also has custody of the largest gold vault in the world, holding about 7,000 tons of gold, more than Fort Knox. But other regional reserve banks, in Chicago, Philadelphia, Boston and San Francisco, also have a strong voice in policy.

The president of each regional reserve bank is selected by the private board of directors of each bank. In turn, the directors are elected by the stockholders, who are private banks in the region.

The Board of Governors of the entire system is based in Washington, D.C. The board consists of seven members selected by the president of the United States and confirmed by the U.S. Senate. Among the governors is a chair and a vice chairman also selected by the president and confirmed by the Senate.

This arrangement gives a total of 19 principal policy makers—7 governors plus 12 regional reserve bank presidents—some appointed by the president and some hired indirectly by private banks.

Things get more complicated from there. Interest rate policy is not made by the governors alone or by the reserve bank presidents. It is set by the Federal Open Market Committee. The FOMC meets eight times per year (about every six weeks). It has 12 members, consisting of all 7 members of the Board of Governors plus 5 of the 12 regional reserve bank presidents.

Still with me? Good, because it gets even more complicated—but you'll understand it all when I'm finished.

Of the five regional reserve bank presidents who can vote on the FOMC, one has a permanent seat. That's the president of the Federal Reserve Bank of New York. The other four rotate from among the remaining 11 regional reserve banks on a one-year term. This rotation is important because some of the regional reserve bank presidents are "hawks" (favoring a rate hike). Some others are "doves" (favoring continued ease). Knowing which are on the FOMC each year is part of what you need to know to forecast policy.

Even with this FOMC formula in mind, there are still surprises. Fed officials often quit or retire before their terms expire (to return to academia or pursue business opportunities). This can lead to surprise appointments by the president or to vacancies, which skew the voting one way or another. As they say in baseball, "You can't tell the players without a scorecard!"

Let's look at the FOMC scorecard and see what it can tell us about future Fed policy.

As of October 2015 there are two vacancies on the Board of Governors. This means there are only five governors on the FOMC: Janet Yellen, Stanley Fischer, Lael Brainard, Jay Powell and Dan Tarullo.

The other five seats are taken up by the following regional reserve bank presidents: Bill Dudley (New York), Charles Evans (Chicago), Dennis Lockhart (Atlanta), John Williams (San Francisco) and Jeffrey Lacker (Richmond).

For all practical purposes, the center of gravity comes down to Yellen, Fischer and Dudley. They are the "Big Three."

The other governors (Brainard, Tarullo and Powell) are relatively new. Jay Powell has been relatively quiet on monetary policy. Lael Brainard and Dan Tarullo shocked markets in October 2015 by breaking with Janet Yellen.

On October 12, 2015, Lael Brainard gave a speech in

Washington, D.C., that was very dovish. She poured cold water on the idea that the unemployment rate was a good predictor of inflation. She said that inflation is nowhere in sight and this is no time to raise rates.

The next day, Dan Tarullo gave an interview on CNBC where he said much the same thing. To have two governors challenge Yellen in two days looked like a revolt in the ranks.

My sources inside the Fed have told me that the Board of Governors doesn't give any particular weight to the views of the regional reserve bank presidents anyway. The chair lets the voting and nonvoting presidents have their say in the FOMC meetings. That tends to dilute the views of the voting presidents. The result is that the Big Three still hold sway.

The lineup changed in January 2016.

Evans, Lockhart, Williams and Lacker went off the FOMC at that point. They were replaced by Loretta Mester (Cleveland), Eric Rosengren (Boston), James Bullard (St. Louis) and Esther George (Kansas City).

Once again, the regional reserve bank presidents are split. Mester, George and Bullard are all hawks, while Rosengren is a dove. However, Rosengren is not as outspoken and does not have the intellectual firepower that Evans brought to the debate this year.

The lineup changed, but the confusion continues. The governors are more dovish (because of the Brainard and Tarullo revolt against Yellen). The regional reserve bank presidents are more hawkish (because Evans left and three hawks are joined).

The entire FOMC, the governors and presidents, is data-dependent. Whatever its members' biases and previously stated views, they will carefully weigh the data and trends at each FOMC meeting. There is no preset timetable either for "liftoff" (another rate hike) or ease (if the economy weakens). The FOMC will take the process one meeting and one data point at a time.

As for the governors on the FOMC, they are a more cohesive group and are all reliably in Janet Yellen's camp if she wants to steer policy in a particular direction. Yellen herself is data-driven but has dovish inclinations. She's revealed her strong support for quantitative easing (QE) in her public speeches, emphasizing slack in labor markets as a rationale for not raising rates.

This Fed background is crucial for assessing market expectations about policy and whether those expectations are well-grounded. Wall Street economists have been excessively optimistic in their growth forecasts for seven consecutive years. This is a dismal track record, and you'd be right to be skeptical about any rosy scenarios for 2016 and 2017.

In the interminable run-up to the start of the Fed's first tightening cycle in 11 years, many analysts used the phrase "one and done" to describe the policy that Janet Yellen would pursue. Apart from having a nice ring to it, this was meant to convey the idea that after the first rate hike, the Fed would pause before hiking again. More to the point, the idea was that the Fed just wanted to get the first rate hike over with, and would move slowly and cautiously through the new tightening cycle.

That's not exactly what happened. The Fed did hike rates in December 2015 and paused (no additional rate hike) at its January 28, 2016, FOMC meeting. Yet the outlook beyond that is far more aggressive than the phrase "one and done" implies.

While Janet Yellen was careful to say that future Fed policy is data-dependent and not on a set schedule, she did, for all intents and purposes, lay out a schedule based on her forecast for economic growth and inflation. The implied tightening cycle for the target Fed funds rate is 100 basis points per year for three years (through the end of 2018).

In keeping with the Fed's declared desire not to disrupt markets, it is also likely that each target rate increase will be 25 basis points (the same measure Greenspan used in his belated tightening cycle from 2004 to 2006, albeit with a slower tempo).

There are eight FOMC meetings per year. Four of those occasions (every other meeting) include press conferences, which are helpful for explaining Fed actions. Yellen (and before her, Bernanke) puts a big emphasis on communication and transparency with regard to Fed policy, part of her misguided notion of setting expectations.

Raising rates 100 basis points per year in 25-basis-point increments means four rate hikes per year, most likely at those FOMC meetings with press conferences.

Taking these parameters into account, the expected policy path in 2016 is 25-basis-point rate increases, on March 16, June 15, September 21 and December 14. In the Fed's view, this pattern could reasonably be extrapolated into 2017 and 2018, until the target Fed funds rate reaches 3.25 percent in December 2018.

That path is a far cry from "one and done," and is highly aggressive in an environment of declining global growth and borderline deflation in the world's four largest economies (United States, Eurozone, China and Japan).

The one thing we can be reasonably certain of is that this will not happen. The Fed's expected path is based on internal models of the interaction of labor markets, growth and inflation. These models are highly flawed and obsolete.

For evidence, we need look no further than the fact that Fed one-year forward growth forecasts have been incorrect by orders of magnitude for nine straight years. A belief that the Fed forecast for 2016 is close to accurate represents the triumph of hope over experience.

One reason Fed forecasts are flawed is the Fed's persistent and misplaced reliance on the Phillips curve (purportedly demonstrating an inverse relationship between unemployment and inflation) and NAIRU (the natural accelerating inflation rate of unemployment).

The Phillips curve is a strong candidate for a starring role in a zombie movie. No matter how many times academics kill it, it keeps coming back to life to scare policy makers. (For evidence, consider the late 1970s and early 1980s, when the United States had back-to-back recessions, rising unemployment and sky-high inflation—over 50 percent cumulative inflation from 1977 to 1981.)

NAIRU resembles a unicorn—that is, a creature that can be described and visualized but does not exist in the natural world. (For evidence, consider how many times the unemployment policy goalposts have been moved by the Fed in recent years—from 6.5 to 5.5 to 5 percent, and now some consideration is being given to 4.8 percent or lower. Like the unicorn, NAIRU is always just over the next hill.)

Given the Fed's consistent forecasting errors and reliance on highly flawed models, we should expect that their current reliance on models will prove misguided. If you use the wrong model, you will get the wrong result every time.

"We Don't Know What We're Doing"

Don't ever think for a minute that the central bankers know what they're doing. They don't.

That's not only my own view; I've heard as much from the mouths of a couple central bankers. I recently spent some time with one member of the FOMC and another member of the Monetary Policy Committee of the Bank of England, which is the equivalent of our FOMC.

They both said the same thing: "We don't know what we're doing. This is a massive experiment. We've never done this before. We try something. If it works, maybe we do a little more; if it doesn't work, we pull it away, and we'll try something else." The evidence of this—besides hearing as much firsthand—is that there have been 15 separate Federal Reserve policies in the last seven years.

If you think about it, Fed policy makers started with forward guidance, which said, "We will keep rates low for an extended period of time."

Then they said, "Oh, 'extended' means all the way to 2013." Then they said, "All the way to 2014."

Then they said, "All the way to 2015," which is when they finally raised rates.

But before that, they said, "Wait a second. The dates don't work. Let's use some numeric concepts."

That's when they started nominal GDP targeting. They changed their tune to say, "We have this threshold of 2.5 percent inflation, not based on actual inflation, but based on projected inflation, as projected by the Fed." Essentially, that meant it could be whatever the central bankers wanted it to be. They also set a target of 6.5 percent unemployment, but when they got down to that level, they said, "Oh, just kidding. We're not going to apply that."

They've had currency wars. They've had Operation Twist. Not to mention QE1, QE2, QE3—except QE3 came in two flavors: $45 billion a month and $85 billion a month.

And then they tapered. But the taper wasn't the first taper because at the end of QE1, they tapered 100 percent, and at the end of QE2, they tapered 100 percent. We have two data points to say tapering doesn't work. I expect this will fail as well.

Just How Nasty a Rate Increase Can Be

It's unfortunate that we have to be spending so much time on the Federal Reserve. It's the place to start if you want to understand a lot of what's going on in the markets. In fact, nothing is more important—but I wish that weren't true.

I wish the central banks could go back to just being boring, opaque, marginal institutions that took care of the money supply and acted as a lender of last resort instead of monstrosities that seem to manipulate and invade every corner of every market in the world. But unfortunately, that is what we have today.

When the Fed manipulates the dollar and dollar interest rates, it's directly and indirectly affecting every market in the world—equities, gold, real estate, other commodities, junk bonds, corporate debt and so on. So even though I wish it wasn't the case, understanding what the Fed will do next is the big question.

It raised rates in December 2015, but what's next?

I'll address that directly, but first, I'd like to give you some background to help you understand what's behind a rate hike and an easing.

From 2013 to 2015, securities around the world were priced as if the Fed were going to raise rates. I've never seen anything more trumpeted and more advertised in my career. There was a good reason for that. Before the December 2015 rate hike, the last time the Fed raised rates was 2006.

In terms of cutting rates, they hit bottom in late 2008 when they got to zero—and they were at zero before the rate hike. It was at zero for seven and a half years. But you have to go back two years before that to find the last time they raised rates, so it's going on 11 years at this point. That's a long time without a rate increase, and people may forget how nasty such an increase can be.

I was in the markets in 1994 when the Fed raised rates, and it was a wipe-out. That's when we had the bankruptcy of Orange County, California, and other dealers went out of business. There was a bond market massacre.

The same thing happened in 1987. A lot of people recall the crash of October 1987, when the stock market dropped 22 percent in a single day. In today's market, that would be the equivalent of over 3,000 Dow points. Imagine the market dropping not *300 points*, which would get everyone's attention, but 3,000 points. That's what happened in October 1987. But before that, in March 1987, there was a bond market crash. The bond market crash preceded the stock market crash by about six months.

These things can get nasty, but it's been a long time since the last one. That's why the Fed has been talking so much about it. You have to go all the way back to May 2013, when the Fed was still printing money and buying bonds (long-term asset purchases, as they call it), when Ben Bernanke first started talking about maybe beginning the taper.

The Fed didn't do anything. It didn't cut purchases and it didn't raise rates—it just talked about it—and still the market threw a taper tantrum fit. We had the actual taper through the course of 2014. Now that the taper is over, QE3 is officially over, so this rate hike had been really advertised for two years.

The reason rates were at zero in the first place is because the Fed was trying to pump up assets. It wanted banks and other borrowers to go out, borrow cheap money, buy houses and stocks and bid up the price of assets. Hopefully, that would make people feel richer, they would spend more money and the economy would get on a self-sustaining path. That last part didn't happen. The asset prices did go up, but the wealth effect did not kick in and the economy is still very weak. The Fed did not get the kind of 3.5–4 percent growth it was really hoping for when it started all this. I think if the Fed had it to do it over, it never would have gone down this path or at least would not have stayed on it this long.

It had encouraged everyone to borrow money and lever up and do maturity mismatches (borrow overnight in the repo market and go out and buy some risky assets like stocks or other assets). Because of that, it wanted to give people lots of warning that it was going to raise rates.

If I'm a dealer, I can borrow money overnight in the repo market and go out and buy a 10-year note, which until recently was at about 2 percent. I have zero cost to funds and I make 2 percent on my 10-year note, but I can leverage that trade 10:1 because I can get a more than 90 percent margin in the repo market.

A 2 percent profit levered 10:1 is a 20 percent return on equity, so with a government security as my asset, it's not like I have to go buy some junk bond. As long as rates are at zero, it's pretty easy to make 10, 20 or even 30 percent returns on equity with a highly leveraged trade.

You might be saying to yourself, "That sounds a little too easy; what's the risk in the trade?" Well, there's no credit risk in the trade because you've got a Treasury note as your asset. The risk is that they may raise short-term rates while you're sitting there with overnight money holding a 10-year note.

All of a sudden the overnight money gets to be more expensive, the trade is upside-down, and you're losing money. The Fed was saying, "We encourage everyone to do these crazy carry trades, do these maturity mismatches, make a lot of money, and rebuild the bank balance sheet. The time will come when we're going to raise rates, but we're going to give you years, literally, to get out of the trade or wind it down or hedge it. Anybody who's caught out, shame on them, as you can't say you weren't warned."

The Fed wanted to raise rates to normalize things. It talked about it for almost two years because it wanted to give people plenty of warning, but the markets didn't listen so well— there's always somebody who doesn't get the message.

As I look around, there's still a lot of leverage in the system— enormous leverage in the stock market, enormous leverage in various carry trades around the world. Chuck Prince, then CEO of Citicorp, said prior to the last world financial calamity that you have to keep dancing as long as the music's playing. There are some people who literally either won't listen to the Fed or don't believe it and are still going to be in these trades.

So the risk is you'll get caught out in the trade, and I expect a lot of market disruption.

All we heard about prior to the Fed raising rates in December 2015 was, "The Fed's going to raise rates, the Fed's going to raise rates." Whatever the particular timing was, that's all anyone was thinking about.

Now that the Fed did raise rates, people have been saying, "Will they tighten more, or will they tighten twice? Will they tighten three times?" That's been the discussion.

Here's a prediction for you. Before the end of 2016, the Fed is going to ease. Now, it may or may not tighten first. It may tighten and then ease, but we're looking into the teeth of a recession. The U.S. economy is heading for a recession. The world is heading for a recession.

The Fed's decision-makers are tightening into weakness. They should've raised rates back in 2011–12. If they had done that, they would have been able to ease today. Two wrongs don't make a right. The fact that they failed to raise rates five years ago doesn't mean they should continue to raise rates today, but they're going to do it anyway.

The problem is they'll be tightening right into a recession. That will make things worse. When it gets bad enough, they're going to have to reverse course and ease. I would look for Fed easing in one of five forms.

It could be QE4, currency wars, "helicopter money," negative interest rates or forward guidance (forward guidance is basically a kind of verbal promise not to raise rates for a long period of time).

Nobody in economics, nobody on Wall Street, nobody on the buy side, nobody in academia, nobody I've seen anywhere has a worse forecasting record than the Fed. I don't say that out of spite or to try to embarrass anyone; it's just a fact. Year after year after year they produce these very high growth forecasts, and every year they're wrong. They're not just wrong by a little bit; they're wrong by orders of magnitude.

So when the Fed says, "Well, we think the economy is healthy enough for a rate increase," that's the first sign that it's not. Now, besides that, there's a lot of data. We're seeing auto-loan defaults go up, real wages are stagnant to down, labor force participation continues to be very low, our trade deficit is getting worse partly because of the strong dollar, emerging markets are slowing down and China and Europe are slowing down.

I think it's nonsense to believe that we could be closely coupled on the way up but somehow, if the rest of the world was going to go down, the United States wouldn't be affected.

Growth was weak when the Fed raised rates. The Fed read the economy wrong and increased rates into a very weak economy.

I still expect the U.S. economy to come close to a recession, to have more deflation, and probably to experience some disruption in equity markets. The one market that might actually rally is the bond market. Ten-year notes are still pretty attractive based on everything we see.

▪ Outlook for 2016 and 2017

If you're going to make a forecast, it's always good to know where you're starting from and then project from there.

When you say "Independence Day" to most Americans, they think of the fourth of July. That's not true for the Federal Reserve. At the Fed, Independence Day was the fourth of March.

Unfortunately, March 4, 2016, may have been the Fed's last Independence Day for a long time!

Why the fourth of March? On March 4, 1951, the Federal Reserve reached an agreement with the U.S. Treasury that restored policy independence to the Fed after nine years of domination by the Treasury.

Beginning in April 1942, shortly after the United States

entered the Second World War, the Fed agreed to cap interest rates on Treasury bonds to help finance the war effort. The cap meant that the Fed gave up its control of interest rate policy.

The cap also meant that the Fed surrendered control of its balance sheet because it would have to buy potentially unlimited amounts of Treasury debt to implement the rate cap. (Such asset purchases had inflationary potential, but in the Second World War, inflation was managed separately through wartime price controls.)

We are now entering a new period of fiscal domination by the Treasury.

The Fed will again have to give up control of its balance sheet and interest rate policy to save the United States from secular stagnation. The Fed will subordinate its policy independence to fiscal stimulus coordinated by the White House and the Treasury. The implications for you are enormous.

The history of the Treasury-Fed Accord of March 4, 1951, is revealing.

Why did the Treasury not restore Fed independence in 1945, when the United States and its allies won the war?

After the Second World War, the Treasury was reluctant to give up its domination of the Fed. President Truman felt strongly that patriotic investors in U.S. bonds should not have to suffer capital losses if rates rose. The White House insisted that the wartime cap on long-term rates be maintained.

The Fed resisted this, but it stopped resisting when the Korean War came. The Treasury used this new war as an excuse to continue the rate cap.

It was not until 1951, with the Korean War in stalemate and a presidential election on the horizon, that the Treasury restored the Fed's independence on interest rates and the size of its balance sheet.

The Fed's independence is again threatened: not by war, but by secular stagnation.

The U.S. economy has grown about 2 percent per year since 2009. This rate is below the economy's potential growth of 3 percent, and well below the pace of past recoveries.

Following the recessions of 1980 and 1981, the U.S. economy grew at about 5 percent for several years before settling back to trend. The U.S. economy had record peacetime expansions in the 1980s and 1990s. That kind of growth is like a distant memory now.

The U.S. debt-to-GDP ratio is the highest since the end of the Second World War (and much higher if contingent liabilities for entitlements are considered debt). While U.S. deficits have declined, they are still adding to the overall debt faster than the economy is growing. The United States is still on a path to fiscal crisis and loss of confidence in the dollar.

Some speculate the Fed is out of bullets to deal with depressed growth. That is not true. Now that the Fed's policy rate is above zero, the Fed has room to cut rates in late 2016 or in early 2017. (More quantitative easing, or "QE4," is unlikely because there's little evidence that QE2 and QE3 achieved much.)

The Fed could also try negative interest rates. But recent evidence from Europe, Switzerland, Japan and Sweden indicates that negative rates don't do any more to help growth than zero rates.

In fact, negative rates may be counterproductive since they signal deflation fears. Such fears can lead to more savings (to make up for low yields) and less spending (based on expectations of lower prices).

That's the opposite of what central banks want. It's a vicious cycle that's hard to break.

The Fed might return to the currency wars and cheapen the dollar, as it did in 2011. This could give the U.S. economy a short-term lift and import some inflation from abroad.

But U.S. gains come at the expense of trading partners whose growth is either already lower than the United States'

(Japan and Europe) or dropping dangerously (China). In a globalized world, there's no escape from a global slowdown.

If monetary solutions don't work, what can be done to restore growth?

We rely on what we call "indications and warnings" to detect momentous policy shifts in advance. Currency wars and the central bank's money printing will not be over soon. Global elites are getting desperate to try something new to stimulate growth.

These indications and warnings now are signaling loud and clear that the Fed must again surrender its independence to the big spenders.

A new global consensus is emerging from elite voices such as Adair Turner, Larry Summers, Joe Biden and Christine Lagarde. The consensus is that the only solution to stagnation is expanded government spending on critical infrastructure, health care, technology, renewable energy and education. (In a Republican administration, more defense spending could be added to the list.)

If citizens won't borrow and spend, the government will! It's Keynesianism 1930s without a monetarist gloss.

More government spending means more government debt. Who will buy the added government bonds? How will the Treasury keep interest rates low enough that a death spiral of higher deficits and higher rates won't push the Treasury bond market to the point of collapse?

The answer is that the Fed and the Treasury will reach a new secret accord, just as they did in 1941. Under this new accord, the U.S. government could run larger deficits to finance stimulus-type spending.

The Fed will then cap interest rates to keep deficits under control. Capping rates will have the added benefit of producing negative real rates if inflation emerges, as the Fed expects.

The Fed could use open market operations in the form

of bond buying to achieve the rate caps. This means the Fed would not only give up control of interest rates, it would give up control of its balance sheet. A rate cap requires a "whatever it takes" approach to Treasury note purchases.

The popular name for rate caps, and Fed bond buying to support government spending, is "helicopter money." The technical names are fiscal dominance and financial repression.

The implications for you are huge.

If deflation persists, rate caps can force bond yields to much lower levels (closer to where German *bunds'* yields are today). Nominal rates and inflation would be in a race to the bottom in an effort to achieve negative real rates. This would produce big capital gains in U.S. Treasury notes.

If inflation emerges, the rate cap might be higher in nominal terms but still low enough to achieve negative real rates. In this scenario, gold would perform extremely well. Treasury note holders would not suffer unduly, because the Fed's rate cap would put a brake on losses.

Nominal interest rates would not be allowed to keep pace with inflation.

In deflation, bondholders have huge gains. In inflation, their losses are capped by the Fed!

Rate caps will not arrive until mid-2017 at the earliest. That's because the current Fed cycle of rate hikes followed by rate cuts has to play out first. Fed rate changes apply to the short end of the yield curve. The Fed might end up in the strange position of imposing rate floors at the short end and rate caps at the long end.

The last time the Fed lost its independence—in 1942—the reason was war. Now a new war on secular stagnation will cause the Fed to lose its independence again.

CHAPTER 8
Today's Currency and Financial Wars

Currency wars are one of the most important dynamics in the global financial system today. I started talking about this years ago in my first book, *Currency Wars.* My point then was the same as it is today: The world is not always in a currency war, but when it is, the wars can last for 5, 10, 15, or even 20 years. They can last for a very long time. There have been three currency wars in the past 100 years.

Currency War One covered the period from 1921 to 1936. It really started with the Weimar hyperinflation. There was a period of successive currency devaluation.

In 1921, Germany destroyed its currency. In 1925, France, Belgium and others did the same thing. What was going on prior to the First World War, before 1914? For a long time before then, the world had been on what's called the classical gold standard.

If you had a balance-of-payments deficit, you paid for your defi-cit in gold. If you had a balance-of-payments surplus, you acquired gold.

Gold was the regulator of expansion or contraction of individual economies. In this system, you had to be productive, pursue your comparative advantage and have a good business environment to actually get some gold—or at least avoid losing the gold you had. It was a very stable system that promoted enormous growth and low inflation.

That system broke down in 1914 because countries needed to print money to fight the First World War. When the First World War was over and the world entered the 1920s, countries wanted to go back to the gold standard but didn't quite know how to do it.

There was a conference in Genoa, Italy, in 1922 where the problem was discussed. The world had started out before the First World War with parity.

There had been a certain amount of gold and a certain amount of paper money backed by gold. Then the paper money supply had doubled.

That left only two choices if countries wanted to go back to a gold standard. They could double the price of gold—basically cut the value of their currency in half—or they could cut the money supply in half. They could do either one, but they had to get to parity either at the new level or the old level.

The French said, "This is easy. We're going to cut the value of the currency in half." They did that.

The Woody Allen movie *Midnight in Paris* shows U.S. expatriates living the high life in France in the mid-1920s. That was because of the hyperinflation of France.

It wasn't as bad as the Weimar hyperinflation in Germany, but it was pretty bad. If you had a moderate amount of dollars, you could go to France and live like a king.

The U.K.'s policy makers had the same decision to make but made it differently than France did. There, instead of doubling the price of gold, they cut their money supply in half. The U.K. went back to the pre–First World War parity. The decision was made by Winston Churchill, who was chancellor of the Exchequer at that time. The move was extremely deflationary.

After you doubled the money supply, even if you don't like that you did, you may feel you have to own up to that and recognize that you've trashed your currency.

So Churchill felt duty-bound to return to the old value. He cut the money supply in half, and that threw the U.K. into a depression three years ahead of the rest of the world. Though the rest of the world ran into depression in 1929, in the U.K. the depression started in 1926.

To go back to gold at a much higher price measured in sterling would have been the right way to do it. Choosing the wrong price contributed to the Great Depression.

Economists today say, "We could never have a gold standard. Don't you know that the gold standard caused the Great Depression?"

I do know that—it contributed to the Great Depression, but not because of gold; it was because of the price. Churchill picked the wrong price, and that was deflationary.

The lesson of the 1920s is not that you can't have a gold standard, but that a country needs to get the price right.

The U.K. continued down that path until, finally, it was unbearable, and it devalued in 1931. Soon after, in 1933, the United States devalued. Then the U.K. devalued again in 1936, as did France.

You had a period of successive currency devaluations and so-called "beggar thy neighbor" policies. The result was, of course, one of the worst depressions in world history. There was skyrocketing unemployment and crushed industrial production and a long period of very weak to negative growth.

Currency War One was not resolved until the Second World War and then, more fully, at the Bretton Woods conference. That's when the world was put on a new monetary standard.

Currency War Two raged from 1967 to 1987. The seminal event in the middle of this war was Nixon's taking the United States, and ultimately the world, off the gold standard on August 15, 1971.

He did this to create jobs and promote exports to help the U.S. economy. What actually happened instead?

We had three recessions back to back, in 1974, 1979 and 1980. Our stock market crashed in 1974. Unemployment skyrocketed, inflation blew up between 1977 and 1981 (inflation in that five-year period was 50 percent, cumulatively) and the value of the dollar was cut in half.

Again, the lesson of currency wars is that they don't produce the results you expect, which are increased exports and jobs and some growth. What they produce is extreme deflation, extreme inflation, recession, depression or other economic catastrophe.

This brings us to Currency War Three, which began in 2010.

Notice I jumped over that whole period from 1985 to 2010, that 25-year period? What was going on then?

That was the age of what we call "King Dollar" or the "strong dollar" policy. It was a period of very good growth, very good price stability and good economic performance around the world.

It was not a gold standard system nor was it rules-based. The Fed did look at the price of gold, though, as a thermometer to see how it was doing.

Basically, what the United States said to the world is, "We're not on a gold standard, we're on a dollar standard. We, the United States, agree to maintain the purchasing power of the dollar, and you, our trading partners, can link to the dollar or plan your economies around some peg to the dollar. That will give us a stable system."

That actually worked up until 2010, when the United States tore up the deal and basically declared Currency War Three. President Obama did this in his State of the Union address in January 2010.

Here we are in 2016, and the currency wars are still continuing. That comes as no surprise to me. A lot of journalists will see, say, the weak yen, and say, "Oh my goodness. We're in a currency war."

And I'll say, "Well, of course we are. We've been in one for six years. And we'll probably be in one for five more years, or even longer."

Currency wars are like a seesaw—they go back and forth and back and forth. In 2011, for example, we saw a very weak dollar. We also saw a very high price of gold. That was the all-time high—about $1,900 per ounce. Since then, the dollar has gotten much stronger and gold has come down a lot.

It's a very simple correlation. If you want to understand gold, the dollar price of gold is just the inverse of the dollar. It's simple, but many investors don't understand the dynamic.

If we have a weak dollar, gold's going to go up. If we have a strong dollar, gold's going to go down.

If you're interested in gold or other hard assets, you need to pay attention to the dollar. Many investors ask me, "What's the dollar really worth?" I always reply, "Compared to what?" Everything is a cross rate. There's a dollar/euro cross rate. There's a dollar/yen cross rate. There's a dollar/yuan cross rate, a dollar/franc cross rate and so on. They're very dynamic because the dollar could be going up against the euro, which, at time of writing, it has been, but at the same time it could be going down against the yuan.

Investors can profit from these dynamics if they can understand them. Any two currencies are part of a zero-sum game. That's another thing that confuses investors. They say, "Oh, the euro's falling apart. The euro's got to go down."

That may or may not be true. But what investors miss is that the Fed wants the dollar to go down too. But the dollar and the euro cannot both go down against each other at the same time.

Lately the dollar's been going up and the euro's been going down. But if you know the Fed wants a weak dollar and you're seeing a strong dollar, what does that mean? It means the Fed has to do something to make the dollar go down. That, in turn, means the euro must go up.

In other words, the dollar and the euro can't go down against each other at the same time. It doesn't work. Once you understand the cross rates are part of a zero-sum game, you can look at all of the cross rates effectively. I think of gold as money too, so I put gold into the cross-rate mix. It's just another currency.

The difference between when we're in a currency war and when we're not is that normally there's stability. I don't mean that we have fixed exchange rates. We don't: we have floating exchange rates. But the central banks agree to keep their currencies within a certain range when the currency wars are off. When the currency wars are on, however, all bets are off. Anything can happen.

They're very dynamic and very complicated, and we watch them very closely in *Strategic Intelligence*. There are a lot of ways for investors to win.

Introducing: My Proprietary IMPACT System

I've developed a proprietary system called "IMPACT" to use the see-sawing currency dynamics of the global currency wars for big, fast gains. IMPACT is an acronym for "International Monetary Policy Analysis and Currency Trading." One of the core system components is a relatively new branch of science known as "complexity theory." Learn how to start using my IMPACT System now by calling 1-866-361-7662 or visiting **www.agorafinancial.info/IMPACT**.

■ The Difference Between Currency Wars and Financial Wars

People sometimes conflate currency wars with financial wars— but they are not the same thing.

A currency war is a battle, but it's primarily economic. It's about economic policy. The basic idea is that countries want to cheapen their currency. Now, they say they want to cheapen their currency to promote exports. Maybe it makes a Boeing more competitive internationally with an Airbus.

But the real reason, the one that's less talked about, is that countries actually want to import inflation. Take the United States, for example. We have a trade deficit, not a surplus. If the dollar's cheaper it may make our exports slightly more attractive. But it's going to increase the price of the goods we buy—whether it's manufactured goods, textiles, electronics, or something else—and that inflation then feeds into the supply chain in the United States.

So, currency wars are actually a way of creating monetary ease and importing inflation. It's part of why Japan is doing Abenomics.

The problem is that once one country tries to cheapen its currency, another country tries to cheapen its currency, and so on, causing a race to the bottom. It's a kind of struggle that's primarily economic.

Financial wars are different. Financial war is just the continuation of traditional war by different means. Instead of using missiles or ships or drones, you use stocks, bonds and derivatives. Another difference is that the goal isn't economic gain; it's economic advantage or political gain.

That means the goals of financial war include damaging your enemies' infrastructure, impairing their markets and increasing their costs or interest rates. In other words, the goal is to damage your opponent's economy.

What does warfare do? It damages the enemy's economy. You transfer wealth from them to you. Financial war is no different. If another nation or group wanted to defeat the United States, they couldn't do it militarily. But they might be able to do it economically.

▤ Financial Wars Are Coming to the Fore

Financial warfare is not a metaphor—it's real. There's real financial warfare going on now. It has been for years, and it will continue in the future.

Think of a traditional Venn diagram: one big circle is the world of national security, intelligence and defense. Another big circle is the world of capital markets, stocks, bonds, commodities, derivatives and so on. Think of the intersection of the two—that's what we're talking about.

That intersection is getting bigger and more important, and there are very few people standing there. There are brilliant practitioners on both sides—on the military side and on the financial side. But the number of people who are really conversing with both worlds is small. That's going to be more and more important to you as an investor, going forward.

I was fortunate enough to participate in a financial war game that was conducted in 2009. I was invited by the Pentagon to be a facilitator and a planner for it. Of course, the Pentagon, our Defense Department, had been doing war games forever. They didn't need any help from me in a traditional war game.

But this was the first financial war game ever done. The weapons were nonkinetic, meaning nothing that would shoot or explode. We could only use stocks, bonds, currencies, derivatives and commodities. We had some of the usual teams, as you might imagine.

There was a U.S. team, a Russian team, a Chinese team and so forth. We also had a team of banks and hedge funds because they're very important players in the space as well.

We spent days—no, months—designing this and played it out over a couple of days in March 2009 at a top-secret weapons laboratory outside of Washington—the applied-physics laboratory.

What was interesting was one of the scenarios that I introduced. Some colleagues, who were playing as the Russian and

Chinese teams, would get together, pool their gold and issue a new currency backed by that gold. Of course, we had the gold in a Swiss vault and the currency issued by a U.K. bank because nobody would trust a Russian or a Chinese bank.

Using those safe jurisdictions to issue this new currency, Russia and China would then say that henceforth, any Russian natural resource exports or any Chinese manufactured exports could only be paid for in this new currency. If you wanted some, you could trade and earn it or you could deposit your gold and they would issue the currency, and then you could use this for transactions with them.

Obviously, this was a stretch. This is not anything that was going to happen tomorrow. But at that time, we were actually ridiculed. We had uniformed military and intelligence experts, and people from the Fed, the U.S. Treasury, think tanks and universities actually ridicule us, saying, "This is ridiculous. Don't you know gold has no place in the monetary system? It's obsolete. Why are you doing this? This just seems like a waste of time."

Be that as it may, we played it out.

I won't take you through every move—I describe it all in my first book, *Currency Wars*. Since 2009, Russia has increased its gold reserves by 70 percent. China has increased its gold reserves several hundred percent. No one knows the exact number because China's not transparent about it.

In 2009, China reported it had 1,054 tons. For the first time in six years, in June 2015, China reported its gold holdings. China reported then that it had 1,658 metric tons of gold in its reserves. Whether today it has 3,000 tons or 4,000 tons, no one knows exactly. But that's the right order of magnitude, and it seems determined to acquire more.

Its actions were actually playing out as we had modeled it for the Defense Department in 2009. China is a very robust actor in financial warfare.

As for the United States, we've been in a financial war with Iran since 2011. The United States has done a couple of things. This is, of course, because of Iran's uranium-enrichment efforts and a drive to get nuclear weapons.

The United States first kicked Iran out of the dollar payment system that's called Fedwire. It's a clearance system run by the Federal Reserve. We said, "Iran, you're out, and your banks are out. Any Swiss or other foreign banks that do business with Iran: you're out too."

That's the way the United States forces other banks to follow its policy—by telling them they can't do business in the United States unless they comply.

Iran said, "Fine, we'll just ship our oil and price it in euros. We don't need your dollars and we don't need your dollar payment system."

There's another, even larger payment system in Europe called SWIFT—Society for Worldwide Interbank Funds Transfers—and you can pay in euros, yen, Australian dollars or any other reserve currency.

The United States then got together with its allies and prevailed on them to kick Iran out of SWIFT. Now the Iranians were stuck. They could ship oil, but they couldn't get paid for it, at least not in any currency they would want. They began a number of workarounds, including acquiring massive amounts of gold from Turkey so they could arrange gold-for-import swaps. They were selling oil to India, for example.

India could pay Iran in rupees and deposit them in an Indian bank account that was outside the payment system I described. So then Iran had rupees, but what can you do with those?

You can buy things in India, but I'm not sure how much curry the Iranians actually needed. Indian merchants were very inventive: because the rupee is a convertible currency, they got dollars, imported goods to India and then sent them to Iran for rupees, converting them back to dollars and taking spreads all along the way. It was very costly to Iran, but it worked.

The Iranians citizens themselves then tried to take their money out of the bank because there was a black market for dollars—some of which were smuggled in from Iraq, which could get dollars. They could pay smugglers in Dubai to bring back the computers and the cellphones and the printers and all the other things they enjoyed.

That caused a run on the bank because people were taking out the little currency they had to go to the black markets. In response, the Iranian government raised interest rates to try to keep the money in the bank, and inflation broke out.

We really came close to destroying the Iranian economy with, as I say, financial weapons—no boots on the ground and no missiles, just a little bit of sabotage here and there, but not much more than that.

We caused high inflation and a run on the bank, contracted Iran's economy and had a very powerful impact on the Iranian economy. Iran was moving toward regime change.

President Obama lifted a lot of these sanctions because the Iranians made some promises.

Don't think that Vladimir Putin wasn't watching when the United States backed away from those financial sanctions, because we have another financial war brewing—a couple of them actually—in the Middle East.

I gave you the Iranian example just to show that these financial weapons are very powerful. The United States uses them aggressively to destabilize countries. Of course, the United States works hand in glove with the IMF to do the same thing.

Financial warfare is real. It's going on, and if you're an investor and you're not aware of it, you're occasionally going to get blindsided.

I can't tell you how many very good fundamental stock

analysts and bond analysts I've met, who've spent, in some case, decades learning their craft and understanding how to analyze markets, get slammed every now and then because Angela Merkel got out on the wrong side of the bed and decided to have a fight with the Greek finance minister.

You can't ignore global macro events if you are a fundamental investor making fundamental decisions because these things are not going away; in fact they're becoming more important.

▦ The New World War Is Already Here—Here's How to Protect Your Money

Financial warfare is not the warfare of the future—it is *already* here and it's going to become a bigger threat as time goes on. Your chance to protect your portfolio is now.

But before we explain how and why it's important, let's begin by analyzing this new kind of war with a definition. Financial warfare, like conventional warfare, is intended to enhance national power, diminish the power of rivals and achieve policy goals. It is actual warfare conducted through banking and capital markets. It is not mere economic policy, as in the case of so-called currency wars, trade wars or embargoes.

Financial warfare can serve many purposes. The 2015 U.S. financial war on Russia, for example, was intended as punishment for its support of rebellion in eastern Ukraine. It can also be used to force behavior of certain kinds. The 2012 U.S. financial war on Iran was intended to force Iran to the bargaining table with regard to its uranium-enrichment activities and pursuit of nuclear weapons.

The financial-warfare battlespace can be offensive or defensive. Offensive capability includes attacks on banks and stock exchanges to steal data, shut down systems or cause financial panics. Defensive capability includes the construction of firewalls, creation of redundant systems and creation of nondigital substitute systems that cannot be hacked.

For example, during a recent financial war game exercise at the Pentagon, I recommended that the SEC and New York Stock Exchange buy a warehouse in New York and equip it with copper-wire hardline phones, handheld battery-powered calculators and other pre-internet equipment. This facility would serve as a nondigital stock exchange with trading posts.

The SEC would assign 30 major stocks each to the 20 largest broker-dealers, who would be designated specialists in those stocks. This would provide market making on the 600 largest stocks, covering over 90 percent of all trading on a typical day.

Orders would be phoned in on the hardwire analogue phone system and put up for bids and offers by the specialists to a crowd of live brokers. This is exactly how stocks were traded until recently. Computerized and algorithmic trading would be banned as nonessential. Only real investor interest would be represented in this nondigital venue.

In the event of a shutdown of the New York Stock Exchange by digital attack, the nondigital exchange would be activated. The United States would let China and Russia know this facility existed as a deterrent to a digital attack in the first place. If our rivals knew we had a robust nondigital Plan B, they might not bother to conduct a digital attack in the first place.

Financial-warfare attacks vary in their degree of sophistication and impact. At the low end of the spectrum is a "distributed denial of service" attack. This is done by flooding a target server with an overwhelming volume of message traffic so that either the server shuts down or legitimate users cannot gain access. In such attacks, the target is not actually penetrated, but it is disabled by the message traffic jam.

The next level of sophistication is a cyberhack in which the target—say, a bank account record file or a stock exchange order system—is actually penetrated. Once inside, the attacking cyberbrigade can steal information, shut down the system or plant sleeper-attack viruses that can be activated at a later date.

In 2010, the FBI and Department of Homeland Security located such an attack virus planted by Russian security services inside the Nasdaq stock market system. You have probably noticed that unexplained stock market outages and flash crashes are happening with increasing frequency. Some of these events may be self-inflicted damage by the exchanges themselves in the course of software upgrades, but others are highly suspicious and the exact causes have never been disclosed by exchange officials.

Here is a recently revealed classified map showing cyberattacks by the Chinese government against U.S. interests. Each dot represents an attack. Notice the concentration of attacks against technology targets in San Francisco, financial targets in New York and military and intelligence targets in the Washington-Virginia area.

The most dangerous attacks of all are those in which the enemy penetrates a bank or stock exchange not to disable it or steal information but to turn it into an enemy drone. Such a market drone can be used by attackers for maximum market disruption and the mass destruction of Americans' wealth *including your stocks and savings.*

In this scenario, an attacker could penetrate the order-entry system of a major stock exchange, such as the New York Stock Exchange, or one of the order-matching dark pools operated by major investment banks, such as the SIGMA X system controlled by Goldman Sachs. Once inside the order-entry system, the attacker would place large sell orders on highly liquid stocks such as Apple or Facebook.

Other system participants would then automatically match these orders in the mistaken belief that they were real trades. The sell orders would keep flooding the market until eventually other participants lowered their bids and began to deflect the selling pressure to other exchanges.

An attack of this type would be launched on a day when the market was already down 3 percent or more, about 550 points on the Dow Jones index. Using exogenous events like that to increase the power of a planned attack is called a "force multiplier" by military strategists.

The result could be a market decline of 20 percent or more in a single day, comparable to the stock market crash of October 1987 or the crash of 1929. You would not have to trade anything or be in the market during the attack; you would be wiped out based on the market decline even if you did nothing.

Another type of highly malicious attack is to penetrate the account-records system of a major bank and then systematically erase account balances in customers' deposit accounts and 401(k)s. If the attack extended to backup databases, you or other customers might have no way of proving you ever owned the deleted accounts.

Some analysts respond to such scenarios by saying that the United States has cyberwarfare attack capabilities that are just as effective as our enemies'. If Iran, China or Russia ever launched a financial cyberattack on the United States, we could retaliate.

The threat of retaliation, they claim, would act as a deterrent and prevent the enemy attack in the first place. This is similar to the doctrine of "mutually assured destruction," which prevented nuclear conflict between the United States and Russia during the Cold War.

This analysis is highly flawed and gives false comfort. MAD worked during the Cold War because both sides wanted to avoid existential losses. In financial warfare, the losses may be existential for the United States but not for Russia, China and Iran. Because they are far less developed than the United States, their markets could be destroyed and it would have little impact on their overall economy or national security.

Many stocks in Russia and China are owned by U.S. and European investors, so any damage would come back to haunt Western interests.

The technological warfare capabilities may be symmetric, but the potential damage is asymmetric, so the deterrent effect on China and Russia is low. There is essentially nothing stopping Russia, Iran or China from launching a "first strike" financial-warfare attack if it serves some other national strategic purpose.

What can you do to preserve wealth when these financial cyberwars break out?

The key is to have some portion of your total assets invested in nondigital assets that cannot be hacked, wiped out or disrupted in financial warfare. Such assets include gold, silver, land, fine art and private equity, which is usually represented by a paper contract and does not rely on electronic exchange trading for liquidity.

For gold, I recommend you have a 10 percent allocation to physical gold if you don't already. Specifically I recommend American Gold Eagle or American Buffalo gold coins from the U.S. Mint. For silver, I've recommended owning what's called a "Monster Box." It's a container of 500 one-ounce silver eagles. This is also available through the Mint.

As for other alternative investments, like fine art, please see the briefing we held in March 2015 called "The Investment Secrets of the Palazzo Colonna," which you can view by logging into our subscriber website and accessing the live briefing archives. There are many recommendations there, including some that will cost you less than $1,000 to get started. We're also exploring avenues for introducing private-equity opportunities to you. There will be more information on that when the opportunities become possible and relevant.

As an investor, you have enough to be concerned about just taking into account factors like inflation, deflation, Fed policy and the overall state of the economy. Now you have another major threat looming—financial warfare, enabled by cyberattacks and force multipliers. The time to take defensive action by acquiring some nondigital assets is now.

My Financial-War Conversation With America's Top Spy

Only one person has ever been director of both the National Security Agency and the Central Intelligence Agency. That person is retired four-star general Michael Hayden.

On June 1, 2015, I had the chance to talk to Mike Hayden on Capitol Hill in Washington, D.C.

We were both there as part of a conclave to discuss the status of Iran-United States negotiations on uranium enrichment and Iran's nuclear-weapons program. We had a chance to talk one-on-one about my specialty, which is financial warfare, and the potential impact on investors. Needless to say, General Hayden's insights were fascinating.

General Hayden's career as a military and intelligence officer spans four decades beginning with his commission as an Air Force officer in 1969.

From 1980 to 1982, he was intelligence chief at Osan Air

Force Base in Korea. From 1996 to 1997, he commanded the Air Intelligence Agency, today part of the Twenty-Fifth Air Force, which is 1 of the 17 separate agencies that make up the U.S. intelligence community.

From 1999 to 2005, he was director of the National Security Agency, based at Fort Meade, Maryland. The NSA is America's lead agency for electronic and technical spying. For many years, the mere existence of the NSA was classified information; intelligence-community members said the acronym NSA stood for "No Such Agency."

In response to the 9/11 attacks, the U.S. Congress in 2004 created the Office of the Director of National Intelligence, with John Negroponte as its first director. From 2005 to 2006, General Hayden was principal deputy director of national intelligence under DNI John Negroponte.

Finally, in 2006, Hayden became the 20th director of the CIA, where he served until 2009. Given Mike Hayden's long career in military and civilian intelligence agencies and his expertise in both electronic intelligence and human intelligence, it is no exaggeration to call him "America's Top Spy."

This was not my first meeting with General Hayden. In an earlier meeting, while he was still at CIA, he told a fascinating story about his time as a military attaché at the U.S. Embassy during the Cold War in what was then the People's Republic of Bulgaria.

He would board a train and simply travel from one end of the country to the other, making mental notes about armored vehicles seen at rail sidings and coal loadings, and other indications and warnings that provided insight into the state of the economy there. He looked for the presence of any Soviet troops.

In one encounter, he was seated in a shared train compartment with three young Soviet soldiers.

They saw his U.S. Air Force uniform and assumed he did not speak Russian. They proceeded to start drinking on the train and spoke in an unguarded manner among themselves, becoming more animated and loquacious as the vodka flowed. Finally, just before disembarking, General Hayden greeted the Soviet soldiers in fluent Russian. Their faces turned white because they realized he understood every word they had said.

On other occasions, Hayden dressed in simple street clothes and listened in on conversations among construction workers to get an idea about consumer prices, food and fuel availability and other basic economic indicators.

Often the best spies are not those in the glamorous James Bond mold, but those who patiently practice simple tradecraft combined with a good knowledge of foreign languages and culture.

Mike Hayden was certainly helped in these efforts by his blue-collar roots in Pittsburgh including time as a taxi driver while working his way through college and graduate school.

My conversation with General Hayden focused on my own specialty, market intelligence, and the ongoing financial wars between the United States and Russia and Iran.

Hayden agreed with me that financial war will be a primary means of warfare in the 21st century. He referred to financial sanctions as "the PGMs of the 21st century," a reference to precision guided munitions.

In effect, asset freezes would replace cruise missiles as a way to disable an enemy.

As I discussed above, the United States was in a financial war with Iran from 2011 to 2013 prior to the start of formal negotiations about Iran's uranium enrichment. Secret negotiations had been going on for years, but the United States wanted to bring pressure to accelerate the pace of negotiations and produce concrete results. The negotiations were intended to avert an attack by either Israel or the United States.

The United States first excluded Iran from the dollar payments system, but Iran simply switched its payments to euros,

Swiss francs and other hard currencies.

Next, the United States and its allies kicked Iran out of the global payments system, called the Society for Worldwide Interbank Financial Telecommunication, or SWIFT.

This meant that Iran could ship oil but could not get paid in hard currency. It also meant Iran had to resort to gold and barter to obtain needed imports of gasoline and other essential goods.

Exclusion from the global payments systems caused Iranians to withdraw their money from local banks so they could purchase smuggled dollars on the black market.

This run on the banks forced the central bank of Iran to raise interest rates. The black market dollar exchange rate showed the Iranian currency had lost half its value.

The result was hyperinflation in Iran. The combination of bank runs, inflation, currency collapse, sky-high interest rates and shortages of imported products was highly destabilizing. At that point, the United States could have tightened sanctions even further, possibly causing regime change in Iran.

Instead, in December 2013, President Obama removed many of the sanctions in exchange for the start of formal negotiations on Iran's nuclear-weapons program. Those negotiations have dragged on ever since and are nearing the point of a final deal that will be put to Congress for consideration. The final deal has not yet been revealed, but the broad outlines are known.

General Hayden calls this a "bad deal" for America because it lacks verification procedures.

He said that U.S. intelligence is good, but not good enough to know if Iran is trying to "break out" of the deal and race to a nuclear weapon. He told me, "Unilateral American intelligence is insufficient to verify compliance. Iran must agree to an intrusive inspection regime. American intelligence is good—it will tell you a lot—but it cannot verify compliance by Iran."

America was winning its financial war with Iran but then

declared a truce before the job was done. Now we are facing an unverifiable nuclear deal with Iran. If the inspections regime breaks down, which it probably will, America may return to financial warfare with Iran. The procedure for reimposing financial sanctions if Iran does not live up to its obligations under a nuclear deal is called "snapback" authority.

America is in another financial war with Russia in response to Russia's annexation of Crimea and its support for separatists in eastern Ukraine. Severe financial sanctions have been imposed on Russia including a ban on refinancing hard-currency corporate debt in U.S. or European capital markets.

The United States and its allies have not yet kicked Russia out of the SWIFT payments system, a process known in financial-warfare circles as "de-swifting." The Russian prime minister, Dmitry Medvedev, has said Russia would regard de-swifting as an "act of war" subject to military retaliation. Russia's ability to retaliate against the United States in a financial war is much greater than Iran's. Russia has a 6,000-member cyberbrigade that is capable of closing down U.S. stock exchanges and banks. Russia would not use these tactics casually, but would nonetheless use them if U.S. economic pressure becomes too severe.

Given this recent history of financial warfare with Iran and Russia, I asked General Hayden if the United States was possibly overusing its financial weapons. Today, these weapons are extremely powerful. But the history of warfare reveals that every offensive weapon is first countered with strong defenses and then eventually made obsolete by improved offensive weapons of the enemy.

With the United States putting financial pressure on Iran, Russia and China, wasn't it likely that these countries would create their own payments systems, develop their own banks and reserve currencies, and turn their back on the U.S. dollar system entirely?

If Russia, Iran, China, Turkey and others no longer relied on U.S. dollars, then control of the dollar system would lose its potency as a weapon. So I was asking if the United States was taking the dollar for granted as a source of strength in financial warfare.

General Hayden agreed this is or will be a problem, if not today, then in the not-too-distant future. He said, "The more you use sanctions, the less effective they become because you motivate your adversaries to develop alternative payment systems. I'm not sure if an alternative payment system will be built before we might want to snap back sanctions on Iran, but if it's not over this ridgeline, it's over the next one."

General Hayden also alluded to what he called "the dynamic of the unpleasant fact." He said this happens when you have to deliver truly bad news to the president. He said a conversation might begin, "Sir, that war we planned starts today." In today's battlespace, that statement could just as well apply to cyberattacks on stock exchanges as to dropping bunker-busting bombs on Iran.

For investors, the implications of this new age of financial warfare are profound. Stock and bond markets have always been affected by wars. But the wars were fought elsewhere—stocks and bonds merely adjusted in price to the new state of the world.

Today, markets are not bystanders; they are ground zero. It's fascinating to meet brilliant military and intelligence officials like General Hayden who are rapidly absorbing the fact that wars are now fought in financial markets rather than on air, sea and land.

The military and intelligence communities are absorbing the new reality, but most investors are still behind the curve. Traditional stocks and bonds are digital assets that can be hacked, wiped out or frozen with a few keystrokes. It's important to allocate part of your portfolio to physical assets that cannot be wiped out in financial warfare.

These assets include silver, gold, fine art, land, rare stamps, cash (in banknote form, not bank deposits) and other physical stores of value. For the portion of your portfolio that is in stocks, it is helpful to consider venture capital and start-up companies where your ownership is in the form of a written contract, not a digital account.

My conversation with General Hayden reinforced my already strong view that financial warfare is here and digital assets such as brokerage accounts and 401(k)s are in the line of fire.

At *Strategic Intelligence*, we keep you informed on the state of financial warfare and make solid recommendations for ways to preserve wealth even as the financial bullets are flying.

▓ Return to the Pentagon

As I noted previously, in my 2011 book *Currency Wars* I gave a detailed description of the first-ever financial war game sponsored by the Department of Defense.

This financial war game took place in 2009 at the top-secret Applied Physics Laboratory, located about 20 miles north of Washington, D.C., in the Maryland countryside.

Unlike typical war games, the "rules of engagement" for this financial exercise did not permit the use of any kinetic weapons such as bombs, missiles or drones.

The only weapons allowed were financial instruments, including stocks, bonds, currencies, commodities and derivatives. The object of each team was to enhance its own power and diminish the power of its rivals.

The game was played out over two days in the main war room of the laboratory using six teams divided into the United States, China, Russia, Europe, East Asia, and banks and hedge funds.

The contestants included about 40 players on the six teams and another 60 participants, including uniformed military, civilian defense officials and observers from the Treasury, the Federal Reserve, the CIA and other government agencies, as well as think tanks, universities and financial-industry professionals.

In that original financial war game, a scenario involving Russia, China, gold and the destruction of the U.S. dollar was played out against a backdrop of geopolitical events including the collapse of North Korea and a threatened Chinese invasion of Taiwan.

Despite much skepticism about the role of gold in the international monetary system expressed by some of the players, events since 2009 have validated the scenarios revealed to the Pentagon at the time.

Russia has more than doubled its gold reserves, and China has increased its gold reserves by more than 300 percent since we first warned the Pentagon about this growing financial threat.

The dollar is still the leading global reserve currency, but its future is increasingly uncertain due to real-world trends that have followed the paths we outlined in that original war game in 2009.

On May 8, 2015, the Pentagon sponsored a new financial-warfare session I was also invited to attend. This time, the financial war took place inside a secure meeting facility at the Pentagon itself. As was the case in 2009, the war game was organized by the Office of Net Assessment, part of the Office of the Secretary of Defense.

The ONA is tasked by the Pentagon with the job of futurology—looking years and decades over the horizon to identify threats to U.S. national security that are not yet on the radar screens of the military commanders.

When we played out the gold attack on the dollar in 2009, we did not believe it would happen immediately but we could see trends moving in that direction and tried to give the Pentagon a glimpse of the future.

Now, six years later, those threats had arrived in the form of Russian and Chinese gold purchases, the launch by China of the Asian Infrastructure Investment Bank, the BRICS contingency reserve fund and other initiatives designed to diminish and eventually eliminate the dollar from large parts of global commerce and banking.

Now it was time to pick up where we had left off and give the Pentagon another look over the horizon.

May 8, 2015, was a sobering time to be at the Pentagon because it was the 70th anniversary of victory in Europe (V-E Day) on May 8, 1945. The celebration of victory was muted by the remembrance of the enormous sacrifices at Anzio, D-Day, the Battle of the Bulge and other battles that led to victory. One recalled the horrors of war and the particular horror of the Holocaust committed by the defeated Nazis.

The Pentagon staged a special flyover using vintage aircraft from the Second World War, collectively known as the Ghost Squadron, which included the only flying B-29 Superfortress bomber, the B-17 Flying Fortress and P-51 Mustang fighters.

It was a warm, beautiful spring day, and we were able to observe the flyover from a pedestrian bridge as we walked from the ONA offices to the secure war room in an adjacent building.

This new financial war game exercise was smaller and more focused than the one in 2009. We had about 20 participants. Our group included representatives from the diplomatic corps, the military, think tanks, universities, the CIA and the National Security Council.

I was one of three individuals from the investment-management community. Our scenario this time was not global but was limited to a confrontation between China and the United States involving disputed jurisdiction in the South China Sea.

There are six nations that have claims in the South China Sea—China, Taiwan, the Philippines, Malaysia, Vietnam and Brunei. These claims overlap to a great extent, setting the stage for disputes and possible war.

The South China Sea is believed to be rich in oil and natural gas reserves in addition to fish and other natural resources. The surrounding nations dispute certain island groups—the Spratly Islands and the Paracel Islands—and are also using reefs, sunken vessels and landfill to create artificial islands, which they are populating with bases and military garrisons.

The United States has treaty obligations to the Philippines and Taiwan, which could result in the United States becoming engaged militarily in the event of a dispute with China. This volatile mix of disputed claims, natural resources and complex treaty networks has the ingredients needed to escalate into a third world war.

All it would take to start a war is some spark such as a collision at sea or an attack based on mistaken identity or misunderstood intentions. A war there is probably just a matter of time.

Our role was not to contemplate the use of aircraft carriers, submarines or missiles in such a confrontation. We were there to consider the use of financial weapons such as disruption of payments systems, cyberattacks on banks and stock exchanges, and trade sanctions that could cut off supply chains and dry up energy imports.

One of the main topics of discussion was the use of sanctions involving access to SWIFT. Contrary to the assumptions of many, SWIFT itself is not a bank or a financial institution. It is more like a phone company or internet service provider, which facilitates communication among its members.

SWIFT has over 10,500 banks and asset managers as members and handles over 5 billion messages each year, amounting to trillions of dollars of payments from one member to another.

SWIFT message traffic is the oxygen supply that keeps the global financial system alive.

As I discussed in detail above, in 2012 the United States and its allies were successful in kicking Iranian banks out of the SWIFT system. This was extremely damaging to the Iranian economy and led to hyperinflation, bank runs, instability and social unrest until President Obama eased these sanctions in late 2013.

Recently, the U.S. Senate has called for the use of SWIFT-related sanctions against Russia. In response, Russia has said it would regard an effort to ban access to SWIFT as an act of war.

In our new financial war game, we asked what would happen if the roles were reversed. Instead of the United States banning its enemies from SWIFT, what if China tried to "de-swift" Taiwan or the Philippines? What if financial weapons developed by the United States were adopted by China and turned against the United States and its allies?

These and other interesting scenarios made for a long and lively day of discussions among our team of experts convened for this exercise in 21st-century warfare.

In addition to contributing to these scenarios, I am also privileged to learn from my expert colleagues in the room. All of us walk away with some knowledge that does not seem to have any individual source but emerges from the ether of a talented assembly working on cutting-edge problems of the utmost importance to national security.

I learned two lessons on May 8, 2015, that I am fortunate to be able to share with you.

The first is that when nations engage in financial warfare, individual investors can be collateral damage. If China tries to attack the United States by closing the New York Stock Exchange, it will be tens of millions of Americans who will suffer an immediate loss of wealth as prices plunge and accounts are locked down or frozen.

The second lesson was that the financial war will be fought in cyberspace using digital technology applied to payments systems such as SWIFT, Fedwire, MasterCard, Visa and Europe's Target2 system.

The answer to both threats—collateral damage and digital warfare—is to have some hard assets in physical form that cannot be attacked digitally. Such assets include physical gold and silver, land, buildings, fine art and rare stamps. These are the things that cannot be erased in a digital attack or frozen when payments systems are disrupted.

There is good evidence that Russian and Chinese plutocrats are already moving in this direction with their purchases of Picasso paintings and high-end condos in Sydney, London and Vancouver.

Americans seem more complacent and are mostly locked into their digital 401(k)s. Some diversification into hard assets seems prudent in light of the emerging threats we discussed inside the Pentagon on V-E Day.

■ The Petrodollar

Of course, there have been a couple of new developments. I mentioned that in December of 2013 President Obama shook hands with Iran and entered into direct negotiations for the first time since 1979.

In effect, Obama anointed Iran as the regional hegemon in the Persian Gulf. This was taken by Saudi Arabia as a stab in the back.

The Saudi–United States relationship goes back to the late 1940s. But in particular, in the mid-1970s, there was a very famous deal struck between Henry Kissinger—who was President Nixon and, later, President Ford's leading national security adviser and secretary of state—and the Saudi king.

In this deal they said that the Saudis agreed to price oil

in dollars. The Saudis didn't have to do that. They could have said, "We'll take gold." There were other currencies at that time, such as the deutschmark, yen and French francs. But they said, "We will only take dollars for oil." That put a prop under the dollar.

The United States agreed to guarantee their national security. We made good on that guarantee in 1991 when Saddam Hussein invaded Kuwait and threatened Saudi Arabia—the United States did respond to that forcefully.

That deal was in place for over 40 years. It was torn up in December 2013. Again, the Saudis took it as a stab in the back. Here was the United States saying to Iran, "Not only are you the regional power, but we're going to let you continue on your path to nuclear weapons." Imagine what that felt like from the perspective of Saudi Arabia.

The Saudis haven't done anything drastic yet, but they are reevaluating this "petrodollar" relationship. The Saudis may say, "Okay, if you don't have our back, if you're not protecting our national security, why should we support your currency and not start pricing oil in euros or perhaps yuan or any other currency to the parties who are actually buying our oil?" That would remove a very significant prop under the U.S. dollar.

Since 2013, there have been new developments. On January 18, 2016, the United States lifted sanctions on Iran. This is a huge snowflake that could set off an avalanche.

Saudi Arabia, long an ally of the United States, considers Iran's rise an existential threat for political, financial and religious reasons. Tensions between Saudi Arabia and Iran are escalating, as witness the recent execution of a senior Shiite cleric in Saudi Arabia and the Iranian retaliation by burning down the Saudi embassy in Tehran.

Yet, major companies around the world, mostly European, can't wait to get back to "business as usual" in Tehran. The United States is trying to stay friendly with Iran and Saudi Arabia. This policy will inevitably fail. The United States clearly favors Iran (despite Iran flouting agreements and working against U.S. interests in many areas).

This United States tilt to Iran will force Saudi Arabia to find a new patron. Obviously the new patron will be China (the largest customer in the world for Saudi oil).

The market implications are clear: Saudi Arabia will de-peg from the dollar (a financial avalanche of major proportions).

The Saudis will then re-peg to a basket (possibly the SDR, or more likely an ad hoc basket including the yuan). From there it's a short step to pricing oil in the basket currency or perhaps the yuan itself. This will cause a major run on the dollar and cause major dollar inflation (even as the "basket price" remains stable).

This could be the biggest shake-up in global currency alignments since the 1970s!

This financial warfare, as I say, is more and more pervasive. The last event I want to call attention to is what's going on in Ukraine.

Russia has taken over Crimea. I think that's a fait accompli: they're not leaving anytime soon. No one in the United States—left, right or center—thinks that the United States should have a military response to this, a traditional military response. No boots on the ground: we're not going to put the 82nd Airborne Division into Sevastopol.

What do you do? You can't just shrug and ignore it. So, of course, the United States immediately used economic sanctions, which are a form of financial warfare. I said at the time—and I've been saying ever since—these financial sanctions are not going to go very far. Why is that?

It takes us back to the 1960s and the 1970s to a doctrine I mentioned above called "mutual assured destruction"—MAD. You may recall it.

This doctrine actually still applies, although it's much

less talked about today. At the time, the United States had enough nuclear missiles to destroy Russia. Likewise, Russia, or the Soviet Union, had enough nuclear missiles to destroy the United States. There was an enormous temptation to shoot first. If you could fire your missiles and destroy the other side, you won. Both sides were aware of that, so they said, "What we need is so-called second-strike capability. That way, if the other side shoots their missiles and devastates our country, we're going to have enough missiles left to shoot back and destroy their country." Therefore, both sides developed a second-strike capability.

This is what the 1960s and 1970s was all about. You can analogize this to two scorpions in a bottle. One scorpion can sting and kill the other, but the victim has just enough strength left to sting back, and they both die.

■ Russia, Ukraine and the Future of Sanctions

In early February 2015, I traveled to Washington, D.C., for a private meeting with top national security, defense and intelligence professionals. Our meeting was focused on a specific aspect of threat finance—the Russian invasion of eastern Ukraine, and the behind-the-scenes financial war that has been going on in response.

Our group of about a dozen experts met behind closed doors at a think tank on M Street in downtown Washington. We operated under Chatham House rules, which means that participants cannot mention or quote other participants by name. But it is permitted to describe the tone and substance of the conversation. Included around the table were subject-matter experts and former officials from the State Department, Defense Department, U.S. Treasury, White House National Security Council, and CIA.

It was the perfect mix of defense, diplomacy, finance and

intelligence. Our mission was to evaluate the economic sanctions currently in place against Russia and to develop recommendations for changes in sanctions policy if needed. These recommendations would later be made public with a view to influencing sanctions policy either in the current or next White House administration.

This is the kind of work that has enormous implications for investors and their portfolios but which is too often unknown to the Wall Street analysts on whom investors rely. At *Strategic Intelligence*, our goal is to synthesize geopolitics with capital-markets expertise so that investors are not blindsided by geopolitical earthquakes that seem far removed from the quotidian concerns of finance.

Our discussion began on a note of frustration from the assembled experts that U.S. economic sanctions had not produced any change in Russian behavior. The United States and most of its allies were unhappy with the Russian takeover of Crimea but were prepared to live with that outcome for various historic and strategic reasons. Crimea has historically been part of Russia, and the Russia Black Sea Fleet, the only warm-water fleet in Russia, was based there. Putin's methods in securing Russian interests in Crimea were blunt, but effective, and NATO seemed willing to treat it as a fait accompli. But Russian support for rebel forces in eastern Ukraine, including the use of Russian troops and heavy weapons, was seen as completely unacceptable. It was a blatant breach of international law and territorial integrity that could not be rationalized in the way that Crimea could.

Despite the egregious nature of Russian involvement in eastern Ukraine, there was no consensus that a NATO military response should result. That battle would be up to the main Ukrainian forces directed by Kiev. But the United States and its Western allies did agree to impose economic sanctions. These were mild at first, involving travel bans and asset freezes on certain Russian oligarchs and officials. When these sanctions failed to modify Russian behavior, they were enhanced to prohibit financing activity of many important Russian companies by Western banks.

The economic impact of the sanctions was severe and undeniable. Russia's GDP dropped precipitously, and the exchange value of the ruble collapsed. There was a drain on Russia's foreign reserves. These were used to prop up Russian companies that could no longer access dollar markets to refinance their debts. Of course, these sanctions came at the same time that global oil prices crashed in late 2014, which made the Russian dilemma even worse. It was in response to these developments that President Obama claimed that the sanctions were "working."

Importantly, there was good evidence that the business interests of Russian oligarchs had been severely impacted. Their revenues were drying up, their stock valuations were down and ultimately their companies could fail if they could not refinance their dollar-denominated debts. This was important because it was believed that desperate oligarchs would put pressure on Putin to force him to seek a reasonable accommodation with the West.

But the sanctions were only working in terms of their economic impact; they were *not* working to alter Russia's behavior. The conflict in eastern Ukraine actually intensified in late 2014 and early 2015, with significant rebel gains against Ukrainian forces. It was this conundrum—sanctions were economically effective but politically impotent—that preoccupied my colleagues. Time and again they asked: what does Putin want? The implication was that Putin was an enigma but if we could discern his hidden preferences a sanctions regime could be devised to frustrate those preferences and, in turn, alter his behavior.

When my turn came to address the group, I cut to the heart of our failed sanctions policy. The entire program was an example of a well-known intelligence failure called "mirror imaging." This arises when an analyst assumes the adversary thinks the way he does. Policies that might change the analyst's behavior are assumed to affect the adversary's behavior the same way. The mirror-image assumption often proves false, and can result in failed policy.

For example, America has its own oligarchs including Warren Buffett, Bill Gates and Larry Page. It is reasonable to assume that if harsh sanctions by others were to seriously impact the economic interests of Buffett, Gates and Page, they would find a way to pressure the White House for sanctions relief, including changes in U.S. policy if needed.

But the obverse isn't true. Pressure on Russian oligarchs is easy to apply, but their ability to influence Putin's behavior is nil. In fact, Putin would not hesitate to imprison or kill them if they were too outspoken. One cannot imagine the White House throwing Warren Buffett in prison for being a policy critic, but a similar outcome is easy to imagine in Russia. Unfortunately, U.S. policy makers had fallen prey to mirror imaging and did not realize that pressuring Russian oligarchs, compared to U.S. oligarchs, would produce different outcomes.

The other area where U.S. policy makers were guilty of mirror imaging is assessing the impact of economic costs. Declining GDP and a crashing currency would send most U.S. politicians running for cover and looking for ways to undo the damage. But Russians were accustomed to adversity and used the Western economic assault as a rallying point. Rather than looking for a way out of the sanctions, Russians took pride in adversity, and were more determined than ever to support the Russian-speaking peoples of eastern Ukraine.

As for the question "What does Putin want?" I said the answer was easy. I explained that Putin wants Georgia, Ukraine and Moldova firmly in the Russian orbit, and he's prepared to use military force to accomplish that. Later he will decide what he wants next.

My question for the group was more difficult: what does

the United States want? The failure of economic sanctions was not only due to mirror imaging, but also to a lack of U.S. strategy. The United States did not have an endgame in Ukraine apart from wishful thinking about the impact of sanctions.

Henry Kissinger advised that countries couldn't formulate policy on a case-by-case basis but need a firm vision of national interests as a context within which to consider policy. Only when goals are known can strategy and tactics be devised.

Kissinger said that countries not only needed to know what they wanted, but needed to know what they wouldn't allow. Would the United States allow Russian dominance in eastern Ukraine? If the answer is no, then the United States needs to pursue regime change in Russia. If the answer is yes, then diplomacy, not sanctions, is the best path to a modus vivendi. The policy problem was that the United States had neither asked nor answered the question. We were lurching day to day with no vision, and no strategy.

Given the clarity of Russian ambitions, and lack of clarity on the part of U.S. strategists, investors should expect further confrontation in Ukraine. There will be good days and bad days. At times a truce may be in effect, but at other times truces will be broken, and hostilities resumed. The Ukrainian government is near bankruptcy but will be propped up by IMF loans. The Ukrainian military appears ineffective against Russian heavy weapons but may receive lethal aid from the United States and NATO.

The United States may consider economic sanctions a branch of diplomacy, but Russia considers them an act of war. So, war it is.

In the end, Russia will prevail because it has the will, the vision and the physical proximity to pursue its interests, while the West does not even have a strong sense of what its interests are. Beyond that, Russia is the eighth-largest economy in the world and produces much of Europe's energy. The world economy is slowing down for reasons unrelated to Russia, but Russia's isolation makes things worse. The appetite for additional sanctions outside of Washington is slight. Russia has absorbed our best shot, and is still standing. Our will to escalate is not there, and Putin knows it.

For investors, this geopolitical dead end for the West creates a classic contrarian investment opportunity. Russian ETFs were among the best performing investments of 2015 but have further to go as the situation in Ukraine is slowly resolved in Russia's favor.

The ETFs to consider are RSX (Market Vectors Russia ETF), and RBL (SPDR S&P Russia ETF), which are both up nearly 10 percent so far in 2016. These investments should be added as a small slice of your portfolio—do not go all in. But they can be an attractive, if volatile, addition to other, more conservative investments.

The RSX and RBL ETFs are all bets on the Ukraine situation moving toward a resolution and on sanctions gradually being lifted. Based on my meetings with the national-security professionals, that seems the most likely path. The United States is not willing to go for the throat, so we will be forced to go for diplomacy. That can only favor Putin and Russia in the end.

▨ My Conversation With Ben Bernanke

On May 27, 2015, I had the privilege of spending time with Ben Bernanke, former chairman of the Federal Reserve System, in Seoul, Korea. We were both there as keynote speakers in an international financial forum sponsored by the leading business publication in Korea.

The theme of the conference was currency wars and their impact on Korea. Our audience was interested in how monetary policy and exchange rate fluctuations affected Korea vis-à-vis its trading partners and competitors, especially China, Japan and Taiwan.

Above all, the audience wanted to learn how Fed policy on interest rates would affect the dollar, and what impact policy would have on developed economies and emerging markets.

In addition to the formal presentations, our event sponsors organized a small VIP reception that included Bernanke and me along with the CEOs of the Korea stock exchange, the Korea Banking Institute, the Korea Federation of Banks and the Korea Financial Investment Association.

There were about 10 of us in all, including financial elites of Korea and some distinguished scholars and economists from Japan; Bernanke and I were the only Americans. The setting was private and allowed us ample time for one-on-one discussions before the main conference commenced.

My conversation with Bernanke began casually enough. In the early 2000s, I had helped to establish the Center for Financial Economics at Johns Hopkins University. The center had selected its director from among the senior monetary economists at the Federal Reserve.

Not long after bringing our director on board, Bernanke tapped him to return to the Fed to serve as special adviser for communications, the person responsible for crafting announcements of Federal Open Market Committee actions that Wall Street economists slavishly dissect after each FOMC meeting for clues about interest rate policy changes.

I chided Bernanke for "picking off" our director. He laughed and said, "We didn't pick him off, we just borrowed him; we gave him back," which was true enough. Our director had just returned to the center after two years at the Fed. That was a good icebreaker before turning the conversation to more serious matters.

I had a copy of Bernanke's book *Essays on the Great Depression* (2000), which contains much of the research on which he built his academic reputation. Bernanke had shown that gold was not a constraint on money-supply creation during the Great Depression, contrary to what many economists and analysts take for granted.

From 1929 to 1933, money supply was capped at 250 percent of the market value of gold held by the U.S. government. The actual money supply *never exceeded 100 percent* of the value of the gold. This meant that the Fed could have more than doubled the money supply without violating the gold constraint.

The implication is that policy failure during the Great Depression was caused by the Fed's discretionary monetary policy, and not gold.

I told Bernanke that I had used his research in my own work on gold in my book *Currency Wars* (2011). When I offered my interpretation of his work, he replied, "That's right."

This confirmation was ironic because the Fed is facing the same challenges today in increasing bank lending and money velocity as it did in the Great Depression.

Gold is not even part of the system today. Bernanke may have identified the money-velocity problem in his book, but as chairman, he had no greater success in solving it than his predecessors.

Bernanke then made a set of remarks that I found both surprising in their candor and refreshing in the extent to which he was willing to take issue with some of what his successor, Janet Yellen, has said recently on the subject of Fed interest rate hikes.

Yellen gave a speech just prior to my meeting with Bernanke in which she said, "I think it will be appropriate at some point this year to take the initial step to raise the federal funds rate."

In contrast, Bernanke told me, "The interest rate increase, *when it comes,* is good news, because it means the U.S. economy is growing strongly enough to bear the costs of higher rates without slowing growth." Unlike Yellen, Bernanke did not tie himself to a particular month or year. He explicitly said the rate hike would come in an environment of strong growth. Today the U.S. economy is close to negative growth and is nowhere near the kind of robust growth that Bernanke associated with a rate increase. The clear implication is that the Fed will be in no position to raise rates anytime soon.

Bernanke also warned that the rate increase had to be clearly communicated and anticipated by the markets. He said, "Markets are not as deep and liquid as they were before the crisis."

The suggestion was that market expectations and Fed actions need to be aligned to raise rates without a market crash. He expressed the hope that "the rate increase may be an anticlimax because the markets anticipate it."

Turning to the international monetary system, Bernanke was also candid and said, "The international monetary system is not coherent." He explained that the current combination of floating exchange rates, fixed exchange rates and moving pegs means that trading partners have no confidence in their relative terms of trade and this acts as a drag on trade, foreign direct investment and capital expenditures.

He said, "Over time, it would be important for the countries of the world to talk more about how to avoid the mixture of fixed and floating exchange rates. We need new 'rules of the game.'"

Of course, international monetary experts know that the phrase "rules of the game" is code for a reformation of the international monetary system, or what some call a global reset. Bernanke was explicit that this reset is needed to end the dysfunction of the current system.

Some aspects of a global reset have already been put in place. For the past several years, the IMF has been attempting to change its quota system to give China more votes at the IMF, more in line with China's 10 percent share of global GDP. Right now China has less than 5 percent of the votes, which is low compared with some much smaller economies in Europe.

The U.S. Congress has refused to approve legislation needed to implement the changes at the IMF. Referring to the closed-door negotiations among the United States, IMF and China that led to the proposed reset in the quotas, Bernanke said, "I participated in this."

This was surprising to me because traditionally matters involving the IMF are handled by the Treasury Department rather than the Federal Reserve. Bernanke's confirmation of his participation made it clear that the Fed, the Treasury, the IMF and China are working hand in glove on the early stages of the reset.

China has grown increasingly frustrated at the delays from Washington. The Chinese have begun building their own version of the IMF in the form of the Asian Infrastructure Investment Bank and other institutions through the BRICS and the Shanghai Cooperation Organization.

Bernanke was dismissive of the AIIB and said, "I don't think it's going to be very important. It's going to be a footnote." I took this to mean that Bernanke expects the IMF voting reforms to move forward, in which case, China will be happy to play by the rules of the existing Bretton Woods institutions rather than try to start its own club independent of the IMF.

This interpretation is consistent with China's large gold acquisitions in recent years. The United States has about 8,000 tons of gold, the Eurozone has about 10,000 tons and the IMF has about 3,000 tons. China would need at least 4,000 tons, probably more, to be a credible member of this elite group.

The AIIB is best seen as a kind of head fake, and Bernanke implicitly confirmed this. China's real goal is to acquire gold, have the yuan included in the IMF's Special Drawing Rights basket and have its IMF votes increased. All of these resets are now well underway.

Bernanke next discussed whether the stock market was in

a bubble. In typical Fed style, he said, "It's very difficult to know." He also seemed relaxed about a sudden market correction.

He said, "What if the stock market dropped 10 or 15 percent? What difference does it make? Is there anything that looks like a systemic risk? I don't see that right now. I don't see anything that looks like a threat."

In other words, the Fed's job is to protect the system as a whole, not to protect investors from sudden drops in stock values. Bernanke could be wrong about a bubble. He certainly missed the mortgage market bubble in 2007 and the systemic risk that emerged in 2008. Whether he's right or wrong about bubbles, he clearly said he's *not* concerned about a 3,000-point drop in the Dow Jones index. Investors are on their own when it comes to that.

Finally, in discussing his legacy as Fed chair, Bernanke turned back to his research on the Great Depression, where our conversation began.

He said the three lessons of the Great Depression were that the Federal Reserve needed to perform as a lender of last resort, increase the money supply when needed and be willing to "experiment" in the style of FDR.

Bernanke defined "experiment" as being willing to do "whatever it takes" to head off deflation and depression. In summing up his own performance, he said, "We tried to do whatever it took. We don't know yet what the long-term implications are." His forecast was that "the Fed will be more proactive in the future."

My impression was that Bernanke knows the jury is still out on his tenure as Fed chairman. There is no doubt that his actions in 2008 and 2009 prevented a worse result at the time. But they may have produced a more dangerous condition today.

There was good justification for QE1 in 2008 and 2009 as an emergency liquidity response to a global financial panic.

This is consistent with the Fed's role as lender of last resort, as Bernanke said.

But QE2 and QE3 were not in response to any liquidity crisis. They were in the category of "experiments," as Bernanke defined them. Experiments are fine in the laboratory but much riskier in the real world. Experiments are a good way to advance science, but every scientist knows that most experiments fail to produce expected results.

Ben Bernanke was generous with his time and candid in his remarks. Still, I was left with an unsettling feeling that he knew that QE2 and QE3 were failed experiments, despite his public defense of them. Growth in the United States has been anemic for six years, and there is good evidence that we are sliding into a new recession.

The Fed can't cut rates now, because it failed to raise them when it had the chance in 2010 and 2011. Markets are probably in bubble territory, which means they could easily fall 30–50 percent.

The Fed will not act during the first 15 percent of a market crash, because it will see that as a normal correction, not a bursting bubble. By the time the Fed is ready to act, it will be too late, just as it was in 2008.

The collapse momentum will feed on itself in ways the Fed cannot control. Bernanke may have learned some lessons from the Great Depression, but it seems he has not learned the lessons of the Panic of 2008.

◾ The Mystery of the Impossible Trinity

When a builder goes to a job site to construct a house, he brings his hammer. The hammer may be the single most useful tool in home construction since it's used for roofing, framing and putting up walls.

Still, we all know it's not the only tool in the toolkit. A

builder wouldn't get very far with just a hammer. He will need a saw, a ruler, a sander and a lot of other tools to get the job done.

Some tools, like a hammer, are used continually. Others, like a chisel, might be used infrequently, but are essential for specialized tasks.

My father always taught me to use the right tool for the job. An expert builder has a lot of tools in his toolkit and knows how to use them to get the job done in an expert manner.

As a reader of *Strategic Intelligence*, you are familiar with the analytic tools we use to get the job done for you.

We use inverse probability (also known as Bayes' rule) to estimate future policy actions when there is little data to go on.

We use behavioral psychology to see why markets are not "efficient" (as academics assume). It also helps us to spot the inefficiencies that can result in great investment opportunities.

We use complexity theory and "indications and warnings" to see the black swans before they fly over and destroy your wealth.

All three of these tools—inverse probability, behavioral psychology and complexity theory—are mainstays in our toolkit.

What makes these tools especially valuable is that they are scarcely used at all on Wall Street or in the wealth-management industry. That gives our work an edge over all the other analysis and research you read and hear about on TV and in the rest of the financial media.

Yet, like a good builder, we need other tools for use in special situations to get the right result for you.

That's why the Impossible Trinity is such an important breakthrough for us. Using it properly unlocks many mysteries about the future of exchange rates, interest rates and global capital flows. Understanding this is the key to protecting and building wealth. The Impossible Trinity is not used at all times and places, but it is the perfect tool for understanding special cases in the ongoing currency wars.

As you know, we don't like to make forecasts without explaining our analysis. We don't like to throw technical jargon around without explaining the meaning in plain English.

We know you like to look behind the scenes and grasp the analysis yourself. That's the best way to make smart investment decisions on your own.

■ What Is the Impossible Trinity?

The Impossible Trinity is a simple rule with deep implications. It was first uncovered by Nobel Prize–winning economist Robert Mundell in the early 1960s.

The rule is that a country cannot have an independent monetary policy, an open capital account and a fixed exchange rate at the same time.

That's it.

You can have any two of those three conditions. You can even have only one or none if you like. But you can't have all three at the same time. If you try, you will fail—markets will make sure of that.

Those failures (which do happen) represent some of the best profit-making opportunities of all. Understanding the Impossible Trinity is how George Soros broke the Bank of England on September 16, 1992 (still referred to as "Black Wednesday" in British banking circles). Soros also *made over $1 billion that day.*

Understanding and using the Impossible Trinity works wonders if you can spot the right conditions and set up your trades in advance of the inevitable policy failures of the central banks.

Here's how it works.

The first part of the Impossible Trinity is an *independent monetary policy.*

This simply means that your central bank can set rates where it wants without regard for what other central banks are doing. If you want to ease to help your economy, and another central bank wants to tighten to prevent inflation, that's fine. Each central bank does its own thing.

The second part of the Impossible Trinity is the *open capital account.*

This refers to the ability of investors to get their money in and out of a country quickly and easily. If you want to invest in China, you'll have to take your dollars, convert these to the yuan, and make the yuan investment in whatever stocks, bonds or direct foreign investment you choose.

Sometimes you don't do this yourself; your broker does it for you. If you buy a Chinese-based exchange traded fund, you may think you're buying a dollar-denominated security on the New York Stock Exchange.

But behind the curtain the ETF sponsor has to go out and buy the actual Chinese stocks to make the ETF work. Either directly or indirectly, your dollars end up in the hands of the People's Bank of China, which issues yuan to complete the local stock purchase.

Or let's say you're a global corporation like IBM or General Electric and you want to invest $1 billion in a factory in Australia or Brazil. The same idea applies.

The investor's dollars end up in the target country's central bank, and the investor gets local currency to complete the purchase. This is one way central banks build up their reserves of U.S. dollars and other hard currencies (the other way they build reserves is from trade surpluses).

So far, so good. Now let's say you want to sell your investment and get your money out of the foreign country.

The process we just described works in reverse. The foreign central bank takes the local currency proceeds from your sale and gives you U.S. dollars from its reserves.

This process of easily getting in and out of a foreign investment, and getting dollars when you want them, is the essence of an open capital account. It's like a revolving door—smooth, fast and easy to get in and out.

But sometimes the revolving door gets stuck with you in it. This happens when a central bank slaps on capital controls and doesn't let your money out of the country. Then the revolving door is more like the Hotel California ("You can check out any time you like, but you can never leave"). When this happens, we say the country has a closed capital account.

The third part of the Impossible Trinity is a *fixed exchange rate.*

This simply means that the value of your currency in relation to some other currency is pegged at a fixed rate.

Of course, formally binding pegs were abandoned in the international monetary system in 1974. This was not long after U.S. president Richard Nixon ended the convertibility of dollars into gold at a fixed rate. Since 1974, all major currencies have technically been floating against others.

But many countries do implement currency pegs informally using central bank intervention and other policy tools.

For example, the Chinese yuan was informally pegged to the U.S. dollar at a rate of about 6.2 to 1 for most of 2014 and 2015. China unexpectedly broke the peg in August 2015 (causing a meltdown in U.S. equity markets) and devalued the yuan to 6.3 to 1. Since then the yuan has been devalued further, and now trades at about 6.48 to 1.

Many countries pursue formal and informal pegs to other currencies, usually the U.S. dollar.

The diagram below represents the Impossible Trinity. In this schematic, the open capital account is labeled "A," the fixed exchange rate is labeled "B," and the independent monetary policy is labeled "C."

The theory of the Impossible Trinity is that it is impossible for a country to achieve A + B + C at the same time. Any country that attempts this is doomed to fail.

**The "Impossible Trinity"
of Capital, Money, and Exchange**

Open Capital Account

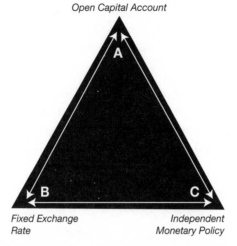

*Fixed Exchange
Rate*

*Independent
Monetary Policy*

▪ Thought Experiment: Freedonia and Sylvania

That's the theory. What about the practice? What's so impossible about the Impossible Trinity?

Consider the case of a country—call it Freedonia—that wants to cut its interest rate from 3 to 2 percent to stimulate growth. At the same time, Freedonia's main trading partner, Sylvania, has an interest rate of 3 percent.

Freedonia also keeps an open capital account (to encourage direct foreign investment).

Finally, Freedonia pegs its exchange rate to Sylvania at a rate of 10 to 1. This is a "cheap" exchange rate designed to stimulate exports from Freedonia to Sylvania.

In this example, Freedonia is trying the Impossible Trinity. It wants an open capital account, a fixed exchange rate and an independent monetary policy (it has an interest rate of 2 percent while Sylvania's rate is 3 percent).

What happens next?

The arbitrageurs get to work. They borrow money in Freedonia at 2 percent in order to invest in Sylvania at 3 percent. This causes the Freedonia central bank to sell its foreign exchange reserves and print local currency to meet the demand for local-currency loans and outbound investment. Printing the local currency puts downward pressure on the fixed exchange rate and causes inflation in local prices.

Eventually something breaks.

Freedonia may run out of foreign exchange, forcing it to close the capital account or break the peg (this is what happened to the U.K. in 1992 when George Soros broke the Bank of England). Or Freedonia will print so much money that inflation will get out of control, forcing it to raise interest rates again (something like this has been happening to Brazil lately).

The exact policy response can vary, but the end result is that Freedonia cannot maintain the Impossible Trinity. It will have to raise interest rates, close the capital account, break the peg or do all three to avoid losing all of its foreign exchange and going broke.

This shows you how powerful the Impossible Trinity is as an analytic tool.

Once you see a country trying to achieve the Impossible Trinity, you can be sure their system will break down one way or another. You can begin to make investment decisions in anticipation of the breakdown.

Conversely, when you see a country avoiding the Impossible Trinity (by not targeting A, B or C in the diagram on the previous page), you can have more confidence in their economic management. That way you can make investment decisions based on that level of confidence.

The Impossible Trinity is a tool to separate countries with good policies from those with bad policies. It is also a tool used to make accurate forecasts based on the sustainability of those policies.

By the way, there is one big exception to the Impossible Trinity. That's the United States.

The One Possible Trinity

The United States sets interest rates independently and has an open capital account. The United States does not officially peg the dollar to any other currency (thus technically not breaking the Impossible Trinity). But it does work with other countries to allow them to informally peg to the dollar. Why does the United States not suffer adverse consequences? Because the United States does not need foreign exchange.

The dollar is the leading reserve currency in the world (about 60 percent of global reserves and about 80 percent of global payments), so the United States can never run out of foreign exchange to pay for things—it can just print more dollars! This is what the French called the dollar's "exorbitant privilege" in the 1960s.

Now you see why so many trading partners are trying to escape from a dollar-denominated global system. The game is rigged against other countries, and in favor of the United States. This is why the game won't last. King Dollar's days are numbered.

Using the Impossible Trinity to spot trends and make investment decisions requires a lot of analysis. There are three policies that can go wrong (A, B and C above), and three ways to fix them (again, A, B and C). That gives nine basic scenarios (3 x 3 = 9), and many more when you consider hybrid or combined policies (a country could devalue its currency and slap on capital controls at the same time).

You don't need to sweat the details or get a Ph.D. in economics to use the Impossible Trinity. That's what we do for you at *Strategic Intelligence*. We're always on the lookout for unsustainable policies that are bound to break.

■ How You Can Use the Impossible Trinity to Profit Today

How can you apply the Impossible Trinity to do forecasting and spot investment opportunities?

China is a good case study. Until the summer of 2014, China was pursuing a version of the Impossible Trinity. It pegged the yuan to the dollar at about 6.2 to 1, it had a partly open capital account and it set interest rates independently from the U.S. Federal Reserve.

At first, China's cheap currency helped exports and led to a massive build-up of U.S. dollar reserves as China recycled its trade surpluses into U.S. Treasury notes.

But, as the Fed tightened policy in 2013 to 2015 (with the "taper" of asset purchases and removal of "forward guidance"), China had to sell dollars and buy yuan in order to maintain the peg. Buying yuan reduces the money supply and is a form of tightening.

This tight monetary policy in China slowed down its economy, and caused foreign investors to move new factories to cheaper countries such as Vietnam and Indonesia.

Chinese investors could see that the Impossible Trinity had to break and started to take their money out of China as fast as they could.

The capital outflows from China were massive. China's foreign exchange reserves have declined for 9 of the past 11 months as of December 2015. China's reserves are down over $600 billion in 2015 alone.

China lost a record $94 billion of reserves in August 2015. At that rate, China would run out of reserves by the end of 2018, and effectively be broke with no way to pay off its dollar-denominated debts.

History says China could be broke even sooner.

Once foreign exchange reserves start to walk out the door, the walk turns into a stampede as investors get their money out. The rout accelerates. Nobody wants to be the last one out of a burning building.

China would probably be broke by 2017 if it didn't do something radical.

Using Impossible Trinity analysis, it was easy to see that China had to impose capital controls (to stop money from leaving), devalue the currency (to slow down the bleeding), or raise interest rates (to attract new money from abroad).

Imposing capital controls (option A) was politically unacceptable. China was trying to join the IMF's world money basket (the SDR) and did not want to anger the IMF, which opposes capital controls.

Raising interest rates (option C) was also a nonstarter because it would have slowed China's economy at a time when it was already slowing.

So, China went for option B (breaking the fixed exchange rate). *It was the only solution.*

Once a country breaks a fixed exchange rate, that's rarely the end of it. More devaluations are usually needed. The conditions that gave rise to the first devaluation in China had not changed. Capital outflows continued. (China lost another $87 billion of reserves in November.)

The IMF pressure for an open capital account also continued. (The Chinese yuan was admitted to the SDR on November 30, 2015, so China had to play by IMF rules on the open capital account.)

Using the Impossible Trinity analysis, here's what we told you in the December 2015 issue of *Strategic Intelligence*:

> For now, China is defending the new peg with more intervention. You should expect further devaluations. You should also expect more market shocks in the near future as China stumbles its way to a freely traded yuan.

And here's what happened: China devalued its currency from 6.3980 to 6.4515 in baby steps between December 4 and

December 11.

Now, look what happened to the U.S. stock market at the same time: major stock indexes tumbled almost 3 percent between December 4 and December 11, in lockstep with the Chinese devaluation!

Our warnings to you in that issue ("Expect further devaluations" and "Expect more market shocks"), played out with a vengeance, causing major losses for investors who did not see it coming.

Fortunately, as a reader of *Strategic Intelligence*, you did see it coming. Do we have a crystal ball? Absolutely not. Instead, we use predictive analytics like the Impossible Trinity.

Now that you understand the Impossible Trinity, and you've seen its predictive power in the real world, we look forward to sharing the insights it provides in future issues of *Strategic Intelligence*.

The Impossible Trinity is your suit of armor in the currency wars. It helps us to predict both potential losses and gains.

For example, Argentina is another case we are following closely.

Argentina tried to pursue the Impossible Trinity just like China. Argentina had pegged its currency, the peso, at an unrealistically high rate to the U.S. dollar.

At the same time, Argentina pursued an independent monetary policy, and officially had an open capital account (in reality, the door was "open" only to favored companies and political cronies). The result was predictable—a flourishing black market in which the peso-dollar exchange rate was only half the official rate.

Argentina now has a new free-market-oriented president, Mauricio Macri. He has already declared his intention to launch a one-time "megadevaluation" of the peso to put the official rate in line with the more realistic black market rate. Macri also wants an open capital account to encourage more direct foreign investment in Argentina.

Using the Impossible Trinity tool, we can already see that if Argentina wants an open capital account (option A), it will either have to let the peso float against the dollar (option B) or give up independent monetary policy (option C).

The most likely outcome is option C. This means that Argentina will closely follow the Federal Reserve when it comes to monetary policy. If the Fed tightens, Argentina will tighten in order not to violate the rules of the Impossible Trinity.

We already use other tools (such as inverse probability) to forecast Fed policy. Now we can combine inverse probability with the Impossible Trinity to forecast Argentina's monetary policy also.

We hope you're as excited as we are about the power of these analytic tools and our potential to help you earn profits and avoid losses in the months ahead.

The BOJ, Currency Wars and Money Printing Gone Wild

On October 31, 2014, staffers at Japan's central bank were sweating bullets.

They'd worked past midnight drafting a proposal to shift the Bank of Japan's dangerous yen-printing experiment into higher gear.

The staffers' boss, BOJ governor Haruhiko Kuroda, was concerned the Japanese public would maintain a deflationary mindset. The public was hoarding cash, expecting prices to drift lower forever. In Kuroda's view, this is a problem in need of fixing.

Kuroda wanted to shock the public out of its deflationary mindset. Nothing short of a revolution in inflation expectations would suffice.

For the two years leading up to 2014, Kuroda had nudged

the Japanese public into expecting higher prices. In anticipation of inflation, Kuroda's theory said, there would be a spending spree. Kuroda thought the spending spree might be enough to revolutionize Japan's consumer psychology.

Ahead of the BOJ's October 31 meeting, Kuroda must have been nervous his policy proposal wouldn't receive a majority vote. He proposed accelerating the yen-printing program begun in 2013. Previously, the Japanese monetary base was growing at an annual pace of about 60–70 trillion yen. Kuroda proposed an acceleration to 80 trillion yen per year.

After a heated two-hour debate, it came down to a cliff-hanger: Kuroda and his deputies were reliable yes votes; two skeptical board members, as expected, voted no; and the four other members split down the middle.

With a 5–4 vote, the BOJ launched a major new battle in the global currency war.

Immediately after the vote became public, the U.S. dollar jumped in value against the yen. Japanese stocks spiked.

The BOJ was heading down a one-way path toward currency destruction.

As I predicted in 2015 based on my work on central banks and currency wars, the yen kept weakening against the U.S. dollar.

Kuroda is a zealot in his belief that he can revolutionize inflationary psychology in Japan. He took the helm of the BOJ in early 2013, vowing to boost inflation and inflation expectations.

He immediately launched the largest quantitative easing program the world had ever seen—twice as big, in GDP terms, as the Federal Reserve's QE3 program. The BOJ pledged to purchase $1.4 trillion of Japanese government bonds over the course of 2013 and 2014 using printed money.

"[The] Bank of Japan was explicit about its goal to increase inflation in order to increase nominal, if not real, GDP," I wrote in *The Death of Money*. "The BOJ explicitly targeted an inflation rate of 2 percent 'at the earliest possible time.'"

Kuroda is increasingly desperate. The prior plan to inflate Japan's base money supply wasn't shocking enough to boost inflation expectations. So Kuroda sought an acceleration in yen printing, got the votes and announced the policy shift on October 31, 2014.

The Bank of Japan is so far down the road to currency destruction that it's now the only sizeable bidder in the Japanese government bond (JGB) market. JGB trading volumes have collapsed. With Japan's shrinking workforce, declining competitiveness and a national debt that requires near-zero interest rates, more and more of the JGB market will be converted into cash deposits. The yen-based money supply will keep growing.

Why is Japan's debt a problem if the central bank stands ready to convert the entire stock of debt into yen?

Here's why: it's only a matter of time before the supply side of the Japanese economy starts viewing yen as hot potatoes to be traded for real assets—a spiraling inflation crisis that the BOJ won't have the flexibility to fight.

Currencies die quickly when producers lose confidence they'll retain value and withhold supply from the market. In *The Death of Money,* I used the term "phase transition" to describe the process:

> When wood burns and turns to ash, that is a phase transition, but there is no easy way to turn ash back into wood. The Federal Reserve believes that it is managing a reversible process. It believes that deflation can be turned to inflation, and then to disinflation, with the right quantity of money and the passage of time. In this, it is mistaken.

Like the Federal Reserve, the BOJ believes it can dial up inflation and dial it back down. But confidence is fragile and will get even weaker with each surge of yen emitted from the BOJ. Many central banks, including the BOJ, are squandering their reputational credibility on wealth-effect experiments. These experiments are leaving central banks with huge balance sheets that cannot be allowed to shrink.

▨ A Currency-Wars "Pearl Harbor"

The most dramatic battle yet in the currency wars took place on January 15, 2015. It was the financial equivalent of a Pearl Harbor sneak attack.

"I find it a bit surprising that he did not contact me," IMF director Christine Lagarde told CNBC's Steve Liesman that day, "but you know, we'll check on that."

You can almost imagine the conversation afterward between Mario Draghi of the European Central Bank and Swiss National Bank president Thomas Jordan.

Mario Draghi: "Did you tell Christine?"

Thomas Jordan: "I thought you were going to tell her."

Mario Draghi: "Wait, I thought you were!"

Switzerland had just abandoned its peg of the Swiss franc to the euro. The result was mayhem, with an immediate 30 percent drop in the value of the euro against the franc and billions of dollars of trading losses by banks and investors around the world.

Several foreign exchange brokers went bankrupt because their customers could not settle their losing trades. The Swiss operated in total secrecy.

Currency wars resemble real wars in the sense that they do not involve continuous fighting all the time. At certain times, there are intense battles, followed by lulls, followed by more intense battles.

But there is nothing new about the Swiss National Bank's move. It's the latest salvo in the currency war that President Obama started in 2010, and it won't be the last. It was in 2010 that the president announced his National Export Initiative designed to double U.S. exports in five years.

The only way to do that was with a cheaper dollar, so the president's policy amounted to a declaration to the world that the United States wanted other countries to let their currencies go up so the dollar could go down. Ten months later, the Brazilian finance minister, Guido Mantega, shocked global financial elites by publicly proclaiming what everyone knew but no one would say—that the world was in a new currency war.

The problem with currency wars is they last a long time— sometimes as long as 15 or 20 years. The reason is they have no logical conclusion, just back-and-forth devaluations and revaluations as countries retaliate against each other.

We have seen this seesaw pattern re-emerge. The weak dollar of 2011 has turned into the strong dollar of 2016. Countries that complained the weak dollar was hurting their exports in 2011 now complain that the strong dollar is hurting their capital markets in 2016.

That's the other problem with currency wars—no one wins, and everyone loses. Currency wars don't create growth; they just steal growth temporarily from trading partners until the trading partners steal it back with their own devaluations.

The surprise revaluation of the Swiss franc on January 15, 2015, was one example of these currency shocks. The Chinese yuan shock in August 2015 was another surprise devaluation.

There are many important pegs left in the international monetary system vulnerable to being broken. Right now, the Hong Kong dollar and the major Arab currencies are all tightly pegged to the U.S. dollar.

If the Fed does not raise interest rates, the result could be a violent reversal of current trends and a weaker dollar as the "risk on" mantra causes capital to flow out of the United States and back to the emerging markets. Either way, volatility is the one certainty.

The other problem with the currency wars is what the

IMF calls "spillover" effects, also known as financial contagion. Many mortgages in Poland, Hungary and other parts of Central and Eastern Europe are made not in local currency but in Swiss francs. The stronger Swiss franc means those borrowers need more local currency to pay off their mortgages.

This could lead to a wave of mortgage defaults and a mortgage-market meltdown similar to what the United States experienced in 2007. This shows how a decision made in Zurich can wipe out a homeowner in Budapest. Financial contagion works just like Ebola. Once an outbreak begins, it can be difficult to contain. It may not be long before the Swiss franc sneak attack infects investor portfolios in the United States.

Financial contagion can also be a two-way street. It not only creates dangers, it creates opportunities for investors who can connect the dots in the currency wars. The easiest conclusion you can draw and act on is this simple truth: do not believe government and central bank lies.

This maxim is not without historical precedent. You've probably heard about Franklin Roosevelt's own sneak currency attack. In 1933, President Roosevelt devised a plan to increase the price of gold in dollars, effectively a dollar devaluation. But he had a problem. If he increased the price of gold while Americans owned it, the profit would go to the citizens, not the U.S. Treasury. He knew that he had to lie to the American people about his intentions in order to pull off the theft of the century.

So Roosevelt issued an emergency executive order confiscating the gold at about $20.00 per ounce and then revalued it to $35.00 per ounce, with the Treasury getting the profits.

On January 15, 2015, the Swiss National Bank pulled a similar stunt. In November 2014, the Swiss citizens had voted on a referendum to require an informal link of the Swiss franc to gold. The Swiss National Bank had argued against the referendum on the ground that it would cause them to break the peg of the Swiss franc to the euro.

The people believed them and voted no on the referendum. But the Swiss National Bank broke the peg anyway. The price of gold spiked as a result, but the Swiss citizens lost the benefit of that because the referendum was a dead letter. The Swiss National Bank lied to the Swiss people about their intentions with regard to the peg.

The lesson of history is that citizens should own some gold, store it safely and not believe government and central bank lies. In fact, we could see more investors fleeing to the safety of gold in the coming months as trust in central bankers wanes.

CHAPTER 9

Gold's Bull Market Isn't Over

▦ A Win-Win Scenario for Gold Owners

Volatility and price drops may be nerve-wracking, but the bull market in gold is far from over. In fact, it has barely begun.

To understand why, it helps to look at two prior episodes in the relationship of gold and money that are most relevant to today. These episodes are a period of extreme deflation, the 1930s, and a period of extreme inflation, the 1970s. History shows that gold does well in both conditions.

Commentators frequently observe that we are experiencing "price stability" or "low inflation" based on the fact that the consumer price index has averaged 2 percent over the past 24 months. However, this average hides more that it reveals.

The economy is experiencing strong deflationary forces as a result of weak employment and deleveraging associated with the depression that began in 2007. Simultaneously the economy is experiencing strong inflationary forces as a result of Fed money printing.

The deflationary and inflationary forces offset each other to produce a seemingly benign average. But below the surface the forces struggle to prevail with some likelihood that one or the other will emerge victorious sooner rather than later.

Inflationary forces often appear only with significant lags relative to the expansion of the money supply. This was the case in the late 1960s and early 1970s. The Fed began to expand the money supply to pay for Lyndon Johnson's "guns and butter" policy in 1965. The first sign of trouble was when inflation increased from 3.1 percent in 1967 to 5.5 percent in 1969.

But there was worse to come. Inflation rose further to 11 percent in 1974 and then topped off at 11.3 percent in 1979, 13.5 percent in 1980 and 10.3 percent in 1981, an astounding 35 percent cumulative inflation in three years. During this period, gold rose from $35 per ounce to over $800 per ounce, a 2,300 percent increase.

The point is that neither the inflation nor the gold-price spike happened overnight. It took 15 years to play out from start to finish. The Fed's current experiments in extreme money printing only began in 2008. Given the lags in monetary policy and the offsetting deflationary forces, we should not be surprised if it takes another year or two for serious inflation to appear on the scene.

Another instructive episode is the Great Depression. The problem then was not inflation but deflation. It first appeared in 1927 but really took hold in 1930. From 1930 to 1933, cumulative deflation was 26 percent. The United States became desperate for inflation. It could not cheapen its currency because other countries were cheapening their currencies even faster in the "beggar thy neighbor" currency wars of the time.

Finally, the United States decided to devalue the dollar against gold. In 1933, the price of gold in dollars was increased from $20 per ounce to $35 dollar per ounce, a 75 percent increase at a time when all other prices were decreasing. This shock therapy for the dollar worked, and by 1934 inflation was back at 3.1 percent, a massive turnaround from the 5.1 percent deflation of 1933. In short, when all other methods fail to defeat deflation, devaluing the dollar against gold works without fail because gold can't fight back.

It is unclear if the world will tip into inflation or deflation, but one or the other is almost certain. The good news for gold investors is that gold goes up in either case, as shown in the 1930s and 1970s. Yet patience is required.

These trends take years to play out, and policies work with a lag. Meanwhile, investors can use recent setbacks to acquire gold at more attractive prices while waiting for the inevitable price increase to occur.

The Long-Term Gold Outlook

My long-term forecast for gold—meaning, over a three-year horizon—is that it will go much higher, based on fundamentals, the amount of paper money in the world and the fact that we're in a global depression.

Money printing by itself won't do any good, but the central banks think it will. That alone should drive gold higher over the longer term because the central banks will keep printing and risk destroying confidence in the paper currencies.

If they had to restore that confidence, that might also mean going back to some kind of gold standard, or at least using the price of gold as a reference point. If deflation is a problem, how do you get inflation? One way to get inflation is to depreciate your currency relative to the gold.

You might say to yourself, "What, hypothetically, would the nondeflationary price of gold be if a gold standard was implemented?" That's not a matter of making a prediction; it's an analytical question. You can do the math on that using available data. The answer is $7,000 to $9,000.

There's no central bank in the world that wants a gold standard. But if we were going to have one and wanted to avoid deflation of the kind we had in the Great Depression, the price of gold would have to at least be $7,000 per ounce, probably higher. It's closer to $9,000 per ounce. I call that the "implied nondeflationary price of gold." That part's easy, actually.

You can do that math because we know how much gold there is and how much paper money there is, and we can make some assumptions about the ratios and confidence levels.

The question then becomes, what would cause central banks to want to go back to some kind of gold standard?

Obviously, it would take a collapse of confidence in paper money. The gold standard would be a desperate move to restore confidence in the system. Then you have to figure out the likelihood of that happening.

The more money central banks print, the closer we get to that confidence boundary and the point where we might actually have to implement a gold standard. That's the kind of instability built into the system. Confidence is fragile. It's something that can be lost very quickly.

How can confidence be destroyed quickly?

Think of a bank run. You wake up in the morning and the bank is on sound financial footing, but some people, for whatever reason, hear a rumor that the bank is actually not sound. So they run down to withdraw all of their money immediately.

Their neighbors, seeing them lined up in front of the bank, say, "I don't know what's going on, but I better get my money before they run out," and they get in line too.

The line gets longer and the buzz causes even more people get in line. Next thing you know, the bank is bankrupt even though it started out the morning perfectly fine. That's the classic scenario of a run on the bank.

We don't have that dynamic today. People don't line up at the bank anymore. They do everything digitally. Plus, we have deposit insurance and other things that mitigate that risk. But the fact of the matter is that psychology hasn't changed at all. A little rumor, even if it's false, or some person getting in line, could start the run on the bank.

Gold, right now, looks to have a floor of around $1,000 an ounce. It's been smashed down to that level four times in recent years.

That said, I did have a conversation recently with Jim Rogers. I think we all know Jim Rogers is one of the greatest commodity investors in history. He said that no commodity is ever going to its final destination without a 50 percent retracement, meaning even if you believe that gold could end up at $7,000 an ounce, which I do, if you see it at $1,900, a 50 percent retracement would take it down to $950.

In other words, it would go all the way down to $950 and then would bounce back. So Jim said, "I have a lot of gold. I'm not selling it. I'm sitting on it. I'm a buyer at $1,000, but I'm not necessarily a buyer at $1,100 because I kind of look for that 50 percent retracement."

That said, if you go back over a five-year period, gold has been much higher. In August 2011, it was about $1,900 an ounce. It's made its way down to around $1,100 an ounce on four separate occasions, and each time, it rallied back. Now, it never got back to the $1,900 level, but it has gone up to around $1,350.

That tells me there's a physical demand out there. Forget about gold futures and paper gold. There's physical demand. When gold gets up to those levels, people do line up. They don't line up to get their money out of the bank; they line up to buy physical gold.

You see this in Asia—in Hong Kong, Thailand, Malaysia and mainland China. You see it even in Australia and other places around the world. I've been to many of those places and spoken to people there, and this is something they tell me about all the time.

This what's called a "recursive function." The plain English name for that is the feedback loop: A happens and that causes B to happen, but B gives you more A, and A gives more B, and B gives you more A, and A gives you more B, and it goes around and around, and the behavior keeps amplifying based on that feedback loop.

▓ Gold Is Money (Once Again)

One of my favorite quotes on the topic of gold is attributed to Lord Nathan Rothschild, a legendary 19th-century banker and gold broker to the Bank of England. He said, "I only know of two men who really understand the true value of gold—an obscure clerk in the basement vault of the Banque de Paris and one of the directors of the Bank of England. Unfortunately, they disagree."

Another favorite quote, even more succinct, is from J. Pierpont Morgan, who said in 1912: "Money is gold, and nothing else."

We also have a modern take on the meaning and value of gold from none other than Ben Bernanke, former chairman of the Federal Reserve. On July 18, 2013, Bernanke said, "Nobody really understands gold prices, and I don't pretend to understand them either."

These quotes illustrate the perennial challenge that investors face in deciding what role gold should play in their portfolios. Few understand how to value gold, and even fewer understand that gold is not really an investment—it is money. Of course, if you want a portfolio that preserves wealth, money is a good place to start.

Saying gold is not an investment may seem strange, especially since I recommend some gold in an investor's portfolio. To illustrate this point, you can reach into your purse or wallet and pull out a dollar bill. You think of the dollar as money, but you do not think of it as an investment. An investment has some element of risk, and typically has some yield in the form of interest, dividends or rent. Money can be turned into an investment by using it to buy stocks, bonds or real estate. But as a dollar bill, it is just money; it has no yield and will still be a dollar tomorrow or next year.

Gold is the same. It has no yield. An ounce of gold today will be an ounce of gold next year and the year after that. It will not mysteriously turn into two ounces. It will not rust or change shape or color. It is just gold. Yet, it is money.

It's true that the value of gold may change when measured in dollars. It is also true that the value of a dollar may change when measured in euros or ounces of gold. But these changes in relative value do not turn these units into investments; they just reflect supply and demand for different forms of money.

If holders of euros have a preference for dollars, the euro may fall relative to the dollar. If holders of dollars or euros have a preference for gold, then the value of gold may rise relative to both. Still, these changes reflect changing preferences for different forms of money, not a return on investment. Though gold is money, investors frequently ignore the fact.

Gold often trades like an investment and is said to be "up" or "down" in dollar value, the same as a stock is said to be going up or down. Gold also trades like a commodity; in fact, the primary trading venue for paper contracts in gold is the Commodity Exchange, or COMEX. In that context, gold typically goes up in dollar terms during inflation, and down in dollar terms during deflation, just like other commodities including oil and copper.

That's why the chart below is so fascinating. It compares the price of gold to the Continuous Commodity Index, an index of major commodities that has been maintained consistently since 1957. The index includes gold, copper, cotton, crude oil, natural gas and 12 other widely traded commodities.

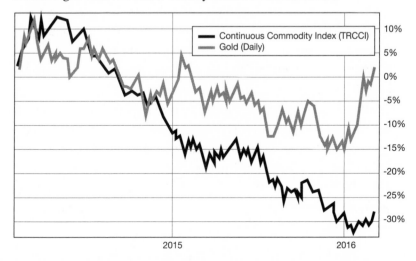

Throughout 2014, the gold price closely tracked the commodity index, as might be expected. The price trend of both was downward, which reflected the strong deflationary trends that began to prevail in 2014. But in November 2014, this correlation broke down and gold began to diverge sharply from the overall index.

That was not the only significant development in gold around this time. As this chart shows, the pace of gold shipments out of the Federal Reserve Bank of New York increased sharply in October and November 2014. Over 90 tons of gold were shipped out of the Fed to their rightful owners abroad in those two months alone. That was more than half the total amount of gold shipped out for the entire year. Bear in mind that prior to 2012 almost no gold had been shipped from the Federal Reserve Bank of New York since the 1970s.

It's a mistake to read too much into a short time series of data such as the gold/GCC correlation or the gold shipments from the Fed. Every analyst knows that correlation of factors does not prove causation. But these two charts do suggest that late last year, gold suddenly stopped trading like an investment or a commodity, and started behaving like what it has always been—money.

Late 2014 was a period when commodities generally declined because of deflation, and currencies generally fell against the dollar as part of the currency wars. The declining currencies were also a symptom of deflation because currency devaluation is a way to import inflation from trading partners in order to stave off domestic deflation.

Only three major assets went up strongly in the past 12 months: U.S. dollars, Swiss francs and gold. The dollar/gold correlation was most striking because they had been inversely correlated since 2011 with the dollar getting stronger, and gold getting weaker. Suddenly gold and dollars were gaining strength together against commodities, euros, yen, yuan and most other measures of wealth.

So is gold a commodity, an investment, or money?

The answer is...

Gold is a chameleon. It changes in response to the environment.

At times, gold behaves like a commodity. The gold price tracks the ups and downs of commodity indexes.

At other times, gold is viewed as a safe-haven investment. It competes with stocks and bonds for investor attention.

And on occasion, gold assumes its role as the most stable long-term form of money the world has ever known.

A real chameleon changes color based on its background. When sitting on a dark green leaf, the chameleon appears dark green to hide from predators. When the chameleon hops from the leaf to a tree trunk, it will change from green to brown to maintain its defenses.

Gold also changes its nature depending on the background.

Right now, gold is behaving more like money than a commodity or investment. It is competing with central bank fiat money for asset allocations by global investors. That's a big deal because it shows that citizens around the world are starting to lose confidence in other forms of money such as dollars, yuan, yen, euros and sterling.

This is great news for those with price exposure to gold. The price of gold in many currencies is going up as confidence in those other currencies goes down. Confidence in currencies is dropping because investors are losing confidence in the central banks that print them.

For the first time since 2008, it looks like central banks are losing control of the global financial system. Gold does not have a central bank. Gold always inspires confidence because it is scarce, tested by time and has no credit risk.

Gold's role as money is difficult for investors to grasp. One criticism of gold is that is has no yield. Gold has no yield because money has no yield. To get yield, you have to take risk.

Bank deposits and so-called money market funds have yield, but they are not money. A bank deposit is subject to default by the bank, as we saw recently in Greece and Cyprus. A money market fund is subject to collapse of the fund itself, as we saw in 2008.

Gold does not have these risks.

Lost confidence in fiat money starts slowly then builds rapidly to a crescendo. The end result is panic buying of gold and a price superspike.

We saw this behavior in the late 1970s. Gold moved from $35 per ounce in August 1971 to $800 per ounce in January 1980. *That's a 2,200 percent gain in less than nine years.*

We may be looking at the early stages of a similar superspike that could take gold to $10,000 per ounce or higher. When that happens, there will be one important difference between the new superspike and what happened in 1980.

Back then, you could buy gold at $100, $200 or $500 per ounce and enjoy the ride. In the new superspike, *you may not be able to get any gold at all.* You'll be watching the price go up on TV but unable to buy any for yourself.

Gold will be in such short supply that only the central banks, giant hedge funds and billionaires will be able to get their hands on any. The mint and your local dealer will be sold out. That physical scarcity will make the price superspike even more extreme than in 1980.

The time to buy gold is now, before the price spikes and before supplies dry up.

What indications and warnings do we see that gold is now behaving like money?

For one thing, gold price action has diverged from the price action of other commodities. This divergence first appeared in late 2014 but has become more pronounced in recent months.

Gold observers know that gold measured in dollars is down significantly from its all-time high in 2011. COMEX gold peaked at $1,876 per ounce on September 2, 2011, and recently traded as low as $1,056 per ounce, on November 27, 2015. That's a 44 percent decline in just over four years. Yet in the same period, broad-based commodities indexes fell even more. One major commodities index fell 53 percent.

The contrast between the behavior of gold and commodities is even more extreme when we narrow the time period. From June 20, 2014, to January 15, 2016, the broad-based commodity index fell 63 percent, while gold fell only 17 percent. *The recent collapse in commodity prices was almost four times greater than the decline in gold prices.*

From mid-January to mid-February 2016, gold rallied 14 percent while commodities still languished near five-year lows.

Right now, investors around the world are losing confidence in Chinese yuan, Saudi rials, South African rand, Russian rubles and a long list of other emerging-market currencies. Investor preferences are shifting toward dollars and gold. This accounts for gold's outperformance of the rest of the commodity complex when measured in dollars.

What is interesting is that when the price of gold is measured not in dollars, but in rubles, yuan or rials, the percentage price increase in gold is even more impressive because those currencies have all declined lately against the dollar.

When you understand that gold is money and competes with other forms of money in a jumble of cross rates with no anchor, you'll know why the monetary system is going wobbly.

It's important to take off your dollar blinders to see that the dollar is just one form of money—and not necessarily the best one for all investors in all circumstances. Gold is a strong competitor in the horse race among various forms of money.

Normally I recommend a 10 percent allocation of investible assets to physical gold for your permanent portfolio. But when short-term trading opportunities arise, certain gold derivatives such as exchange-traded funds (ETFs) are a great way to get dollar price exposure to gold and book 100 percent profits (or more).

Aside from gold acting like money, our intelligence collections and inferential models suggest that something even more profound may be going on. Russian and Chinese gold-acquisition programs have been going on for years; that story is well-known to our readers.

But those acquisitions have now passed the point that Russia and China need to have a seat at the table in any new international monetary conference. Both countries have caught up to the United States in terms of the all-important gold-to-GDP ratio. Yet massive gold acquisitions by Russia and China continue. Can something else be going on?

At a minimum, Russia and China are using gold to hedge the dollar value of their primary assets. In the case of China, those assets consist of $3 trillion of U.S. Treasury and other dollar-denominated debt. In the case of Russia, those assets consist of oil and natural gas, both of which are priced in dollars on world markets.

For China, the hedge is simple. If the United States inflates the value of the dollar, China will lose on its debt holdings but will make large gains on its gold. Converting some portion of its dollar reserves to gold is a good way for China to hedge its exposure to dollars.

For Russia, the case is more convoluted. In the short run, Saudi Arabia is suppressing the dollar value of oil, which hurts Russian receipts since Russian oil is also priced in dollars at the world price. But this deflation has also tended to keep gold prices low in recent years.

When Russia sells oil at a low dollar price, it immediately converts the dollars to gold, also at a relatively low dollar price. When inflation returns, the dollar price of Russia's gold will soar, thereby compensating it for the "lost dollars" or the earlier sales of oil.

What China and Russia have in common is they are both protecting themselves against dollar and oil-price manipulation by converting their export sales into gold. While investors may have missed this development, other central banks have not. The withdrawals from the Federal Reserve represent efforts by central banks in Germany, Netherlands and elsewhere to take physical possession of their gold in advance of a systemic monetary breakdown.

The correlation of dollars and gold, the divergence of gold from commodities, the repatriation of gold from the Fed and continued large acquisitions of gold by China and Russia are all visible from the data. The conclusion that gold is beginning to behave like money, rather than a commodity, and that Russia and China are using gold to hedge dollar exposures in oil and Treasury securities respectively are reasonable inferences using our models.

Based on the monetary history of the past century, we are probably at the end of the useful life of the current (dollar-based) international monetary system and fast approaching a new one.

But here's the good news.

No matter what happens in the world—through great disasters and extreme crisis—there are always people who not only survive, but thrive.

When you look at America's hardest times—the Great

Depression, the Second World War and the stagflation of the 1970s, for example—there were always a few who made fortunes. They saw the crisis coming and took the right steps beforehand to prepare.

Wealth was simply transferred from unprepared Americans to those who took action.

This time will be no different.

And one of the best ways to ensure you'll be on the winning side of this massive wealth transfer is by owning gold.

I've actually just released a new book, *The New Case for Gold*, that goes into much more detail about owning gold.

But is something else going on—something that is not apparent in the data and for which the inference would be less certain? Could Russia and China be trying to corner the market in gold?

Leaving aside blatant government intervention such as FDR's 1933 gold confiscation, there has not been a successful effort to corner the gold market since Jay Gould and "Big Jim" Fisk tried it in 1869. Even that corner was broken when the U.S. Treasury unexpectedly sold large quantities of gold after Fisk and insiders had assured Gould that the Treasury would not do so.

The Hunt brothers infamously tried to corner the silver market in 1979 and 1980. That corner was broken by a combination of scrap silver flooding the market in the form of tea sets and silverware, and changes in exchange regulations that increased margin requirements and hurt the Hunts' ability to maintain their leveraged futures positions.

A Russian corner of the gold market would not be leveraged on futures exchanges because Russia is a cash buyer of physical gold. Russia is also immune from U.S. regulation: the United States has no enforcement powers in Russia. As in the cases of Gould, Fisk and the Hunt brothers, patience and stealth are needed at the beginning of a successful corner. Russia has both.

▓ Gold Is an "Invisible Gorilla"

You may have heard the phrase "the 500-pound gorilla."

It's used to describe something that is obvious to everyone in the room but that no one wants to acknowledge or discuss. It's a metaphor for an unpleasant or potentially damaging reality that most people prefer or ignore or deny entirely.

The usual outcome is that the 500-pound gorilla eventually makes its presence known by wreaking havoc in the room and destroying the plans of those who ignored it.

But have you heard of the *invisible gorilla?*

The invisible gorilla is the name given by social scientists to a kind of selective perception. (Spoiler alert: The video experiment that gave rise to the "invisible gorilla" name is available online here: **www.theinvisiblegorilla.com/videos. html.** Try it on yourself if you like before reading the rest of this chapter, where I discuss the results.)

The invisible gorilla is shorthand for selective perception. In other words, we see certain objects and don't see certain others based on our mental frames and biases. If we are totally focused on one problem, our brains will "shut down" on the perception of other events to give us the mental bandwidth to solve the problem. The issue is that the things we shut out may be more important than the things we're focused on. That's when we get blindsided by the gorilla.

In the original experiment (conducted in 1999 by psychologists Daniel Simons and Christopher Chabris), subjects were asked to watch a short video of two teams passing a basketball.

One team is dressed in white shirts; the other team is dressed all in black. The subject is asked to count the number of times the white team passes the ball.

It's challenging because the teams are passing two balls using some razzle-dazzle passing tricks.

The video begins, and the subjects are completely focused on the white shirts (the actions of the black-shirt team are irrelevant).

In the middle of the video, a scientist in a black gorilla suit walks onto the basketball court, looks straight at the camera, beats his chest and moves off the court. The gorilla is clearly visible for nine seconds.

When the video is over, subjects are asked to tell how many times the white-shirt team passed the ball (the correct answer is 15). Then comes the point. The experimenter asks the subjects, "But did you see the gorilla?"

Amazingly, over 50 percent of the experimental subjects did not see the gorilla!

How could over half the subjects watch a short film of basketball and not see a gorilla that was clearly visible on the basketball court?

The answer is selective perception. The experimental subjects were totally focused on the white shirts. Their minds shut out anything that was black.

But when their minds went blank on the color black, they not only shut out black shirts but also black gorillas! The gorilla was "invisible" to more than half the subjects, even though it was in plain sight on the video.

Interesting stuff.

But how does it affect you as an investor? What impact does an invisible-gorilla experiment have on your net worth and portfolio allocation?

The answer is that selective perception is not limited to basketball videos. It's hardwired into our brains.

Invisible gorillas are everywhere, and investors don't see them unless they work hard to ignore what Wall Street wants us to see. You have to focus on what really matters in the world.

For example, investors tend to obsess over the day-to-day gyrations in the stock market and the month-to-month policy decisions of the Federal Reserve.

Wall Street and Washington want you to focus on the

"white shirts" in stocks and bonds.

What do they *not* want you to see? What is the invisible gorilla in global markets?

The answer is gold.

The facts on gold are as obvious as the gorilla in the video. World output is about 2,000 tons per year. China, India, Iran and Russia alone have been buying about 3,000 tons per year for the past seven years. The jewelry industry absorbs over 1,000 tons per year. (I consider jewelry to be gold bullion in decorative form, what I call "wearable wealth.")

Additional thousands of tons are being purchased by countries other than the "big four" mentioned above and by savvy individuals in Europe, Asia and Latin America. (U.S. citizens don't understand gold and are not large buyers.)

This excess of buying over output means existing gold stocks from vaults in London, New York and elsewhere are being depleted at a rapid rate. Actual physical-gold shortages and high-profile failures to deliver physical gold by banks and dealers are imminent.

Is it too late to invest in gold? That's where the invisible gorilla comes in.

Investors have been conditioned for 40 years *not to think about gold*. Investors have been told it's a "barbarous relic." Investors have been told, "Gold has no yield." Investors have been told, "There's not enough gold to support a monetary standard."

Sounds familiar?

These canards from Washington and Wall Street are like the scientists telling the experimental subjects, just look at the white shirts and ignore the black ones. Or in this case, ignore the gold shirts and miss the golden gorilla.

I've never seen a better setup for gold. Physical supplies are scarce. Leveraged accounts are short. Gold stocks have been trashed.

And no one is paying attention.

This is a great entry point for gold investors.

■ Gold Manipulation

A lot of people think about gold as a percentage of a country's total reserves. They are surprised to learn that the United States has 70 percent of its reserves in gold. Meanwhile, China only has about 1 percent of its reserves in gold. People look at that and think that's an imbalance. But those are not very meaningful figures in my view.

The reason is that a country's reserves are a mixture of gold and hard currencies, and the currencies can be in bonds or other assets. The United States doesn't need other currencies. We print dollars, so why would we hold euros and yen?

The United States doesn't need them, so it makes sense that the country would have a very large percentage of its reserves in gold. China, on the other hand, has greater need for other currencies.

A better metric, in my opinion, is to look at a country's gold holdings as a percentage of GDP. GDP is a representation of how big a country's economy is. It's the gross value of all the goods and services.

There are different measures of money supply—M3, M2, M1 and M0. In a money economy, however, you can say that the country's gold holdings are the real money. That's why I call gold M-subzero.

The IMF officially demonetized gold in 1975. The United States ended the convertibility of gold in 1971. Gold disappeared officially in stages in the mid-1970s. But the gold never went away.

Today, the United States has about 8,000 tons. We haven't sold a significant amount of gold since 1980. We dumped a lot of gold in the late 1970s to suppress the price, but none after that. So one of my questions for central bankers is "If it's such a ridiculous thing to have, why are we hanging onto it?" But that's a separate question.

Right now, China does not have enough gold to have a seat at the table with other world leaders. Think of global politics as a game of Texas hold 'em.

What do you want in a poker game? You want a big pile of chips.

Gold serves as political chips on the world's financial stage. It doesn't mean that you automatically have a gold standard, but that the gold you have will give you a voice among major national players sitting at the table.

For example, Russia has one-eighth the gold of the United States. It sounds like Russia's a small gold power—but its economy's only one-eighth as big. So it has about the right amount of gold.

U.S. gold reserves at the market rate are about 2.7 percent of GDP. That number varies because the price of gold varies—but it's around 2.7 percent. For Russia, it's about 2.7 percent. For Europe, it's even higher—over 4 percent.

In China, that number is 0.7 percent officially. Unofficially, if you give the Chinese credit for having, let's say, 4,000 tons, it raises them up to the U.S. and Russian level, but they want to actually get higher than that because their economy is growing.

Here's the problem: If you took the lid off of gold—ended the price manipulation and let gold find its level—China would be left in the dust. It wouldn't have enough gold relative to the other countries, and because its economy's growing faster and because the price of gold would be skyrocketing, it could never acquire it fast enough. It could never catch up. All the other countries would be on the bus while the Chinese would be off.

When you have this reset, and when everyone sits down around the table, China's the second-largest economy in the world. It has to be on the bus. That's why the global effort has been to keep the lid on the price of gold through manipulation. I tell people, if I were running the manipulation, I'd be embarrassed because it's so obvious at this point.

The price is being suppressed until China gets the gold that they need. Once China gets the right amount of gold, then the cap on gold's price can come off. It doesn't matter what price gold is because all the countries will be in the same boat. As of right now, however, they're not, so China has to catch up.

There is statistical, anecdotal and forensic evidence piling up for this. All of it is very clear. I've also spoken to members of Congress, the intelligence community, the defense community and very senior people at the IMF about it.

■ What's in It for the United States?

China is our largest trading partner. It's the second-largest economy in the world. The United States would like to maintain the dollar standard.

I've described some catastrophic scenarios where the world switches to SDRs or goes to a gold scenario, but at least for the time being, the United States would like to maintain a dollar standard. Meanwhile, the Chinese feel extremely vulnerable about the dollar. If we devalue the dollar, that's an enormous loss to them.

That's why, behind the scenes, the United States needs to keep China happy. One way to do that is to let China get the gold. That way, China feels comfortable. If China has all paper and no gold, and we inflate the paper, it loses. But if it has a mix of paper and gold, and we inflate the paper, China will make it up on the gold. So it has to get to that hedge position.

Gold is liquid, but it's a fairly thin market. If I call JPMorgan and say, "Hey, I want to buy 500 tons of gold," I can't do it. That would be a huge order. An order like that has to be worked between countries and central banks behind the scenes.

It's done at the Bank for International Settlements, in Basel, Switzerland. That's the acknowledged intermediary for gold transactions among major central banks and private commercial banks.

That's not speculation. It's in the footnotes of the annual BIS report. I understand it's geeky, but it's there. They have to acknowledge that because they actually get audited. Unlike the Fed and unlike Fort Knox, the BIS gets audited, and it has to disclose those kinds of things.

The evidence is there. The Chinese are saying, "We're not comfortable holding all these dollars unless we can have gold. But if we are transparent about the gold acquisition, the price will go up too quickly. So we need the Western powers to keep the lid on the price and help us get the gold until we reach a hedged position. At that point, maybe we'll still have a stable dollar."

The point is that there is so much instability in the system with derivatives and leverage that we're not going to get from here to there. We're not going to have a happy ending. The system's going to collapse before we get from here to there. At that point, it's going to be a mad scramble to get gold.

▧ The Threat of Paper-Gold Default

So much of the gold market today is paper gold. We all know dozens of different ways to get involved in paper gold. So much of it is manipulated, which we no longer have to speculate about. It's very well-documented. But the whole paper-gold market rests on some physical gold. It's like an inverted period with a little tiny bit of gold at the bottom, and a whole big inverted pyramid of paper gold resting on top of that.

What's happening is that the physical gold at the bottom of that inverse pyramid is getting smaller. You would say, "Gee, there are 2,000 tons of mining output per year, maybe a little more, and the gold that exists doesn't go anywhere, so why isn't that little brick getting bigger instead of smaller?" The answer is that investors have to distinguish between the total supply and the floating supply.

The total supply gets bigger every year by about 2,000 tons. People don't throw gold to the bottom of the sea. They don't blow it up with explosives. They hoard it. That means all the gold that's been mined is still around, and new gold keeps coming into the system.

The total supply grows every year, and when you move gold bars from the GLD warehouse in London to the Chinese warehouse in Shanghai, the impact on the total supply is zero. A lot of people say that, and they're right. But the floating supply shrinks. Now, what do I mean by the floating supply?

The **floating supply** is the physical gold that is available for re-hypothecation, collateral and so on, which support the paper transactions. The floating supply can be leased, it can be in a warehouse and it can be sold forward on an unallocated basis.

When you take gold from the GLD warehouse and put it in Shanghai, there's no impact on the total supply, but you have shrunk the floating supply. I've seen this firsthand.

I was in Switzerland in 2014, and I met with VIA MAT, which is one of the big four secure logistics firms in the world—along with G4S, Brinks and Dunbar.

These are the firms that handle physical gold. They're not dealers or bankers. They bring in armored cars and freight planes and use vaults. These are the people handling the actual stuff.

I met with the head of gold, precious metals and fine art for VIA MAT outside of Zurich. He told me that they're building vaults as fast as they can. They're actually negotiating with the Swiss Army. If you know anything about the Swiss Army, it's as if behind every rock in Switzerland there's a hidden entrance to a cave or an artillery piece. The whole country is an armed camp.

Over the years, the Swiss have hollowed out some of these mountains in the Alps and built these extensive warehouses, storage facilities and tunnels. All can withstand nuclear attack. Some of them are obsolete, and the Swiss are getting to the point where they don't think they need as many.

So, VIA MAT is in negotiation with the army to lease these nuclear bomb–proof mountains. The executive told me that VIA MAT is building vault space as fast as it can because it's running out of capacity.

I asked him, "Where's the gold coming from?" To which he replied, "UBS, Deutsche Bank, Credit Suisse and customers are taking it out of the banks and giving it to us."

Now, there's another example where the total gold supply is unchanged. Let's say I have 4,000 ounces of gold with UBS, and I call them up and say, "Please send the gold to VIA MAT."

In that case you have to send an armored car, pick the gold up, drive it down the street, drop it off with VIA MAT and get a receipt. It's the same 4,000 ounces, but I've now reduced the floating supply because VIA MAT is not doing anything with it. It's not a bank, and it doesn't lease the gold out like UBS might.

VIA MAT just watches the gold for you. UBS, on the other hand, is taking my gold and selling it 10 times over as unallocated gold on a London Bullion Market Association forward contract.

How does this end? It ends sooner rather than later when someone goes to a bank like UBS and says, "I want my gold, please," and the bank is unable to give it to them. They're not going to be able to get their hands on it. This is happening a lot now in small ways.

There are stories are out there including from pretty well-known people, like Kyle Bass and others, where the bank tells them, "We're sorry, you have to come back in a few weeks." Then you go back in a few weeks, and they say, "There's your gold."

Obviously it took them a few weeks to get the gold; otherwise they would have let you in in the first place. There's a lot of that going on behind the scenes, but none of it has really broken the system. The quantities of gold haven't been particularly large.

People don't find it in their interest to talk much about this, but it is happening. But what if there was a failure to deliver gold by a major dealer like HSBC or JPMorgan? That would be a shockwave.

I think it would set off panic buying in gold. Inflation expectations would get out of control. That could be a catalyst for the next crisis.

There are linkages you must consider too. I talked to a top employee at Goldman Sachs last time I was in China, and he's anticipating what he calls a demand shock in China. He's anticipating a situation where 200 million people run out to buy all the gold they can.

I said, "Well, that's interesting, because your firm is calling for $1,000 gold. You're the head of commodities trading. Why are you telling me you're expecting a demand shock when you're calling for $1,000 gold?"

That's when his associate said, "That's our research department. We don't listen to them."

I found that revealing. Goldman Sachs' research was telling every institution in the world at the time that gold was going to $1,000. Meanwhile, the head of commodities trading at Goldman Sachs was telling me he's positioning for a demand shock.

It pulls the rug out from under the idea that firms like Goldman Sachs are evil, monolithic forces manipulating the world. I know that's not true because I've known a lot of these people very well. It's also revealing in the sense that here's a major dealer who doesn't listen to his own research department.

The main point, however, is that there are major risks in the market right now. A threat I've already described, like a Chinese credit shock, could start this gold demand shock that the guy described to me. That could feed into a failure to deliver physical gold somewhere else in the system, maybe Switzerland or London, and then, quickly, the situation would spin out of control.

Where would it go from there?

The first thing that would happen is people would start to panic buy gold. The price would start to run up and then up still higher. Instead of increasing by $10 per ounce, it would go up $100 per ounce. At that point, everyone on CNBC would say, "Well, that's a bubble." But it could continue increasing $100 the next day and $200 the day after that. Within a week or 10 days, it would be up $1,000, and then everyone's calling it a bubble, but it keeps going.

Then, people might start selling stocks and taking money out of the banks to buy gold. What would that do? That would start to take the stock market down. From there, interest rates could start to go up.

In turn, maybe a bank like UBS is in a swap agreement with some hedge fund. It's a fixed-income swap, viable versus fixed, and it has nothing to do with gold or stocks. But one's given the other some Treasury collateral, and, as interest rates are spiking, there's a margin call. Then the bank says, "You're supposed to have 10 percent margin, and your collateral's worth less. Send us some money because you have to top up your margin."

The hedge fund sells what it can to meet the margin costs. At that point, the hedge fund is selling good stocks to raise cash to meet a margin call on a fixed-income swap, none of which has anything to do with gold. That's how cascades unfold.

Like an earthquake that causes a tidal wave, the damage has moved out from the source, and it's hitting communities all along the coastline that are very far removed from the original earthquake. But these are the ripple effects that you see in a highly interconnected system.

At that point, stocks would be crashing, gold would be spiking, the repo market would be drying up and the Fed would most likely be on the phone, trying to keep it all together. Soon after, there might be a run on money market funds.

These are all real-world scenarios and real network effects. The problem spreads quickly to areas far removed from the source of the problem. The essence of contagion is that the problem is never confined to the catalyst. It just spreads and spreads and spreads, and finds different channels, all of which lead to dead ends.

■ It's Time to Prepare for "Zero Hour"

If you're a fan of the 1964 James Bond movie *Goldfinger*, you recall the plot involved an effort to detonate a nuclear device inside Fort Knox. The purpose was not to blow up the gold, but to make it radioactive and unusable. This would greatly increase the price of other usable gold.

The villain of the movie, Auric Goldfinger, had already cornered the market on physical gold. When the nuclear device detonated, he would be the biggest winner from the spike in gold prices.

Of course, Bond, played by Sean Connery, famously foiled the plan by disabling the nuclear detonator with exactly seven seconds left on the clock!

While most James Bond fans recall the climax, fewer recall how Goldfinger was able to corner the physical gold market in the first place. He was an international gold dealer and owned a private gold refinery in Switzerland. Goldfinger would smuggle gold into Switzerland (sometimes in the body panels of his Rolls Royce) and then process it into pure gold bars at his Swiss refinery.

I recently visited Switzerland myself and had dinner with the head of the largest gold refinery in the world, located near Lugano, close to the Swiss border with Italy. The refinery chief is a friend whom I have met before. I jokingly refer to him as "Goldfinger." But he's no villain—he's one of the good guys when it comes to gold!

I call him Goldfinger to protect his privacy. I know of no single individual in the world with a more detailed working knowledge of physical gold flows. My meetings with him are always a source of unique insights into his dealings with central banks, Chinese buyers, gold miners and other players in the secretive world of physical gold.

A few years before my recent visit, Goldfinger said he had never seen a tighter supply situation for physical gold.

His refinery was running triple shifts—24 hours per day—and had orders for all the gold it could produce, 20 tons per week. About half went to China and half to longstanding customers such as Swiss watchmakers and jewelers. New business was simply turned away.

Now, a refinery receives gold in three main forms: existing gold bars from London Bullion Market Association vaults; so-called "scrap" (consisting of rings, bracelets, necklaces, etc.); and doré (semirefined gold bars from mining companies).

The scrap and doré were between 60 and 90 percent pure gold; the existing bars (the standard 400-ounce "good delivery" bars under LBMA rules) were about 99.0 percent pure. The object of the refining was to turn it all into 99.99 percent pure gold ("four nines" purity) and recast it into one-kilo bars (the new global standard bar established by Chinese buyers).

Goldfinger said his problem was sourcing the gold. In over 30 years in the gold business, he had never had difficulty sourcing gold. Now it was a persistent struggle to find any.

At our recent dinner, he confirmed that the supply scarcity had not changed. He was getting more scrap from Southeast Asia (Malaysia, Indonesia and Thailand). This was due to economic distress in those countries caused by the Chinese slowdown and emerging-markets capital outflows after the Federal Reserve started to tighten policy in May 2013. The Fed had put the world into "risk off" mode, and capital was leaving emerging markets. Locals were feeling the pinch, and had started selling their gold jewelry to raise dollars.

On the other hand, good-delivery bars were becoming more scarce. Vaults in London (such as the vault holding gold for the GLD exchange-traded fund) were being stripped bare. Goldfinger knew this because each LBMA good-delivery bar is stamped with the name of the refinery that produced it and the date it was produced.

Bars are generally stored in a vault on a "last-in-first-out" basis. Newer bars are removed first. The older bars (some with dates from the 1980s) are not moved out until the vault is almost empty. Goldfinger was now seeing more of those older bars come in for refining.

He told me he had recently returned from China, where he had visited Chinese refineries and gold mines. His tour was somewhat restricted by Chinese Communist officials, but as a prominent gold executive himself, he was able to see far more than most outsiders.

He said Chinese gold demand was voracious. The Chinese were buying over 450 tons per year produced from their own gold mines, and another 1,400 tons per year of imports. Chinese gold exports were zero.

Thus the Chinese were acquiring about 1,850 tons per year. This rate of acquisition has persisted for at least seven years. China has acquired about 13,000 tons of gold since 2009. Even if one assumed China started from a low base in

2009 (say, 3,000 tons), China's total gold hoard today (public and private) would be about 16,000 tons, considerably more than the United States' and about the same as India's.

In every city Goldfinger visited, his hosts took him to gold boutiques and gold emporia that sold gold to retail investors. This gold included not only bars and coins, but also jewelry, ornaments, statues and other decorative items. Some of these objects had been re-refined locally from the "four nines" bars sent to China by Goldfinger's refinery. They added alloy to make the malleable four-nines gold more durable for everyday use in jewelry.

The Chinese have recently built a network of state-of-the-art gold refineries of their own. Goldfinger visited some of these new gold refineries. He said the equipment was first-rate, and the refineries were as efficient as any in the world. These Chinese refineries did not compete directly with the Swiss refineries. Instead they mostly processed China's gold output from its own mines.

Chinese-refinery gold bars, like others, were stamped with the seal of the particular refinery that produced them. Goldfinger said that he had only ever seen three Chinese bars outside of China, and he believed these bars had been smuggled out. This is further proof that Chinese gold exports are practically nil.

Based on his observations and conversations, Goldfinger estimated that about 70 percent of total Chinese production and imports went to private retail consumption, and the remaining 30 percent to official gold held by the People's Bank of China or one of the Chinese sovereign wealth funds.

This was highly revealing. My own prior estimates (in the absence of better information) were that official gold was about 50 percent of the total. Lowering my estimate to 30 percent in line with Goldfinger's would put Chinese official gold at about 4,800 tons. (China admits to having about 1,700 tons of official gold at the People's Bank of China, but this figure is well-known to be a deception because most of China's official gold is "off the books" and parked at the State Administration for Foreign Exchange.)

Assuming that China's goal is to equal or exceed the official gold position of the United States (about 8,000 tons), China must still acquire over 3,200 tons to surpass the United States.

Chinese retail demand is unlikely to diminish anytime soon because the Chinese stock and real estate bubbles have popped. Everyday Chinese investors have few alternative investments other than gold.

The bottom line is that the Chinese shopping spree for physical gold is far from over. At current rates of gold consumption, the Chinese demand for gold will remain strong at least until 2021.

The problem as Goldfinger saw it was that the Chinese may well want the gold but the world was running out of supply. There is only one way to balance out a supply/demand problem of this type. The price of gold has to go up by a lot, initially past $2,000 per ounce, and ultimately much higher.

Our conversation next turned to the role of central banks, other than China's, in the gold market. I asked Goldfinger what he knew about the request by Germany to have some of its physical gold returned from custody at the Federal Reserve Bank of New York to vaults in the Frankfurt headquarters of the German central bank, the Deutsche Bundesbank.

The total amount of gold originally stored by Germany in New York is 1,500 tons. Germany was seeking the return of 300 tons from the New York Fed.

This request had been made in 2013, and had been the subject of enormous speculation in financial blogs and websites. In principle, the gold could have been returned to Germany in a matter of weeks or a few months at most using air deliveries arranged with secure logistics providers such as Brinks.

In fact, the Bundesbank revealed that the process would take seven years. This immediately led to speculation that the New York Fed did not have the gold and was dragging out the delivery process until it could locate enough bullion.

The truth is somewhat more nuanced. The New York Fed certainly did have enough gold on hand to satisfy the German request. The problem was that much of the gold was subject to leasing arrangements. There is a well-developed gold-leasing market in New York and London, but no similar market in Frankfurt.

(At this point in the conversation, Goldfinger said, "Yes, there is no established leasing market in Frankfurt, but if they [the Bundesbank] want to lease it to me, I'll take it!" Right there was confirmation that refiners do in fact take gold bars from central bank vaults and melt them down, *leaving central bank vaults partly empty.*)

The Federal Reserve Bank of New York needed years to deliver the gold to Germany not because of logistical problems, but because the gold was tied up in complicated leasing arrangements that needed to be unwound slowly in order not to cause a shock to the physical gold market that could cause prices to spiral upward and out of control.

But Goldfinger told me another reason the Bundesbank had acquiesced to such a long delivery timetable. He said that the gold in the New York vaults was what he called "Fed melt," a term I had never heard before. Fed melt was a disparaging way to describe the quality of the Fed's gold bars.

These bars had originally belonged to member banks of the Federal Reserve System (created in 1913). The private bank gold was consolidated in the regional reserve banks and ultimately shipped to the Federal Reserve Bank of New York in stages between 1913 and 1934. This gold was re-refined as late as the 1940s into bars that do not meet LBMA good-delivery standards (they had lower purity and were more irregular as to weight, size and shape).

The United States had about 20,000 tons of official gold in 1950, but by 1980 this official gold hoard had been reduced to the current level of about 8,000 tons. The 12,000-ton reduction was due to U.S. trade deficits under the old Bretton Woods system (ended in 1971), which allowed trading partners to cash in dollar reserves for gold.

Some of the reduction in the U.S. gold hoard was due to U.S. gold-dumping efforts in the late 1970s (after Bretton Woods) in a futile attempt to suppress the price of gold as the United States teetered on the brink of hyperinflation.

But while the official U.S. gold hoard was shrinking dramatically, much of the physical gold *never went anywhere*. It simply remained in the New York Fed vault. Ledger entries were made to reflect the new ownership. Now that the gold actually was leaving, the bars being delivered were ones that had been sitting in the vaults for over 50 years, sometimes longer.

Goldfinger said the Bundesbank was surprised and displeased with the low quality of the Fed's gold. They contacted him and insisted that the Fed melt be re-refined, assayed and cast into new bars of four-nines quality, the same as the Chinese. Once the Bundesbank realized how expensive and time consuming this process was they agreed to slow down the deliveries from New York.

(The funniest story of the evening was when Goldfinger revealed that the Bundesbank briefly considered putting a small gold refinery in the basement of the central bank's headquarters in Frankfurt to reduce outside refinery costs. In the end, they desisted due to the utter impracticality of the plan.)

Ultimately, the Bundesbank will get its 300 tons of gold back, but it will take time in order both to not disrupt the gold-leasing market and to spread out the costs of re-refining the gold to modern standards. Eventually "Fed melt" will be a thing of the past, at least in Germany.

One thread that ran through my conversation with Goldfinger was the concept of floating supply. In the physical-gold market, the floating supply is the amount of gold available for leasing or immediate delivery in connection with paper-gold transactions in futures, options, ETFs, unallocated sales and other leveraged transactions.

One ton of physical gold in the floating supply can support as much as 100 tons of paper-gold transactions. This enables short sellers to suppress the price of gold by selling paper contracts even though they have no physical gold to sell.

Of course, for every seller there must be a buyer. If 100 tons of short sales of gold are made against each ton of physical gold, then someone in the market must have bought 100 tons of paper gold. Those paper-gold buyers are just as much a part of the inverted paper-gold pyramid as the sellers.

The reason the inverted pyramid does not tip over is that the buyers do not demand physical delivery from the sellers. Paper-gold buyers are content to count their paper profits (or losses) and roll over their paper-gold futures contracts (earning steady profits from calendar spreads in contango).

Dealer banks are content to earn bid/offer spreads and arbitrage profits in paper gold while taking relatively little directional risk in the gold price itself. None of the gold bank dealers, gold futures traders or gold investors has much interest in disrupting these comfortable relationships.

In contrast to the floating supply is the **total stock**. This is simply the sum of all the above-ground gold in the world, whether it's official gold, private bullion or scrap. Today the floating supply is perhaps only 10 to 15 percent of the total stock.

As gold moves through Goldfinger's refinery, from West to East, from London to Shanghai, the total stock is unchanged but the *floating supply is shrinking*. Gold in London and New

York vaults is generally available for leasing and other leveraged paper-gold transactions, but gold in Chinese vaults is not.

(The Chinese gold is put in what is called "deep storage," where it is unavailable for leveraged transactions and may not see the light of day for centuries.)

As Goldfinger looks out over his refinery operations, he is *literally watching the floating supply disappear before his eyes.*

Yet, paper-gold transactions continue to grow. More and more paper trading is being supported with less and less physical gold. This leverage is inherently unstable and is destined to collapse in a buying panic and superspike in gold prices sooner rather than later.

This end-game scenario is just a matter of time. Goldfinger and I call this "Zero Hour." When the buying panic hits, gold will soar past $2,000 per ounce (if it's not there already) and spike to $3,000 per ounce, then higher, in a matter of weeks or months at most.

But when? This is the ultimate question that Goldfinger and I discussed as our dinner in Lugano neared its end. The idea that the paper-gold pyramid might tip over has been discussed for years. Yet, far from spiking, the price of gold fell 45 percent between 2011 and 2015. What would it take to create the upward gold-price momentum that both Goldfinger and I foresee?

For years, gold bugs implored futures traders to "stand for delivery" on the COMEX. If every long in the futures market put in a notification that they wanted to take physical delivery instead of closing out or rolling over their contracts, the result would be one of the greatest short squeezes and price spikes since Big Jim Fiske and Jay Gould tried to corner the private gold market in 1869. (Fiske and Gould's corner failed when the U.S. Treasury unexpectedly made public gold available to bail out the shorts.)

But this scenario is unlikely to play out in the way the gold bugs wish for several reasons. The first is that the COMEX has emergency powers to prevent longs from taking delivery in a way that disrupts the orderly functioning of the market. The COMEX rulebook makes it clear that a futures exchange is for hedging, price discovery and legal speculation *but is not a source of supply.* (Physical delivery is permitted, but only enough to keep the paper price "honest." The irony, of course, is that the paper price is anything but honest due to manipulation.)

Another rule allows COMEX officials to change the rules as needed in emergencies (something the Hunt brothers experienced when they tried to corner the silver market in 1980).

The fact that longs know they cannot take delivery in the end is a major deterrent to the attempt.

But there's another reason the gold longs don't squeeze the gold shorts: it's *illegal.* Most major participants in the gold market (banks, dealers and hedge funds) are regulated by one or more of the Federal Reserve, U.S. Treasury, SEC and CFTC. Applicable laws contain strict antifraud and antimanipulation rules including jail time in cases of willful and knowing violations. A hedge fund manager who is long on gold may want to kick over the inverted paper-gold pyramid but will refrain from doing so if he fears prosecution by the U.S. government.

(Of course, there's great irony in the fact that gold longs fear prosecution while there have been no antimanipulation prosecutions aimed at the gold shorts. Part of this is because of what's called "selective prosecution" designed to favor gold-price suppression. Another reason is that the chief manipulator is probably China, which is effectively beyond the reach of U.S. investigation and prosecution.)

Again, our question was, what would trigger the super-spike in gold prices? Why can't price suppression continue indefinitely, as it has for the past five years? What if China ultimately agrees to perpetuate price suppression by making some of its gold stock available for leasing?

The answer is found in avalanche theory, our name for the science of complexity. You know as a *Strategic Intelligence* reader that we use the science of complexity to analyze capital markets. The study of complex physical systems reveals that minute, even imperceptible changes in initial conditions can result in dramatically and exponentially different outcomes.

A single snowflake can turn a seemingly stable snowpack into a roaring avalanche that destroys everything in its path. Once the snowpack is arranged in an unstable way (like the gold market today) a single snowflake can unleash carnage. Of course, a single snowflake is so small you never see it coming.

What this means is that the superspike in gold prices will not come from any of the obvious sources but from an unexpected source. This could be the bankruptcy of a medium-sized gold dealer. Suddenly, customers would have to race to the physical-gold market to cover unmet deliveries from the failed dealer. It could be a proposed law that would impose onerous new reporting obligations on gold dealers. Just as gun sales spike every time Washington considers gun control, gold sales would spike if new gold controls were introduced.

The catalyst for a gold price spike could be something that has nothing to do with gold. It could be from an exogenous shock such as a new world war or a pandemic that caused people to flee to gold to safeguard wealth in the ensuing panic.

It doesn't matter. Once the avalanche begins, there's no stopping it.

At that point, the hedge funds *can* demand physical delivery of gold without fear of prosecution. If a hedge funds tries to start an avalanche, it's manipulation. But if the avalanche starts from another source, then a hedge fund piling on is "normal" market conduct. (Wouldn't you demand physical delivery if a full-scale buying panic broke out?)

Since every gold-market participant knows there's not enough physical gold to go around, everyone will demand physical gold at once. No one wants to be left holding the bag.

The point is that the stage is set. The gold market is in a critical state, like an atomic bomb about to detonate. Gold is scarce, and the floating supply is shrinking. Open interest in paper-gold contacts is expanding. Demand for physical gold is seemingly insatiable while the supply of physical gold is drying up. It will take very little to trigger a buying panic. It could happen tomorrow.

In fact, the buying panic may have started already in a quiet way. We all know the roar of an avalanche when it's in full cascade. But few can hear the slow slide at the beginning after the critical snowflake hits, before the snowpack completely separates from the mountain.

Right now, the price of gold is showing significant strength, especially considering the continued weakness in other commodities such as oil, copper and silver. This indicates that gold is no longer trading as a "commodity" but is beginning to trade as money. This can be thought of as a vote of no confidence in central bank money after seven years of failed monetary experiments.

Investors are expressing a preference for gold as money over other forms of money such as dollars, euros and yen. This is a trend that bears watching. The avalanche may already have begun.

As our dinner ended and we settled the check, I asked Goldfinger one final question. "If you didn't know me and I wasn't an existing customer, would you sell me a few tons of gold if I called you?"

Goldfinger's answer was chilling. "If you weren't an existing customer, I wouldn't take the business. I don't have any gold to spare. I might not even return your call."

When the panic does happen, you can forget about trying to buy gold. There won't be any, at least not for you. Some central banks and major dealers may be able to get some, but mints, small dealers and retail outlets will not be able to get any. The time to get gold is now, before the panic.

I recommend you have a 10 percent allocation to physical gold if you don't already. Here, again, I recommend American Gold Eagle or American Buffalo gold coins from the U.S. Mint. The American Eagle is 22-karat gold, and the American Buffalo is 24-carat gold. The Eagle is more durable than the Buffalo because it has some alloy, but both have one ounce of gold. You should not buy so-called "collectible" gold coins or older coins, because dealers charge a premium that is not worth it in terms of numismatic value.

Stick with new or relatively uncirculated Eagles or Buffalos. Prices are usually at the daily market price for one ounce of gold plus a premium, which can range from 4 to 8 percent, depending on the dealer. Storage should be with a reliable, insured, nonbank vault near your home or in a home safe. The best security is to not let anyone know you have the coins in the first place.

■ Physical Gold Versus Gold Miners

I've always talked about owning physical gold. By that I mean gold bullion, not paper gold. I've also never recommended gold-mining stocks—for two reasons. Number one is that stocks are very idiosyncratic. Gold is generic—it's an element—but mining stocks are not.

Miners are anywhere from extremely well-run companies to complete frauds. You can make money in the well-aligned companies, and you can lose your shirt in the frauds. There are bad mining companies out there, so you have to be very careful.

Having said that, if you're equipped to do the proper due diligence, it may be the right time to look at some high-quality gold-mining stocks. I would suggest looking at some of the larger players. The reason is because they've been beaten down so much. When you're down 90 percent, one of two things is going to happen. You're either going to go to zero, or you're going to bounce back big.

You've got to watch out for the companies that will go to zero. There is a predatory aspect to it too. Many investors may say, "Gee, these stocks are down so far, why not buy them?"

The answer: Why not wait until they go bankrupt and buy the assets even cheaper? That's the shark mentality. But you have to do the research, do the diligence, read the balance sheets and know what you're doing as an analyst.

Don't Buy Another Ounce of Gold Until You Read This!

I'm one of the few people to do the simple math that shows why gold is headed to $10,000 per ounce. This is one proof point for owning the 10% allocation to physical gold I recommend in this book.

But given the beaten-down state of the mining sector, I believe a lucrative opportunity has presented itself. I call them "penny gold" trades. And historically, windows of opportunities like them have been short—so you'll have to act fast on this. I've worked with my top geologist to create what we call the M.I.D.A.S. Touch. It's our proprietary approach for identifying the safest and biggest gains in this niche of the gold market. You can get more information about how this system works and how you can start using it by calling 1-866-361-7662 or visiting **www.agorafinancial.info/DontBuyGold9**.

CHAPTER 10

The Best Way to Understand the Global Financial System

■ It All Started When I Was a Young Boy...

My background is fairly eclectic. Some people say I could never decide what I wanted to be when I grew up, but I started as a lawyer. But before I went to law school, I got a graduate degree in international economics from the School of Advanced International Studies in Washington.

The interesting thing about that is I was studying international economics at a time when the world was still on a gold standard, so I was taught about gold in an academic context in an economics course.

That hasn't been true since. I was really the last generation, almost the last student, to learn about gold in the monetary sense. Literally a year after I left grad school, the IMF officially demonetized gold, and so, for several generations since then, if you've wanted to learn about gold, you've had to go to mining college or else be self-taught.

After that, I went to law school then got a second graduate law degree, this one in taxation. Soon after, I started my career as an international tax counselor at Citibank. I had the opportunity to travel around the world at a fairly early stage in my career, which was a great experience and allowed me to apply what I had learned about international economics in a banking-law context.

Over the course of my career, I made a move to investment banking and later made a move to hedge funds. In those areas and in those firms I learned a lot about government securities. I worked for one of the so-called primary dealers.

The Federal Reserve conducts monetary policy by increasing or reducing the money supply. It does that by buying and selling bonds. If it buys bonds from dealers, it pays for them with printed money. If it wants to reduce the money supply, it sells bonds and removes the money from the system. It needs someone to trade those bonds with, and it has an approved list. It won't trade with just anybody.

There are about 20 banks in the world that it's willing to trade with. The firm I worked for at the time was one of the banks, a so-called primary dealer.

After that, I joined a hedge fund and learned about derivatives. My career has evolved as I moved in the industry from commercial banking to investment banking to hedge funds and derivatives, but all the while I've kept my hand in international economics.

More recently, I was involved on the national-security side, particularly in the aftermath of 9/11, which I talk about in my books.

In *The Death of Money,* I talk about a study of insider trading and events of the 9/11 attacks, and in *Currency Wars,* I talk about a war game—the first financial war game ever done.

I've been able to combine both my background in international economics and law on the one hand with geopolitical expertise on the other to the benefit of *Strategic Intelligence* readers like you.

▧ I've Lost Everything Twice

Other personal experiences—two in particular—have helped form the goal of *Strategic Intelligence.*

If there was a middle of the middle class, that's what my family was when I was growing up. We weren't wealthy, but we weren't poor either. We had Chevrolet cars, a split-level house in New Jersey and a very *Leave it to Beaver* kind of upbringing.

At the age of 12, my family had the rug pulled out from under us financially. My father always supported the family with a job on the railroad, but he was also entrepreneurial and started a gas station. It was a partnership with his brother.

They borrowed some money to join a franchise operation. Unfortunately, there were price wars going on at the time, causing that business to fail and enter into bankruptcy. This was in the early 1960s. At the time, the bankruptcy laws were a lot tougher then than they are today, and we lost everything. We lost our house and our car.

We had to pack up and move. Picture that scene from *The Grapes of Wrath* when the Joad family gets in their old Model A and heads west on Route 66 looking for better times in California after the Oklahoma Dust Bowl. That was like what we went through moving to a place 80 miles away that we could actually afford. The rent was $35 a month in a bungalow that my grandmother owns.

I was the oldest of six. We went from a very comfortable middle-class existence to being on the edge of poverty. Financially, it was devastating. Some people who have heard this story say, "How did you put eight people—six kids and two adults—in a two-bedroom bungalow?"

Well, it wasn't easy, but we made it work. I ended up on a porch, very windswept and freezing cold in the winter. And my closet was a nail in the wall. I would take my sweatshirt off at night and hang it on the nail.

I didn't blame anybody. I understood that there are circumstances beyond everyone's control. At the same time, my attitude was, "I need to take my life in my own hands." I had taken too much for granted; I had had a very comfortable existence thanks to my parents.

Suddenly things weren't so comfortable. I made a vow to myself that I was going to take charge and not let this thing happen to me again. I wasn't going to be a victim, in other words.

Again, I wasn't blaming anyone. I understood that things change, but I wanted to be more alert to financial circumstances and try to understand them. If I understood things I couldn't control, I reasoned, I wouldn't be caught off guard.

That was a very seminal experience for me. I decided that my ticket out or my way forward was education. I got my undergraduate degree, a graduate degree in economics and, as I mentioned, two law degrees. That got me on my way and into financial services.

■ Long-Term Capital Management

In the late 1990s, I joined Long-Term Capital Management as a lawyer. That was another very critical experience for me.

The firm made billions of dollars, and I was one of the partners there, so I shared in that. Here I was, working with 16 finance Ph.D.s. We had two Nobel Prize winners there too.

We actually had complaints from business schools that we were hiring so many finance Ph.D.s that there wasn't anyone left to teach in academia. Our firm had the founders of modern financial theory.

We had former vice chairman of the Federal Reserve David Mullins Jr. We had two Nobel Prize winners, Myron Scholes and Bob Merton, who had invented the Black-Scholes options formula. There were many others, some of whom were less well-known, but one of them occupied the office next to Janet Yellen at Berkeley. It was the crème de la crème of finance Ph.D.s.

I invested my money in the fund. My thought was, "These guys know more about investing than I do. I could try to buy stocks on my own, but compared to these geniuses, what do I know?" So I put all of my money with them.

At the time I was making $1 million a year. I was one of the highest-paid lawyers on Wall Street. Well, you probably know how the story ended. In 1998, that fund went down 92 percent and we all got back eight cents on the dollar. I was wiped out financially for the second time in my life: first time when I was 12, second time when I was 47 years old.

I had to pick myself up again and rebuild things. Once again, I didn't blame anybody. I made the decision, so I wasn't going to point fingers. But I was dissatisfied intellectually.

I felt I did my job, but the Ph.D.s didn't do their jobs. They were the risk managers. They were the modelers. They were the inventors of modern finance. Why didn't their models work?

That's when I decided to set out on a kind of intellectual odyssey to understand what went wrong.

When Genius Failed

To be clear, LTCM was not just another hedge fund failure. We had $1.3 trillion of swaps when we were bailed out at the last minute. As I mentioned, we were given eight cents on the dollar.

Wall Street put in $4 billion of cash to take over our balance sheet. I like to tell people that they didn't bail us out, they bailed themselves out, because the next step would've been when LTCM went to zero; all those trades would've gone back to the counterparties and would've been no good from their point of view. Then they would've failed too.

It's interesting; we all knew that Lehman Brothers would be the next firm to fail in 1998. It ultimately did fail in 2008.

It was literally hours away from failing in 1998, though, along with Morgan Stanley and all the other banks.

It was sort of like a plane coming in for a nosedive and about to hit the ground; then somebody grabbed the joystick and got it back in the air at the last second. We were just hours away from closing every financial market in the world.

That's how severe it was for the world financial system. That's how devastating it was to me personally. From that experience, I realized there was something wrong with modern financial theory. I knew there was something wrong with risk management on Wall Street. If they knew what they were doing, LTCM never would've happened.

It took me 10 years. I spent five years figuring out what was wrong in the existing models. Then it took me five more years to figure out what did work. I said, "Well, if those other models don't work, what is the model that does work? What is the way to approach financial markets?"

I spent time taking courses in applied mathematics, physics, network theory, graph theory and complexity theory. It was good timing too, because by the time of the Panic of 2008, I was able to see the crisis ahead of time.

I gave a series of lectures in 2005, 2006 and 2007 warning about it very explicitly.

I said that the crisis is coming, that it will be bigger than 1998 and more devastating. I'm glad to say that thanks to my understanding of risk and complexity I did not lose any money in 2008. But I only saw it coming because of my experiences in 1998 when I had a disastrous loss. Paying tuition for an education enabled me to see what was wrong with modern finance.

■ Complexity Theory

My use of complexity theory in understanding risk in capital markets arose as a direct consequence of my involvement with

Long-Term Capital Management.

After the collapse and rescue, I chatted with one of the LTCM partners who ran the firm about what went wrong. I was familiar with markets and trading strategies, but I was not expert in the highly technical applied mathematics that the management committee used to devise its strategies.

The partner I was chatting with was a true quant with advanced degrees in mathematics. I asked him how all of our trading strategies could have lost money at the same time, despite the fact that they had been uncorrelated in the past. He shook his head and said, "What happened was just incredible. *It was a seven-standard-deviation event.*"

In statistics, a standard deviation is symbolized by the Greek letter sigma. Even nonstatisticians would understand that a seven-sigma event sounds rare. But I wanted to know how rare. I consulted some technical sources and discovered that for a daily occurrence, a seven-sigma event would happen less than once every billion years, or less than five times in the history of the planet Earth!

I knew that my quant partner had the math right. But it was obvious to me his model must be wrong. Extreme events had occurred in markets in 1987, 1994 and now 1998. They happened every four years or so.

Any model that tried to explain an event as something that happened every billion years could not possibly be the right model for understanding the dynamics of something that occurred every four years.

From this encounter, I set out on a 10-year odyssey to discover the proper analytic method for understanding risk in capital markets. I studied physics, network theory, graph theory, complexity theory, applied mathematics and many other fields that connected in various ways to the actual workings of capital markets.

In time, I saw that capital markets were complex systems

and that complexity theory, a branch of physics, was the best way to understand and manage risk and to foresee market collapses. I began to lecture and write on the topic including writing several papers that were published in technical journals. I built systems with partners that used complexity theory and related disciplines to identify geopolitical events in capital markets before those events were known to the public.

Finally I received invitations to teach and consult at some of the leading universities and laboratories involved in complexity theory including Johns Hopkins University, Northwestern University, Los Alamos National Laboratory, Singularity University and Applied Physics Laboratory.

In these venues, I continually promoted the idea of interdisciplinary efforts to solve the deepest mysteries of capital markets. I knew that no one field had all the answers, but a combination of expertise from various fields might produce insights and methods that could advance the art of financial-risk management.

I proposed that a team consisting of physicists, computer modelers, applied mathematicians, lawyers, economists, sociologists and others could refine the theoretical models that I and others had developed, and could suggest a program of empirical research and experimentation to validate the theory.

These proposals were greeted warmly by the scientists with whom I worked, but were rejected and ignored by the economists. Invariably top economists took the view that they had nothing to learn from physics and that the standard economic and finance models were a good explanation of securities prices and capital-markets dynamics.

Whenever prominent economists were confronted with a "seven-sigma" market event they dismissed it as an "outlier" and tweaked their models slightly without ever recognizing the fact that their models didn't work at all.

Physicists had a different problem. They wanted to collaborate on economic problems but were not financial-markets experts themselves. They had spent their careers learning theoretical physics and did not necessarily know more about capital markets than the everyday investor worried about her 401(k) plan.

I was an unusual participant in the field. Most of my collaborators were physicists trying to learn capital markets. I was a capital-markets expert who had taken the time to learn physics. One of the team leaders at Los Alamos, an MIT-educated computer science engineer named David Izraelevitz, told me in 2009 that I was the only person he knew of with a deep working knowledge of finance *and* physics combined in a way that might unlock the mysteries of what caused financial markets to collapse.

I took this as a great compliment. I knew that a fully developed and tested theory of financial complexity would take decades to create with contributions from many researchers, but I was gratified to know that I was making a contribution to the field with one foot in the physics lab and one foot planted firmly on Wall Street. My work on this project, and that of others, continues to this day.

▓ LTCM and Cognitive Diversity

In November 2015, our entire global *Strategic Intelligence* team held a summit at Rancho Santana in Nicaragua.

One of my analysts came up to me and said, "You know, I tried group meetings in our own office... and they haven't been as creative or productive as what we've done here."

I'm a geek, so I said, "You know what? That doesn't come to me as a surprise. I'll give you a scientific reason for why that's true."

The explanation has a lot to do with complexity theory and why my friends at Long-Term Capital Management lost $4 billion in a matter of weeks.

At LTCM, we had 16 Ph.D.s. We had more IQ points than you could imagine. These people actually had 150–170 IQs. That's about three times as smart as I am. When you get those types of scores, you're not too far from Leonardo da Vinci.

These men were the fathers of modern financial theory. They had written the original papers in the '70s and '80s. One of the guys was down the hall from Janet Yellen when she was at Berkeley; two of them won the Nobel Prize in economics and invested in the swaps market and fixed-income arbitrage in the '80s. They were legends.

But they had a blind spot. And it caused LTCM to fail and almost caused every market in the world to close. We were hours away from that happening in 1998. Few people know that. It was midnight on Sunday. We were trying to get a deal done before Tokyo opened that day. We did that, issued a press release and restored confidence. The Federal Reserve was involved.

But if we hadn't done that—and we were a lot closer to failure than people realize—markets would not have opened.

What was the problem? Why did 16 Ph.D.s get it wrong?

What the LTCM group lacked, and what our global-research team meeting in Nicaragua has, is cognitive diversity. It's a very powerful thing.

If you have five people from one country, there's a lack of cognitive diversity. When everyone on a board thinks alike, there's no one around to see what everyone may be missing. If you have five people from five different countries, it's going to be a fascinating group. You'll hear things you'd never hear otherwise. Where it really gets interesting is in the interaction.

This is where complexity theory comes in. The technical term for what comes out of a meeting with high cognitive diversity, like the one we held at Rancho Santana, is called an "emergent property." That means something that comes out of a complex system that cannot be inferred from having perfect knowledge of all of the components.

For example, at our meeting, we researched, discussed and applied the idea of the Impossible Trinity, a concept we covered in the January 2016 issue of *Strategic Intelligence* and that I discussed in chapter 8.

Yet if, before our meeting, I had every piece of information and data about who was going to be in attendance at our meeting, where it would be, what the format would be and so on, I would have had no basis for saying, "Aha, we will come up with the idea of the Impossible Trinity for our next monthly issue at our meeting." Instead, it was an emergent property; it arose spontaneously from our meeting because of the interaction.

▦ Similarities Between Today and 1998

I think it's important to know that no two crises are ever exactly the same. But we can learn a lot from history, and there are some elements today that do resemble prior crises. Right now, as we sit here in 2016, the damage of 2008 is still fresh in a lot of people's minds. It was eight years ago, but there's nothing like the experience of being wiped out, and a lot of people saw their 401(k)s erased.

It wasn't just stock prices but real estate, housing, unemployment and students graduating with loans who were not going to be able to get jobs. There was a lot of trauma and distress.

That's still clear in people's minds, even though it was, as I say, eight years ago. But what's going on right now, in my view, more closely resembles that 1997–98 crisis than the one in 2007–8.

Let's skip over the dot-com bubble in 2000 because that was clearly a bubble with an associated market crash but not a severe recession. We had a mild recession around that time, and then of course that played into the volatility due to 9/11. It was painful if you were in some of those dot-com stocks, but that wasn't a real global financial crisis of the kind we saw in 1998 and again in 2008.

What are some of the characteristics of 1998 that I think we are seeing now?

What was interesting about that time was that the crisis had started over a year earlier—July 1997 in Thailand. It ended up in my lap at LTCM in September 1998 in Greenwich, Connecticut. That was 15 months later and about halfway around the world.

How did a little problem that started in 1997 in Thailand end up in Greenwich, Connecticut, 15 months later as ground zero?

The answer is contagion. Distress in one area of financial markets spread to other seemingly unrelated areas of financial markets.

It's also a good example of how crises take time to play out. I think that's very important because with financial news, the internet, the web, and Twitter, Instagram, Facebook, chat and e-mail, there's a tendency for people to focus on the instantaneous and ignore trends.

That's what I call the curse of the two-second attention span. If there is a crisis, it's going to take 12 or 14 or maybe 18 months to play out. When people hear that, they go to sleep, then they wake up the next day and say, "Well, nothing bad happened today; I guess everything's fine." That could be a mistake. Don't expect the kinds of things in this book to turn around and bite us tomorrow morning. It might actually take a year. But a year is not that long a period of time. It's certainly not too soon to start thinking about it and start getting prepared.

What happened in 1997–98 was that U.S. interest rates were going up. A lot of people had borrowed dollars and invested in markets like Thailand. There were lots of projects—golf courses, hotels, real estate, Oriental projects, tours, certain Thai corporate names—not just in Thailand but all over South

Asia. You may remember the story of the Asian tigers. Some of those countries—Thailand was one of them—had pegged their local currency to the dollar.

If you were a dollar investor and you bought the Thai baht and made investments in the country, the government was promising you that the baht would still be worth the same amount of dollars.

So investors said: "That's pretty good. It takes away my exchange risk. I've got all this upside. I can borrow cheap money, put it to work in a faster-growing market, take out my exchange risk and make a lot of money."

That was an earlier version of what we call the carry trade today. What happened was that as U.S. rates started to go up, there was capital flight. Investors wanted to get their money out of Thailand. Meanwhile, Thailand was trying to defend the baht.

That meant that Thailand sold dollars from their reserves and bought baht in order to maintain the peg. It was pretty apparent at a certain point that the Thai central bank couldn't keep doing that. The demand for getting dollars out of Thailand was so great it began to overwhelm the bank's reserves.

Finally, Thailand broke the link to the dollar. Then it devalued its currency, which meant that investors could still get dollars but fewer of them for each baht. That started a panic, and everybody wanted to get out of Thailand.

The crisis didn't stay in Thailand, however. All of a sudden, investors looked around and saw other countries in the region that had their currency pegged to the dollar, countries that had some attractive investment opportunities but that looked unsustainable.

Next thing you knew, there was a run on the bank in Indonesia. Everybody wanted to get his or her money out. That led, of course, to unemployment, layoffs, busted projects, bankruptcies and riots in the streets of Indonesia. This was a few months later, but still, people were killed—there was literally blood in the streets. After that came South Korea.

This was happening over the course of June, July, August and September and well into the fall. It was playing out country by country—exactly like Ebola spreads.

In fact, the mathematics of financial contagion are exactly like the mathematics of disease or virus contagion. That's why they call it contagion. One resembles the other in terms of how it's spread.

That's when the International Monetary Fund got involved. The IMF started working up bailout projects. By December, it looked as if things had settled down. We at Long-Term Capital, in Greenwich, were sitting around in the early part of 1998 making plans to expand our operations in Asia.

We said, "Hey, look at all this financial distress." We were looking at buying Asian Pulp and Paper, because we thought there were good bargains to be had in Indonesia. Far from thinking, "We're the next in line," we were thinking, "With our $4 billion in cash, what a great opportunity to maybe pick up some deals in Asia." Needless to say, we didn't know what was coming.

Then, of course, by the spring, the crisis hit Russia. To this day, a lot of people say: "Oh, Long-Term Capital, I remember that story; those are the guys who lost all their money in Russian debt."

That's not true. We did lose about $100 million because of Russia. But our total losses were *$4 billion*. Not to mention the $1 trillion of swaps that we had with the rest of Wall Street. Russia was just a slice of that.

At this point, it was August 1998, and there were a lot of Russian derivatives because a lot of people wanted to buy Russian securities. It wasn't easy to buy them directly, so Credit Suisse and others started creating basket derivatives where the return would be indexed to the performance of certain Russian securities.

But of course, when that's done, the leverage increases be-cause there's a certain amount of those securities but if I start writing derivatives, I can write 5, 6 or 10 times the amount of securities in derivatives and let everybody make the same bet. So when Russia went down in August 1998, that was a shock.

Russia not only defaulted on its external debts—it's one thing when you default on your external, dollar-denominated debt, which it did—but it actually defaulted on its internal, ruble-denominated debt. In theory, there was no reason to do that because it could have printed rubles. Yet, Russia let its currency crash.

The ruble collapsed even more rapidly than it has recently. It started a global financial panic. Everybody wanted his or her money back. People had to sell good securities to raise cash to meet margin calls on bad securities.

Then, all of a sudden, the good securities weren't so good anymore because everybody was dumping them, trying to raise cash.

I saw another example of this dynamic in the early stages of the 2007–8 panic.

I was in Japan in September 2007, right after the mort-gage crisis started. It was a full year before Lehman Brothers. Remember, Lehman Brothers and AIG didn't happen until September 2008. The Tokyo stock market was going down. I remember my Japanese friend said: "Wait a second, Jim, we don't understand what's happening. You Americans have a mortgage problem, but we don't understand why that should affect the Tokyo stock market."

The reason the Tokyo stock market was going down was because the two were linked. That is, when you're in financial distress, when you're in trouble, you don't sell what you want; you sell whatever you can to raise cash to quell the trouble.

U.S. hedge funds and U.S. investment banks were getting margin calls on their mortgage-backed securities position.

They didn't want to sell those securities because there was no market or they would suffer enormous losses. Instead, they were selling Japanese stocks, which were pretty liquid. They were selling Japanese stocks to raise cash to meet the margin calls on the mortgages. That's how contagion works.

That's how all these markets are linked. It happened in 2007–8; it happened in 1997–98. By August, everybody was selling everything. Everybody wanted his or her money back. Credit spreads were widening. That's where Long-Term Capital lost its money because it was basically "the bank of volatility."

We would sell a security that looked a little rich, we would buy one that looked cheap, and there would be some spread between the two. You could be pretty confident that over time, the spread would come in. As those securities got closer to maturity the pricing would converge.

They were essentially two different flavors—two different maturities—of the same security. There was a securities swap that was denominated in the same currency.

Whatever it was, it was enough in common that your expectation was that any spread between the two instruments—the long and the short—would converge. Well, they didn't converge; they diverged. They widened. The more the panic grew, the worse the spreads widened and the more money we lost.

We were heading for a complete crack-up until Wall Street injected the $4 billion. They didn't do that to bail us out. They were bailing out themselves. They were, in effect, buying our balance sheets so that they didn't have to suffer the defaults, which would have happened if the company had actually filed for bankruptcy.

That's true of most bailouts. The people putting up the money are not doing a charitable act. They're really protecting their own interests because they're on the other side of some trade that they don't want to see go down.

The lesson is simple. Don't underestimate the power of contagion.

▓ Six Major Flaws in the Fed's Economic Models

For now, the U.S. dollar is the dominant global reserve currency. All markets, including stocks, bonds, commodities and foreign exchange, are affected by the value of the dollar.

The value of the dollar—in effect, its "price"—is determined by interest rates. When the Federal Reserve manipulates interest rates, it is manipulating, and therefore distorting, every market in the world.

The Fed may have some legitimate role as an emergency lender of last resort and as a force to use liquidity to maintain price stability. But the lender-of-last-resort function has morphed into an all-purpose bailout facility, and the liquidity function has morphed into massive manipulation of interest rates.

The original sin with regard to Fed powers was the Humphrey-Hawkins Full Employment Act of 1978, signed by President Carter. This created the "dual mandate," which allowed the Fed to consider employment as well as price stability in setting policy. The dual mandate allows the Fed to manage the U.S. jobs market and, by extension, the economy as a whole, instead of confining itself to straightforward liquidity operations.

Janet Yellen, the Fed chair, is a strong advocate of the dual mandate and has emphasized employment targets in the setting of Fed policy. Through the dual mandate and her embrace of it, and using the dollar's unique role as leverage, she is a de facto central planner for the world.

Like all central planners, she will fail. Yellen's greatest deficiency is that she does not use practical rules. Instead she uses esoteric economic models that do not correspond to reality. This approach is highlighted in two Yellen speeches. In June 2012, she described her "optimal control" model, and in April 2013, she described her model of "communications policy."

The theory of optimal control says that conventional monetary rules, such as the Taylor rule or a commodity-price standard, should be abandoned in current conditions in favor of a policy that will keep rates lower for longer than otherwise. Yellen favors use of communications policy to let individuals and markets know the Fed's intentions under optimal control.

The idea is that over time, individuals will "get the message" and begin to make borrowing, investment and spending decisions based on the promise of lower rates. This will then lead to increased aggregate demand, higher employment and stronger economic growth. At that point, the Fed can begin to withdraw policy support in order to prevent an outbreak of inflation.

The flaws in Yellen's models are numerous. Here are a few:

1. Under Yellen's own model, keeping rates "lower, longer" is designed to improve the economy sooner than alternative policies. But if the economy improves sooner under her policy, she will raise rates sooner. So the entire approach is a lie. Somehow people are supposed to play along with Yellen's low-rate promise even though they intuitively understand that if things get better the promise will be rescinded. This produces confusion.

2. People are not automatons who mindlessly do what Yellen wants. In the face of the embedded contradictions of Yellen's model, people prefer to hoard cash, stay on the sidelines and not get suckered by the bait-and-switch promise of optimal-control theory. The resulting lack of investment and consumption is what is really hurting the economy. Economists call this "regime uncertainty," and it was a leading cause of the length of the Great Depression of 1929–41, if not the cause of the depression itself.

3. To make money under the Fed's zero-interest-rate policy, banks are engaging in hidden off-balance-sheet transactions, including asset swaps, which substantially increase systemic risk. In an asset

swap, a bank with weak collateral will "swap" that for good collateral with an institutional investor in a transaction that will be reversed at some point. The bank will then take the good collateral and use it for margin in another swap with another bank. In effect, a two-party deal has been turned into a three-party deal with greater risk and credit exposure all around.

4. Yellen's zero-interest-rate policy constitutes massive theft from savers. Applying a normalized interest rate of about 2 percent to the entire savings pool in the U.S. banking system, compared to the actual rate of zero, reveals a $400 billion-per-year wealth transfer from savers to the banks. This has continued for six years, so the cumulative subsidy to the banking system at the expense of everyday Americans is now over $2 trillion. This hurts investment, penalizes savers and forces retirees into inappropriate risk investments such as on the stock market. Yellen supports this bank subsidy and theft from savers.

5. The Fed is now insolvent. By buying highly volatile long-term Treasury notes instead of safe short-term Treasury bills, the Fed has wiped out its capital on a mark-to-market basis. Of course, the Fed carries these notes on its balance sheet "at cost" and does not mark to market, but if it did, it would be broke. This fact will be more difficult to hide as interest rates are allowed to rise. The insolvency of the Fed will become a major political issue in the years ahead and may necessitate a financial bailout of the Fed by taxpayers. Yellen is a leading advocate of the policies that have resulted in the Fed's insolvency.

6. Market participants and policy makers rely on market prices to make decisions about economic policy. What happens when the price signals upon which policy makers rely are themselves distorted by prior policy manipulation? First you distort the price sig-

nal by market manipulation, and then you rely on the "price" to guide your policy going forward. This is the blind leading the blind.

The Fed is trying to tip the psychology of the consumer toward spending through its communication policy and low rates. This is extremely difficult to do in the short run. But once you change the psychology, it is extremely difficult to change it back again.

If the Fed succeeds in raising inflationary expectations, those expectations may quickly get out of control, as they did in the 1970s. This means that instead of inflation leveling off at 3 percent, inflation may quickly jump to 7 percent or higher. The Fed believes it can dial down the thermostat if this happens, but it will discover that the psychology is not easy to reverse, and inflation will run out of control.

The solution is for Congress to repeal the dual mandate and return the Fed to its original purpose as lender of last resort and short-term liquidity provider. Central planning failed for Stalin and Mao Zedong, and it will fail for Janet Yellen too.

▧ Self-Organized Criticality

Let's say I've got a 35-pound block of enriched uranium sitting in front of me that's shaped like a big cube. That's a complex system. At the subatomic level, neurons are firing off—but it's not dangerous. You'd actually have to eat it to get sick.

Say I were to take the same 35 pounds, however, and mold part of it into the shape of a grapefruit, and take the rest of it and shape it into a bat. If I were to put them in a tube and fire them together with strong explosives, I'd kill 300,000 people because I would've engineered an atomic bomb.

It's the same uranium in both cases. My point is that the same basic conditions arrayed in a different way—what physicists call self-organized criticality—can go critical, blow up, and destroy the world or the financial system.

That dynamic, which is the way the world works, is not understood by central bankers. And it's not just central bankers. I've talked to monetary economists and staffers. They look at me and can't even process what I'm saying.

They don't get complexity theory or the critical-state dynamics going on behind the scenes because they're using equilibrium models.

An equilibrium model basically says that the world runs like a clock. Every now and then, according to the model, there's some perturbation, and the system gets knocked out of equilibrium. All you do then is apply policy and push it back into equilibrium. It's like winding up the clock again.

Unfortunately, that is not the way the world works. Complexity theory and complex dynamics tell us that a system can go into a critical state.

▦ The Problem With Equilibrium Models

I've met any number of governors and senior staff at the Federal Reserve. They're not dopes. A lot of people like to ridicule them and say they're idiots. They're not idiots, though. They've got the 160 IQs and the Ph.D.s.

Every year, however, the Fed makes a one-year forward forecast. In 2009, it made a forecast for 2010. In 2010, it made a forecast for 2011. And so on. The Fed has been wrong seven years in a row by orders of magnitude.

It'll say it projects 3.5 percent growth, and growth actually comes in at 2 percent. Then it'll lower the forecast to 3 percent, and growth actually comes in at 1.9 percent.

It's the same thing with the IMF. The IMF forecasts have been wrong seven years in a row too. When I hear these forecasts and I hear commentators say, "We're projecting 3 percent growth next year based on the IMF forecast," I just laugh. How many years in a row can you be wrong and still have any credibility?

But they're not dopes—they are really smart people. I don't believe they're evil geniuses trying to destroy the world. I think they're dealing in good faith. If they're so smart and they're dealing in good faith, though, how can they be so wrong for so long?

The answer is they've got the wrong model. If you've got the wrong model you're going to get the wrong result every single time. The Federal Reserve, policy makers, finance ministers and professors around the world use equilibrium models.

They treat the world like a car engine that works fairly well until it gets a little bit out of sync. At that point, you just need to tweak it and then it will run fine again. As I've said, unfortunately, the world is not an equilibrium system.

Now, we pay attention to those models because the Fed pays attention to them. If you're trying to figure out what the Fed's decision-makers are going to do, you need to know how they think. And they're using these equilibrium models.

I don't believe the models are accurate, but I do believe the Fed thinks they're accurate. So the second derivative of that is to watch them because it's a good guide to policy. My own view is that you can't use equilibrium models in a nonequilibrium world. The world is a complex system.

What are examples of the complexity? There are lots of them.

One of my favorites is what I've been calling the avalanche and the snowflake. It's a metaphor for the way the science actually works, but I should be clear, it's not just a metaphor. The science, the mathematics and the dynamics are actually the same as those that exist in financial markets.

Imagine you're on a mountainside. You can see a snowpack building up on the ridgeline while it continues snowing. You can tell just by looking at the scene that there's danger of an avalanche. It's windswept, it's unstable and if you're an expert, you know it's going to collapse and kill skiers and wipe out the village below.

You see a snowflake fall from the sky onto the snowpack. It disturbs a few other snowflakes that lay there. Then the snow starts to spread, then it starts to slide, then it gains momentum until, finally, it comes loose and the whole mountain comes down and buries the village.

Question: whom do you blame? Do you blame the snow-flake, or do you blame the unstable pack of snow?

I say the snowflake's irrelevant. If it wasn't one snowflake that caused the avalanche, it could have been the one before or the one after or the one the next day.

The instability of the system as a whole was a problem. So when I think about the risks in the financial system, I don't focus on the "snowflake" that will cause problems. The trigger doesn't matter.

A snowflake that falls harmlessly—the vast majority of all snowflakes—technically fails to start a chain reaction. Once a chain reaction begins it expands exponentially and can "go crit-ical" (as in an atomic bomb) and release enough energy to de-stroy a city. However, most neutrons do not start nuclear chain reactions, just as most snowflakes do not start avalanches.

In the end, it's not about the snowflakes or neutrons, it's about the initial critical-state conditions that allow the pos-sibility of a chain reaction or avalanche. These can be hypoth-esized and observed at large scale, but the exact moment the chain reaction begins cannot be observed. That's because it happens at a minute scale relative to the system. This is why some people refer to these snowflakes as "black swans": they are unexpected and come by surprise. But they're actually not a surprise if you understand the system's dynamics and can estimate the system's scale.

It's a metaphor, but really the mathematics are the same. Financial markets today are huge, unstable mountains of snow waiting to collapse. You see it in the gross notional value of derivatives.

There are $700 trillion worth of swaps. These are derivatives off balance sheets, hidden liabilities in the banking system of the world. These numbers are not made up. Just go to the BIS annual report, and it's right there in the footnote.

Well, how do you put $700 trillion into perspective? It's 10 times global GDP. Take all the goods and services in the entire world for an entire year. That's about $70 trillion when you add it all up. Well, take 10 times that, and that's how big the snow pile is. That's the avalanche that's waiting to come down.

Diligence, research and patience in asset selection are all required to earn consistent profits—especially in today's volatile automated markets. If you cut corners, act impulsively or make bets without considering the odds, you should expect to lose money.

But what about the situations where you do everything right and still come up short?

Imagine trying to invest intelligently in emerging markets. You know it's risky, but there are ways to mitigate the risk. You look for countries with strong reserve positions, positive trade balances, good rule of law and a sticky kind of comparative advantage. You look for a conservative central bank that tries to preserve currency values and avoid inflation and currency wars.

Once you've done all of that (or been advised by someone who has), you make your investment. Then, *boom*, you may be down 30 to 50 percent on your investment before you know it.

You did everything right and still lost a lot of money in the blink of an eye. Why?

When this happens, it is usually due to the emergence of some "Knightian uncertainty" (named after economist Frank Knight, who distinguished between risk, which can be measured, and uncertainty, which cannot).

At *Strategic Intelligence*, we say a loss of this type is due to an "emergent property" of a complex dynamic system. Both Knightian uncertainty and emergent properties fall into the snowflake-and-the-avalanche category I just explained. You know when you've been buried in an avalanche, but you never see the snowflake that started it all. It's an event you don't expect and don't see coming.

As we explain in the special report *30 "Snowflakes" That Could Trigger the Next Financial Avalanche (www.agora financial.info/snowflakes)*, a snowflake comes in all shapes and sizes. It can be an outbreak of a deadly disease like Ebola. It can be a multiple catastrophe like the earthquake–tsunami–reactor meltdown that struck Fukushima, Japan, in March 2011. It can be a political event such as an assassination, a coup d'état, or the Arab Spring.

Regardless of the particular circumstances, a financial avalanche is always a shock because no one sees the snowflake that caused it.

▓ What Backs the Dollar

All of your assets, whether they're stocks, bonds or other types of assets, are denominated in dollars. A lot of people say the dollar is not backed by anything, but that's not true. The dollar is backed by one thing—confidence.

If confidence in the dollar is lost, that means that people almost simultaneously decide that the dollar is not a store of value. They want to get out of dollars and into other things. That's what I mean by a collapse in confidence in the dollar. When that happens, your dollars won't save you. You're going to need the other things, especially gold, fine art and land. There are some stocks that will preserve value too if the underlying assets themselves are tangible assets.

The problem I see is that the policy makers, the central bankers in particular, take confidence for granted. Using equilibrium models that have little relationship to the real world

is bad enough, but if they use them to pursue a certain policy that destroys confidence in the dollar, then we'll have the kind of crisis I'm predicting.

▓ Thomas Kuhn and Paradigm Shifts

The vast majority of the people working at the Federal Reserve are not uneducated—they're miseducated. They are very smart people who have worked very hard to learn the wrong things.

They've learned things that don't exist in reality. Let me back that up because that's a big statement. When I lecture on complexity or on finance in general I include a digression on the history of science first.

There's a case study laid out in a book by Thomas Kuhn called *The Structure of Scientific Revolutions*. Kuhn coined the phrase "paradigm shift." I'm sure you've heard paradigm shift a million times. It's often misused, or it's used as a cliché. Maybe somebody wears brown shoes instead of black shoes and a person says, "There's been a paradigm shift," when all that has really happened is somebody changed their shoes.

The way Thomas Kuhn intended it is that the paradigm is bigger than the model. We construct a model of reality as a tool kit for whatever kind of analysis we're doing. Your paradigm is the way you see the world, the big picture that forms the model that supposedly corresponds to the reality.

For about 1,500 years, from the 1st century A.D. to the 16th century A.D., all the smartest people in the world—or anybody who thought about it—believed that the sun revolved around the Earth.

It was called the geocentric view. The church believed it, but you don't have to blame the church. This was science—because it was obvious. You woke up in the morning and the sun was over there, and then it moved across the sky and went down over there, and then you went to bed. The next day it came up over there again. So, clearly, the sun was revolving around the earth; that was very obvious.

They came up with a model that explained that the Earth is the center of the universe and that the sun, the planets, the moon and the stars revolve around the Earth. They modeled concentric circles of the sun, moon, planet, and stars all revolving around the Earth, which was the center of the universe. This was science for 1,500 years. People modeled it and wrote equations explaining it.

It wasn't mythology. They could write scientific equations to know what planet was going to be where on what day. Mathematicians, scientists and astronomers were doing this for 1,500 years.

What happened, however, was that by the late 15th century, scientific data started to improve. This was around the time of Galileo and telescopes. Scientists and astronomers started to notice that the planets weren't exactly where the model said they were supposed to be. The data was coming in at odds with the model.

As a scientist, what you're supposed to do is question the model. But that's not what they did. What they did was embellish the model to account for the anomalies. They said, "Well, there are big circles, which are called cycles. But if the planet's off the cycle a little bit, then there must be an epicycle, or a little circle. So it's doing a big loop, but while it's doing a big loop it's also doing these little, counterclockwise loops." And they kept embellishing it. They wrote new equations for all of this. It is all well-documented.

Finally, Copernicus came along and said, "Maybe the Earth is not the center of the universe; maybe the sun is the center of at least the solar system. And maybe the planets—including the Earth—revolve around the sun."

Then Kepler came along and said, "And maybe the orbits are not circular—maybe they're elliptical."

And after him came Tycho Brahe, who used his telescope to take observations. By the end of the 16th century, Copernicus, Brahe, and Kepler had created a new model, the heliocentric model, where the sun is the center of the solar system and the planets and the moon revolve around it in elliptical orbits.

And guess what? It works. That's the model.

That's an example of how, for 1,500 years, all the smartest people in the world, using very good math, physics and astronomy were completely wrong.

The men and women at the Federal Reserve and IMF have 170 IQs and advanced Ph.D.s. But what good is all of that brain power if you've got the paradigm wrong?

They're using equilibrium models, normally distributed risk, mean reversion, Monte Carlo simulations and other things that are the financial equivalent of thinking that the sun revolves around the earth.

What a small minority and I are doing is coming along and saying, "No, the sun doesn't revolve around the Earth; the Earth revolves around the sun." The best models for understanding capital markets are complexity theory, physics, phase transitions, network theory, graph theory and other applied mathematics that go along with those.

Let's say you're a really smart 25-year-old, and you're trying to get a Ph.D. in finance. Perhaps you're reading *Strategic Intelligence* or *The Daily Reckoning* and you say, "You know, I think they're onto something. I think this complexity theory means something."

But your professor, your Ph.D. thesis advisor, is a 55-year-old who spent the last 40 years learning about equilibrium models. They don't want to back away from it. It's very hard when you're 55, 60 years old to say: "Hey, everything I've been doing for the last 40 years is pretty much wrong."

If you, the smart 25-year-old Ph.D. student, ask your MIT professor if you can write your thesis on complexity theory, they'll say no. Instead of being the first student to write on complexity theory, you need to be the 9,000th student doing some minute little tweak on the same equilibrium models that we've been doing for the last 50 years.

If you're the outlier who wants to pursue the new science, you're not going to get your Ph.D., or you're not going to get it from a prestigious school. You won't be taken under the wing of a prominent thesis advisor or get published either.

And, perhaps most important, you're not going to get a job. That's when you, the bright 25-year-old, give up and write something the professor likes instead. That's how, even in the face of new ideas and new science, bad science perpetuates itself—all because of nostalgia. Fortunately, the old models are eventually replaced, but it takes time.

CHAPTER 11

The Beginning of the End for the Dollar

I talk a lot about the coming collapse of the international monetary system. It sounds provocative, maybe even apocalyptic, but it's not meant to be. The international monetary system actually has collapsed three times in the past 100 years.

It collapsed in 1914 when the classical international gold standard was abandoned. It collapsed again in 1939 when something called the gold-exchange standard was abandoned. And then it collapsed in 1971 when President Nixon abandoned the convertibility of dollars into gold. That's three collapses in 100 years. They happen about every 30 or 40 years, and it's been about 40 years since the last one.

That doesn't mean the system is going to collapse tomorrow morning like clockwork. It does suggest, however, that the useful life, if you will, of the international monetary system is about 30 or 40 years. We're at the end of that period, so we shouldn't be surprised if it collapses again.

I do make the point that when these collapses occur it's not the end of the world. It doesn't mean that we all go live in caves and eat canned goods. What it does mean is that the major financial trading powers of the world sit down around a table and they rewrite the "rules of the game."

■ Critical Thresholds for Quitting the Dollar

There is something called a "hypersynchronous Ising model" that illustrates how the dollar can collapse. It demonstrates how confidence can be lost and how tenuous and dangerous the dollar's situation is today, contrary to what policy makers say.

Let me give you a very plain-English explanation of it. Imagine you were in a room of 300 people listening to a lecture on complexity theory. Everything was going smoothly until, suddenly, four people got up and ran out of the room as fast as they could.

What would you do?

I dare say you would do nothing. You'd think that was odd or rude. Maybe you'd figure they got a text message, or something urgent came up where they were late for something and had to go. Meanwhile, you'd stay in your seat to listen to the rest of the wonderful lecture.

Now, what if it was the same exact situation, except 100 people suddenly got up and ran out of the room as fast as humanly possible. What would you and the people seated around you do? I dare say you'd be right behind them!

You wouldn't know why. Maybe you'd think that place is on fire, but you wouldn't stick around to find out. The collapse of the dollar will be no different.

The point of the illustration is to show what's called the "T-Factor" or "critical threshold." The critical threshold is the point at which your behavior changes based on the behavior of others.

Where is it? It's probably different for every one of you. Going back to our illustration, for some people, 10 people running out of the room would be enough to convince them to run out right behind them.

For another person, maybe 200 people running out wouldn't be enough to convince them there's a danger. The thresholds are all over the place. They change all the time.

Some days people are bolder, and some days they're more fearful. Some days people are tired, and other days they're energetic.

We all have different thresholds. Think of the complexity of just that room of 200 people. Now, extrapolate that dynamic to the whole world and you get some idea of how complex systems work.

Take a look at this table:

Sub-Critical and Critical States
(Simplified Hypersynchronous Ising Model)

Assume 100 People repudiate the dollar in each casein total population of approximately 310,00,000 people.

T= Critical Threshold for each cohort

Case 1 Sub-critical State	Case 2 Critical State
1,000 people / T=500	1,000 people / T=100
1 million people / T=10,000	1 million people / T=1,000
10 million people / T= 100,000	10 million people / T= 100,000
100 million people / T=10 mil.	100 million people / T=10 mil.
200 million people / T=50 mil.	200 million people / T=50 mil.

In case 1, I'm assuming that the starting place is that 100 people will repudiate the dollar. What does that mean, "repudiate the dollar"? It means that they no longer want dollars. They no longer trust dollars as a store of value. They may get them because they got paid or sold something. They dump the dollars and buy some hard assets. It could be gold, other precious metals, fine art or land.

The next 1,000 people have a critical threshold of 500. That means 500 people have to quit the dollar before they're convinced to quit too.

The next million people have a critical threshold of 10,000. In other words, 10,000 people have to quit the dollar before they quit.

These numbers on the right of the table are the thresholds at which the numbers on the left also repudiate the dollar.

In case 1, 100 people quit the dollar. What happens? The answer is nothing. Nothing happens because you haven't hit the threshold for the next 1,000 people.

A hundred people quitting the dollar is like four people running out of the room in my example. It's not enough to get anyone to do anything, and so the dollar is stable.

If you move to case 2, what I call the "critical state," you'll notice that I've lowered the threshold from 500 to 100 for the first group. I've also lowered the threshold from 10,000 to 1,000 for the second group. All the rest is unchanged. I haven't changed the information for the other 310 million people. All I've changed are the preferences of three one-thousandths of 1 percent of the population.

Now what happens?

When 100 people quit the dollar the threshold for 1,000 people to also quit is hit.

When those 1,000 people quit the dollar the threshold for 1 million people to quit also is hit.

At 1 million people quitting the dollar, you're way past the threshold for 10 million more people to quit it too.

At 10 million people quitting the dollar you've hit the threshold for *100 million* people quitting the dollar.

You can see what happens. The dollar collapses because no one wants dollars.

Here's the point. If case 1 was stable, case 2 is a catastrophic collapse. The only difference is three-thousandths of 1 percent of the people. You didn't have to change 300 million people's minds. You only had to change a tiny, tiny fraction. This is completely characteristic of complex systems.

Minute changes in initial conditions cause catastrophically different outcomes in the system as a whole. This is the world we live in.

This is an actual model that describes the economy—not the one the Fed is using. Are we at this point? Not yet, and we won't know when we're there until it's too late.

I can tell you, however, we're getting closer with the Fed's money printing, the banks' derivative creation, the increase in the scale of the system and the concentration of assets. We're getting closer to that critical state and the point at which the entire system collapses.

It's happening slowly and invisibly, but you can see the momentum. That momentum is going to build until suddenly we get to the point where there is a new global reserve currency, which, of course, will be highly inflationary. Investors need to get out of the dollar system, and there are a number of ways to do that.

You can buy gold, silver, land, fine art, carefully selected hedge funds, some mutual funds and select energy, transportation, natural resource, water and agriculture stocks. There are plenty of companies that have hard assets underneath that will survive the coming inflation.

It's a fairly dire forecast, but it doesn't make me a "doom and gloomer." I'm just realistic about what I see. It doesn't mean you have to live in a cave. I don't. I wake up every day. I'm an investor, a writer, an advisor and an analyst. There are always things to do to protect your wealth.

I wouldn't discourage anyone from being an active investor, but just be smart about it and know what's coming.

The Future of the International Monetary System

Earlier, I laid out four crisis scenarios, including financial warfare, inflation, deflation and collapse. But there are also four different scenarios for the future of the international monetary system.

The Kumbaya Solution

One future scenario is a world of multiple reserve currencies where the dollar is still used. In the last 10 years, the dollar has gone from 70 percent of global reserves to 60 percent. Imagine that continuing below 50, down to 45. Maybe the euro increases to 35 percent of global reserves and the roles of the Swiss franc and the Japanese yen as global reserve currencies increase as well. I call this the "kumbaya solution"—where all of these currencies get along.

I think that's extremely unstable because the system would not be anchored to anything. Instead of one central bank, like the Fed, behaving badly, we'd have five or six central banks behaving badly.

Societal Collapse

The second scenario is simply collapse—as in, societal collapse. You'd see civilization falling apart.

You might see the president using executive orders to implement neofascist policies. Look at your local police force. When I was a kid, cops would walk the beat and get kittens out of trees.

Today, they're wearing body armor, helmets, night-vision goggles, flash-bang grenades, battering rams, and automatic weapons. They drive around in armored personnel carriers. They're using drones, surveillance, and so on.

We have a heavily militarized police force in every county and town in America. Under government direction, that militarization could be used to keep social order. These are the kinds of scenarios you're looking at if the system collapses.

A New Gold Standard

The third scenario is a gold standard. There's not a central bank in the world that wants a gold standard, but central banks may be forced to accept one to restore confidence. That's a possibility. If they go back to a gold standard, they'll have to get the price right and there will be a calculation.

It will be arranged depending on how much gold backing you want, depending on if you're talking about M0, M1 or M2, and depending on which countries are involved.

Special Drawing Rights

The fourth scenario is a world of SDRs. I believe this is the most likely outcome.

The SDR sounds geeky. The name is by design. Global financial leaders pick strange names for what they're doing so people don't understand what it is.

Luckily, the SDR isn't complicated. It's very simple. The Fed has a printing press and can print dollars. The European Central Bank has a printing press and can print euros. The IMF has a printing press and can print Special Drawing Rights. The SDR is simply world money. The IMF didn't want to call it world money because that sounds a little scary, but that's what it is.

SDRs are not new; in fact, they've been around since 1969. The IMF can print them, and in the next liquidity crisis, they will do so. In 2009, they printed hundreds of billions of dollars' equivalent of SDRs. Not very many people noticed.

SDRs will be involved in a bigger way when the next crisis hits, and we could see the SDR become the new global reserve currency. That doesn't mean the dollar will go away. It just means the dollar will be a local currency like a Mexican peso or a Turkish lira. We will have them for getting a taxicab or going out for drinks, but it won't be used for the big things.

When I say the big things, I mean the price of oil, the settlement or balance of payments between countries, probably the financial statements of the 100 or so largest corporations in the world. In the future, maybe you'll get your annual report from IBM or Volkswagen or General Electric and it'll be in SDRs.

I think this is so important that I've devoted an entire chapter to SDRs and how you can own them.

Triffin's Dilemma And The Future Of SDRs

Robert Triffin was a Belgian economist who lived from 1911 to 1993. He was regarded as one of the leading authorities on gold, currencies and the international monetary system during his career. He made many notable contributions to international economics, but his most famous was the articulation of what became known as "Triffin's dilemma."

The paradox of Triffin's dilemma was pointed out in the early 1960s, yet its implications are just now coming into full view. Far from a relic of the past, Triffin's dilemma is the key to understanding the future of the international monetary system.

Triffin's dilemma arose from the Bretton Woods system established in 1944. Under that system, the dollar was pegged to gold at $35.00 per ounce. Other major currencies were pegged to the dollar at fixed exchange rates. The architects of the system knew that these other exchange rates might have to be devalued from time to time, mostly because of trade deficits, but the devaluation process was designed to be slow and cumbersome.

A country that wanted to devalue (for example, the U.K. in 1967) first had to consult with the International Monetary Fund. The IMF would typically recommend structural changes—changes to fiscal policy, tax policy and other areas designed to cure the trade deficit.

The IMF also stood ready to offer bridge loans of hard currency to help the deficit-hit country withstand temporary stresses while it implemented the structural changes. Only if the structural changes failed and the trade deficits were persistent would the IMF allow devaluation.

That was the process for countries other than the United States. As far as the United States was concerned, the link between gold and the dollar was fixed for all time and could never be changed. The dollar/gold link was the anchor of the entire system.

This fixed link between the dollar and gold made the dollar the most prized reserve currency in the world. That was the hidden agenda of Bretton Woods. With the dollar as the main reserve currency, the U.K. pound sterling, a competing reserve currency, would eventually fall by the wayside.

The U.K. relied on Imperial Preference among its trading partners in the British Commonwealth to gain trade surpluses, and also relied on the willingness of those Commonwealth partners to hold sterling in their reserves. The Bank of England assumed Commonwealth members would not ask to convert the sterling to gold. Imperial Preference came under attack by the General Agreement on Tariffs and Trade, which was also part of Bretton Woods. (Today, GATT is known as the World Trade Organization.)

Bretton Woods was a one-two combination punch designed by the United States to destroy the British Empire. GATT undermined Imperial Preference. The dollar-gold link undermined sterling. It worked. The U.K.'s trade deficits persisted, and the Commonwealth partners demanded their gold. Eventually, the pound sterling was devalued, and the empire dissolved. It was replaced by a new age of U.S. Empire and King Dollar.

There was only one problem, and Robert Triffin pointed this out. If the dollar was the lead reserve currency, then the entire world needed dollars to finance world trade. To supply these dollars, the United States had to run trade deficits.

The United States sold a lot of goods abroad, but Americans quickly developed an appetite for Japanese electronics, German cars, French vacations and other foreign goods and services.

Today, China has replaced Japan as the main source of exports to the United States; still, Americans have not lost their appetite for imports financed by printing dollars.

So the United States ran trade deficits, the world got dollars and global trade flourished. But if you run deficits long enough, you go broke. That was Triffin's dilemma. Any system based on dollars would eventually cause the dollar to collapse because there would either be too many dollars or not enough gold at fixed prices to keep the game going. This contradictory system was unsustainable.

The system broke down in the 1970s. The solution then was to abolish the dollar-gold peg in 1971 and demonetize gold in 1974. But there was a third part of the solution that had been invented in 1969—the IMF's Special Drawing Right.

The SDR was a new kind of world money printed by the IMF. The idea was that it could be used as a reserve currency side by side with the dollar. This meant that if the United States cured its trade deficit, and supplied fewer dollars to the world, any shortfall in reserves could be made up by printing SDRs.

In fact, SDRs were printed and handed out repeatedly during the dollar crisis from 1969 to 1980. But then a new King Dollar age was started by Paul Volcker and Ronald Reagan, with some help from Henry Kissinger, the king of Saudi Arabia and private bankers like my old boss Walter Wriston at Citibank.

Under the new King Dollar system, U.S. interest rates would be high enough to make the dollar an attractive reserve asset even without gold backing. Remember those 20 percent interest rates of the early 1980s?

Henry Kissinger also persuaded Saudi Arabia to keep pricing oil in dollars. This "petrodollar deal" meant that countries that wanted oil needed dollars to pay for it whether they liked the dollar or not.

The Arabs deposited the dollars they received in Citibank, Chase and the other big banks of the day. The bankers, led by Wriston at Citibank and David Rockefeller at Chase, then loaned the money to Asia, South America and Africa.

From there, the dollars were used to buy U.S. exports like aircraft, heavy equipment and agricultural produce. Suddenly, the game started up again, this time without gold. This new age of King Dollar lasted from 1980 to 2010.

Still, it was all based on confidence in the dollar. Triffin's dilemma never went away; it was just in the background waiting to re-emerge while the world binged on new dollar creation and forgot about gold. The United States ran persistent large trade deficits during this entire 30-year period, as Triffin predicted. The world gorged on dollar reserves, with China leading the way in the 1990s and early 2000s.

The new game ended in 2010 with the start of a currency war in the aftermath of the Panic of 2008. Trading partners are again jockeying for position, as they did in the early 1970s. A new systemic collapse is waiting in the wings.

The weak dollar of 2011 was designed to stimulate U.S. growth and keep the world from sinking into a new depression. It worked in the short run, but now the tables are turned. Today, the dollar is strong, and the euro and yen have weakened. This gives Japan and Europe some relief, but it comes at the expense of the United States, where growth has slowed down again.

The new dollar-yuan peg has contributed to a slowdown in China. There's just not enough global growth to go around. The major trading and finance powers are cannibalizing each other with weak currencies. Soon the United States and China may devalue relative to Europe and Japan, but that will just move the global weakness back to them.

Is there no way to escape the room? Is there no way out of Triffin's dilemma?

A new gold standard might be one way to solve the problem, but it would require a gold price of $10,000 per ounce to be nondeflationary. No central banker in the world wants that, because it limits their ability to print money and be central economic planners.

Is there an alternative to gold? There is one other way out. That's our old friend, the SDR. The brilliance of the SDR solution is that it solves *Triffin's dilemma*.

Recall that the paradox is that the reserve-currency issuer has to run trade deficits, but if you run deficits long enough, you go broke. But SDRs are issued by the IMF. *The IMF is not a country and does not have a trade deficit.* In theory, the IMF can print SDRs forever and never go broke. The SDRs just go round and round among the IMF members in a closed circuit.

Individuals won't have SDRs. Only countries will have them in their reserves. These countries have no desire to break the new SDR system, because they're all in it together. The United States is no longer the boss. Instead, you have the "Five Families" consisting of China, Japan, the United States, Europe and Russia operating through the IMF.

The only losers are the citizens of the IMF member countries—people like you and me—who will suffer local-currency inflation. I'm preparing with gold and hard assets, but most people will be caught unaware, like the Greeks who lined up at empty ATMs in June 2015.

This SDR system is so little understood that people won't know where the inflation is coming from. Elected officials will blame the IMF, but the IMF is unaccountable. That's the beauty of SDRs—Triffin's dilemma is solved, debt problems are inflated away and no one is accountable. That's the global elite plan in a nutshell.

CHAPTER 12

The Only Way to Own the New World Money

In my newsletter *Strategic Intelligence*, we call the SDR world money. This world money has existed for some time, but it's about to become a lot more important.

In 1944, John Maynard Keynes proposed a form of world money, which he called the "bancor," at the Bretton Woods international monetary conference.

In 1961, Nobel Prize winner Robert Mundell said, "The optimum currency area is the world," laying the theoretical foundation for world money in his classic article "A Theory of Optimum Currency Areas."

In March 2009, Treasury Secretary Timothy Geithner supported greater issuance of SDRs in the depths of the financial crisis.

And as recently as October 2015, the former undersecretary general for economic and social affairs of the United Nations, José Antonio Ocampo, wrote an op-ed calling for new issues of SDRs with a disproportionate share going to emerging markets.

The list of prominent international monetary elites calling for greater use of SDRs as world money keeps growing. It's critical for you to understand this new trend.

The SDR has the power to reduce the dollar to the status of a local currency no different than the Mexican peso.

Understanding SDRs will also help you avoid losses from inflation and profit from new investments that will be created by their use.

Much has been written about the collapse of the dollar. We define collapse as a spontaneous loss of confidence in the dollar as a store of value resulting in sudden hyperinflation.

The source of such hyperinflation is not money printing (that happened already) but the rapid turnover of money. Those who lack confidence in dollars as a store of value will quickly dump dollars for other assets.

In this scenario, the alternative to the dollar can be as familiar as gold or land. It could be one of the new digital assets such as Bitcoin. The dollar alternative could even consist of natural resources such as oil or water.

When it comes to hyperinflation, the alternative doesn't matter that much.

What matters is that investors will dump dollars as fast as they get them. The resulting turnover (what economists call velocity) will feed on itself and lead to skyrocketing dollar prices. You shouldn't think of hyperinflation as prices "going up" (although that is literally true).

A better understanding is that assets, goods and services have a constant real value, while the dollar itself is collapsing. That dollar devaluation is the real source of "higher prices."

After all, gold is gold, land is land and water is water. When you see hyperinflation, you are really seeing the collapse of the dollar relative to everything that dollars can buy.

Two Ways to Collapse: Suddenly or Slowly

A collapse can happen at any time due to the scale, density and inherent instability of the financial system. The immediate cause of such a sudden loss of confidence is unknowable.

It could be a war, natural disaster or epidemic. It could

also be a less visible dynamic such as a change in the amount of liquidity a small group of investors wants that cascades out of control. Markets will go "no bid" as asset bubbles burst all around.

The cause doesn't matter. What matters is that it can happen quickly. None of us will know the hour or the day. Your only safe haven is to prepare now and be vigilant for indications and warnings.

This sudden-collapse scenario is definitely possible (and you need to prepare for it). Still, it is not necessarily the most likely way for the dollar to fail as the leading reserve currency.

A more likely path (and the one the elites are planning) is a slow, steady, step-by-step decline. In many ways, the slow collapse is more dangerous to your financial health than the swift crash.

In a sudden collapse, you'll know it's happening. Even if you're not prepared today, there may still be time to join the scramble for gold (albeit at a higher entry point).

When the ship is sinking, you don't have to be the first person in the lifeboat; just don't be among those who find the last lifeboat is gone. A slow decline is more dangerous because you won't know it's happening.

Policy makers, leaders and media will keep up the pretense that all is well. You may be lulled into keeping your wealth in markets that are going nowhere.

Elites will be pulling the props out from under the dollar, but you may not see it coming. This is not a hypothetical scenario. There is ample evidence for it.

Consider the Japanese Nikkei stock index. It was 40,000 in December 1989. Today, it's about 20,000, down 50 percent *almost 30 years after the crash.* Or, take the U.S. Nasdaq stock index. It was 5,000 in January 2000 and is about 5,100 today. That index has *gone almost nowhere in 15 years.*

TV talking heads and Wall Street wealth managers ignore

such unpleasant truths. They tell you that stocks are up 200 percent since the lows of March 2009. That's fine if you woke up from a 10-year nap in 2009 with a huge pile of cash, invested everything in stocks and sold them all yesterday. Nice job!

Far more common is an investor who rode the wave down, rode it back up again and completed a nerve-wracking round trip with his retirement savings but is no further ahead after fees and inflation.

Even more likely is an investor who sold near the 2009 lows, bought back in at recent highs and is ready to be fleeced again by Wall Street in the next collapse. Sound familiar? Hopefully, that's not you, but it could be someone you know.

Bond markets don't offer much relief. Short-term Treasuries have almost no yield. Long-term Treasuries offer 2 percent if you're prepared to bet on no inflation for 10 years. If inflation comes, you'll be crushed. You can score some capital gains on 10-year notes if rates fall in the short run (which I expect), but that's a trading strategy, not a retirement plan.

High-yield corporate debt is loaded with credit risk at this stage of the cycle. The defaults will pile up as we enter a global recession.

Yet, despite this dismal investment landscape, financial cheerleaders still wave their pompoms and urge you to buy stocks and bonds "for the long run." Their assurances that all is well have been echoing for 20 years and may echo for 20 more.

Meanwhile, the financial foundation built on the dollar is rotting away.

▓ The Dollar Has Already Had Its "1914 Moment"

The historical precedent for the slow loss of reserve-currency status is the strange case of sterling.

The story begins with an event far removed from the

counting rooms of London: the assassination of Archduke Franz Ferdinand, heir to the throne of the Austro-Hungarian Empire, by a Serbian terrorist in Sarajevo on June 28, 1914.

That act of political terrorism set in motion a chain of ultimatums and mobilizations that resulted in the First World War. Over 16 million people were killed for no ascertainable reason. The Russian, Ottoman, German and Austro-Hungarian empires all collapsed as a direct consequence of the war.

But one empire that did not fall, at least not right away, was the British Empire. In June 1914, the world viewed from Westminster was a global enterprise zone in which British military, diplomatic and financial power reigned supreme. There were competing powers, of course, but the U.K. was the most powerful politically.

Also, London was the unquestioned financial capital of the world. The pound sterling was the leading global reserve currency. And it was backed with gold held by the Bank of England. Sterling was "money good" on five continents.

When the First World War began, all of the major belligerents immediately suspended the conversion of their currencies into gold except the U.K. The conventional view was that countries needed to hoard gold and print money to pay for the war, which is why they suspended convertibility. The U.K. took a different approach.

By maintaining the link to gold, London maintained its credit standing. This enabled the U.K. to borrow to pay for the war.

It was John Maynard Keynes who convinced the U.K. to remain on the gold standard. And it was Jack Morgan, son of J. P. Morgan, who organized massive loans in New York to support the British war effort.

Initially, there were huge outflows of gold from the United States to the U.K. Even though the U.K. remained on the gold standard, investors sold stocks, bonds and land in the United States.

Then they converted the proceeds into gold and shipped the gold to the Bank of England. But this gold outflow from the United States soon ran its course. There were only so many portfolio assets that the British could sell to get gold.

The House of Morgan saw to it that gold flows remained orderly and the United States lived up to its financial obligations. Then, in November 1914, *the flow of gold suddenly reversed.*

The British needed U.S. exports of food, wool, cotton, oil and weapons. All of this had to be paid for in either gold or pounds sterling that could be converted into gold.

The gold that had flowed east from New York to London now began to flow west from London to New York. From November 1914 until the end of the war in November 1918, there were massive gold inflows to the Federal Reserve Bank of New York and its private member banks.

It was at this stage that the dollar emerged as a new global reserve currency to challenge the supremacy of sterling. The process of the dollar replacing sterling began in November 1914. But there was no immediate or sudden collapse of sterling.

Throughout the 1920s, the dollar and sterling competed side by side for the role of leading reserve currency.

Scholar Barry Eichengreen has documented how the dollar and sterling took turns in the leading role, with the lead shifting back and forth several times. But by 1931, the race was becoming one-sided. The dollar was starting to pull away.

Winston Churchill had blundered by pegging sterling to gold at an unrealistic rate in 1925. The superstrong sterling that resulted decimated U.K. trade. It also put the U.K. in a depression three years before the rest of the world. U.K. trade deficits caused Commonwealth trading partners such as Australia and Canada to get stuck with huge unwanted reserves in sterling.

The rise of the dollar and the steady decline of sterling continued through the 1930s until the start of the Second World War, in 1939. At that point, the U.K. suspended the convertibility of sterling into gold.

The international monetary system broke down for the second time in 25 years. Normal trade, currency exchange and gold convertibility remained suspended until the international monetary system could be reformed.

This reform took place at the Bretton Woods international monetary conference held in New Hampshire in July 1944. That conference marked the final ascendency of the dollar as the leading global reserve currency. From 1944 to 1971, major currencies, including sterling, were pegged to the dollar. The dollar was pegged to gold at $35.00 per ounce.

Bretton Woods was the definitive end to the role of sterling as the leading reserve currency. The conference enshrined the dollar in that role—a position it has held ever since. The point of this history is to show that the replacement of sterling by the dollar as the leading reserve currency was not an event, but rather a process.

The process played out over 30 years, from 1914 to 1944. It involved a seesaw dynamic in which sterling would try to reclaim the crown, only to lose it again.

With hindsight, it is possible to see that the turning point took place in November 1914, when gold outflows from the United States reversed and became inflows. Those inflows continued until 1950 despite two world wars and the Great Depression. *Yet no one saw the collapse at the time.*

From the Bank of England's perspective, November 1914 may have seen gold outflows, but no one believed the process of decline was inevitable or irreversible.

The belief in London was that Britain would win the war, maintain the empire and preserve sterling's position as the most valued currency in the world. Britain did win the war, but the cost was too great. It lost the empire, and sterling lost its role as the leading reserve currency.

The question for you today is whether the U.S. dollar has

already had its November 1914 moment. Is it possible that the collapse of the U.S. dollar as the leading reserve currency has already begun?

Yes, it has.

Looking at the massive flows of gold to China, the rise of a dollar competitor in the form of the SDR and the inclusion of the Chinese yuan in the SDR basket, it is difficult not to conclude that the dollar collapse has already begun.

Yet, like the collapse of sterling a century ago, the decline of the dollar will not necessarily happen overnight. It will likely be a slow, steady process (at least in the beginning stages).

This is bad news if you don't understand this process and stay too long at the dollar party. It can be good news for you if you understand the process and adjust now to the rise of the SDR.

I'm going to give you some more history on SDRs and how they're valued, and show you an exclusive new way to profit from the inclusion of the yuan in the SDR—one that my *Strategic Intelligence* team has created just for you.

▦ 1969: The Genesis of the New World Money

The Bretton Woods system was administered by the newly formed International Monetary Fund. Members could apply to the IMF for swing loans if their reserve position was in distress.

The IMF would provide dollar reserves but would demand structural reforms in return. The idea was that the structural reforms would return the deficit country to a surplus. Then the surplus could be used to repay the loan.

It was viewed as a stable equilibrium system where countries might swing back and forth between surplus and deficit based on comparative advantage and the terms of trade.

The IMF was there to make sure the swings were not disorderly and the system did not break down. The anchor of the entire system was the U.S. dollar, pegged (forever, it was believed) to gold.

Although this system performed reasonably well for the first 20 years, some stresses and design flaws were apparent from the start. Initially, the world suffered a "dollar shortage." Gold was scarce, but so were dollars.

If the dollar was the leading reserve currency, how could global trade and finance grow if there were not enough dollars to go around?

In the late 1940s, the United States had the only dollar printing press. It also held over 20,000 tons of gold. The rest of the world held few dollars and little gold. World finance was like trying to start a poker game where one player held all the chips and the others couldn't ante up. The system was stuck.

In the 1950s, the United States began to pump out dollars at a prodigious rate, first through the Marshall Plan and then through Korean War spending.

Gradually, the gears became unstuck. Countries like Germany and Japan began earning dollars by exporting Volkswagens, transistor radios and other consumer goods that war- and Depression-weary Americans wanted.

By the 1960s, the "dollar shortage" turned into a "dollar glut." The global economy was performing well, and U.S. trading partners ran up huge dollar surpluses. These trading partners (France, Italy, Netherlands and Japan) began cashing in their dollars for gold from Fort Knox.

Between 1950 and 1970, the U.S. gold hoard dropped from 20,000 tons to 9,000 tons. Still, the United States continued to run budget deficits (to pay for defense against the Soviet Union) and trade deficits (to feed Americans' appetite for cheap imports).

It was at this point that the Belgian economist Robert Triffin articulated what became known as Triffin's dilemma, as discussed earlier.

The idea was simple. In a world based on dollars as the leading reserve currency, the United States would have to make dollars available to the world to finance trade and investment. But if the United States pumped out dollars through its deficits, eventually the United States would go broke, run out of gold or both.

Triffin predicted the Bretton Woods system would collapse because the United States could not supply the world with enough dollars without bankrupting itself in the process.

He was right. By 1968, the steady drain of gold from Fort Knox had become a run on the bank. Efforts to suppress the price of gold (via the infamous London Gold Pool) failed.

Trading partners like France could make risk-free profits by cashing in dollars for gold at $35.00 per ounce, then turn around and sell the gold on the open market for $40.00 per ounce.

The world had too many dollars and was dumping them for gold as fast as it could.

The IMF (under U.S. direction) needed a solution. The United States would have to adopt structural reforms to fix its deficits in order to save the dollar. But such U.S. austerity implied a return of the "dollar shortage" and a global recession.

There was not enough gold at the official price to fill the shortage. No one wanted to raise the price of gold (which really meant devaluing their currency) because this would be inflationary. No other currency was strong enough to replace the dollar.

What the world needed was a *new form of money* to provide liquidity while the United States went on a financial diet. This was the genesis of the special drawing right, invented by the IMF in 1969.

Contrary to what financial elites would have you believe, SDRs are easy to understand in concept and practice. They are fiat money, pure and simple. Today, SDRs are backed by nothing. And they can be issued in unlimited quantities by the IMF.

Interestingly, SDRs did not start out that way. The original SDR was valued at 0.888671 grams of gold (which equals 1/35th of an ounce, or $1.00 at the time). This value was supported by the IMFs own gold hoard of almost 5,000 tons in 1969. In this sense, the SDR was like the dollar (backed by gold with a fixed value in gold) but could be created from thin air by the IMF.

The SDR was the solution to Triffin's dilemma.

The United States could practice austerity to repair its trade and budget deficits, but the world would not run short of liquidity, because the IMF could provide its members with SDRs. Since the IMF is not a country, it does not have a trade deficit and theoretically could never go broke.

That was the theory of SDRs, but the practice turned out differently. The international monetary system got worse, not better.

The United States did not fix its deficit problems. In fact, they deteriorated because of spending on the Vietnam War and Lyndon Johnson's Great Society. The run on Fort Knox continued as Switzerland, France and Spain drained U.S. gold supplies.

In 1971, the United States closed the gold window, preventing further exchanges of dollars for gold. In 1973, the IMF abandoned the gold value of the SDR. Fixed exchange rates were abandoned in stages by IMF members between 1970 and 1974.

By 1975, the original Bretton Woods system was completely gone. There was no gold standard and no system of fixed exchange rates.

What ensued was a period of near hyperinflation from 1975 to 1980.

By January 1980, the market price of gold touched $800 per ounce, equal to a 95 percent devaluation of the dollar when measured in gold.

In the midst of this turmoil, the IMF began issuing SDRs. The first issuance was from 1970 to 1972, consisting of SDR 9.3 billion.

The second issuance was from 1979 to 1981, consisting of SDR 12.1 billion.

There was a gap of almost 30 years before the third issuance in 2009. This consisted of a general issue of SDR 161.2 billion and a special issue of SDR 21.5 billion in August and September 2009, respectively.

■ Have Financial Panic, Will Issue SDRs

As of today, the total amount of SDRs issued is SDR 204.1 billion, equal to about $280 billion at the current dollar value of SDRs.

The issuance of SDRs is closely associated with financial panic.

The first issue was around the time Nixon closed the gold window.

The second issue was during the period of near hyperinflation in the U.S. dollar. The third issue was in the immediate aftermath of the Panic of 2008.

This shows that SDRs are not used for ordinary stimulus in recessions. SDRs are used to deal with liquidity crises.

They are also used when crises of confidence in the international monetary system occur. SDRs are like a secret weapon that global elites deploy as needed to prop up the global financial system.

This was confirmed to me personally by Zhu Min, the deputy managing director of the IMF, in a conversation we had in 2013.

This means the next time there is a global financial panic— and we can be sure one is coming sooner rather than later— SDRs will be used to put out the fire. The central banks in the

United States, Europe, China and Japan are tapped out.

Their balance sheets have never been repaired after printing money to squash the panic in 2008. The only clean balance sheet left in the world is the IMF's.

In the next panic, you should expect SDRs to be issued in the trillions to provide liquidity. That issuance, when it comes, will mark the end of the dollar's reign as the leading reserve currency.

▧ What Most People Don't Get About SDRs

Most people think that SDRs are backed by a basket of currencies. They are not. The so-called basket is nothing more than a list of currencies used for the purpose of calculating the value of SDRs.

Inclusion of a currency in the SDR basket is based on four criteria:

1. the volume of international payments in the currency;
2. the amount of reserves held in that currency;
3. an open capital account so the currency is freely convertible to other SDR currencies; and
4. transparency and consistency in meeting IMF accounting and reporting standards.

On October 1, 2016, the list of currencies and their weights in the SDR basket will be euros (31 percent), Japanese yen (8 percent), pounds sterling (8 percent), Chinese yuan (11 percent) and U.S. dollars (42 percent). Until then, the 2010 weights stand.

Calculating the dollar value of one SDR is a three-step process starting with basket weights set by the IMF. Next, a specific amount of each currency is placed in the basket based on average dollar exchange rates over a base period.

For example, 0.4230 euros is included in the basket to give the euro a 37.4 percent weight, taking into account the fact that one euro was worth about $1.13 during the base period.

Finally, these currency amounts are converted to dollars at the exchange rate on a given valuation date.

The resulting dollar equivalents are added to determine the dollar value of one SDR. This method is illustrated in the chart titled "Method for Calculating the Value of SDRs" below, available on the official IMF website.

Method for Calculating the Value of SDRs
as of December 30, 2010

Currency	(1) Initial new weight (share)	(2) Illustrative currency amount [1]	(3) Exchange Rates on [2] 12/30/10	(4) U.S. dollar equivalent
Euro (€)	37.4	0.4230	1.32500	0.560475
Yen (¥)	9.4	12.1000	81.63000	0.148230
£ Sterling	11.3	0.1110	1.54350	0.171329
U.S. dollar	41.9	0.6600	1.00000	0.660000
SDRl=US$ [3]				1.54003

Source: 13F's from June 30, 2015

This shows that one SDR equaled about $1.54 on December 30, 2010.

Like any currency, the dollar value of an SDR moves daily. It is also subject to market forces. Today, one SDR is worth about $1.41, down significantly from the $1.54 value in 2010.

This reflects the recent strength of the dollar (since the nondollar currencies in the basket are all worth fewer dollars).

The SDR has gone down for the same reason gold, euros, oil and other currencies and commodities have gone down— the strong dollar.

The construction of the SDR valuation basket is reviewed every five years by the IMF's Executive Board. But it can be changed more or less frequently at the Executive Board's discretion.

Prior to the yuan's inclusion in the SDR basket, the last review became effective on January 1, 2011. The next review was scheduled to be completed by December 31, 2015, with an effective date of January 1, 2016.

However, the Executive Committee decided that they wanted to grant the Chinese yuan inclusion in November 2015.

The new effective date for the revised basket is October 1, 2016.

The reason for this ad hoc change in the effective date had to do with including the Chinese yuan in the exclusive club of SDR reference currencies.

■ A New Face at the Global Poker Game

Aside from the inclusion of the yuan that was announced in November 2015, membership in the exclusive SDR currency club had changed only once in the past 30 years.

That change took place in 1999, and was purely technical due to the fact that the German mark and French franc were being replaced by the euro.

Leaving aside this technical change, the SDR has been dominated by the "Big Four" (United States, U.K., Japan and Europe) since the IMF abandoned the gold SDR in 1973. This is why inclusion of the Chinese yuan is so momentous.

Including the yuan is a "seal of approval" by the world's major financial powers, led by the United States. It means China is a financial superpower and deserves a seat at the table when the international monetary system is reset.

You can think of this as a four-person poker game where a fifth player just sat down at the table with a large pile of chips. The poker game will now take on a new dynamic.

China does not strictly meet all the IMF criteria for inclusion in the SDR club. But use of the Chinese yuan in global trade does satisfy the test.

The yuan's share of global payments has been steadily rising, from less than 1 percent in 2013 to about 2 percent in 2014. Yuan use is currently approaching 3 percent, as shown in the charts below.

Yuan's Share in Global Payments

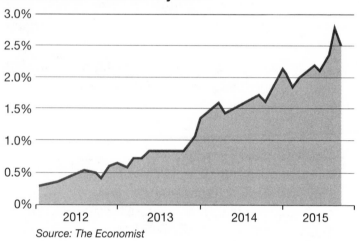

Source: The Economist

RMB's Share as an International Payments Currency

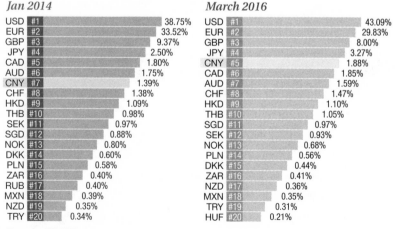

Jan 2014		March 2016	
USD #1	38.75%	USD #1	43.09%
EUR #2	33.52%	EUR #2	29.83%
GBP #3	9.37%	GBP #3	8.00%
JPY #4	2.50%	JPY #4	3.27%
CAD #5	1.80%	CNY #5	1.88%
AUD #6	1.75%	CAD #6	1.85%
CNY #7	1.39%	AUD #7	1.59%
CHF #8	1.38%	CHF #8	1.47%
HKD #9	1.09%	HKD #9	1.10%
THB #10	0.98%	THB #10	1.05%
SEK #11	0.97%	SGD #11	0.97%
SGD #12	0.88%	SEK #12	0.93%
NOK #13	0.80%	NOK #13	0.68%
DKK #14	0.60%	PLN #14	0.56%
PLN #15	0.58%	DKK #15	0.44%
ZAR #16	0.40%	ZAR #16	0.41%
RUB #17	0.40%	NZD #17	0.36%
MXN #18	0.39%	MXN #18	0.35%
NZD #19	0.35%	TRY #19	0.31%
TRY #20	0.34%	HUF #20	0.21%

Source: SWIFT

Use of Chinese yuan surpassed Australian, Canadian, Singapore and Hong Kong dollars, as well as Swiss francs, by 2014. It also recently passed the Japanese yen. This makes the yuan the fourth most used currency in the world, after U.S. dollars, euros and sterling.

Where the Chinese yuan doesn't meet IMF standards is in having an open capital account. China has also not always been transparent in its reporting of reserve positions.

Market confusion and turmoil in 2014 and 2015 was caused by China's efforts to move in the direction required by the IMF.

For two years prior to August 2015, China informally pegged the yuan to the U.S. dollar at a rate of about 6.2 to 1.

Maintaining the peg requires continuous market intervention by the People's Bank of China (the central bank). Market forces tried to drive the yuan lower. This forced the PBOC to sell dollars and buy yuan to maintain the peg.

This operation drained about $500 billion from China's $4 trillion in reserve assets in a matter of months. It is inconsistent with an open capital account in which market forces, not PBOC intervention, determine the value of the yuan.

But suddenly, in August 2015, China devalued the yuan in two steps, to a level of about 6.4 to 1. This was a shot heard round the world.

The devaluation led directly to meltdowns in U.S. equity markets as the resulting strong dollar threatened to hurt U.S. exports and jobs. A stronger dollar also hurts earnings of U.S. companies with overseas operations. This damage became apparent in 2015 third-quarter corporate earnings reports.

From China's perspective, the devaluation was a step in the direction of an open capital account. But from the world's perspective, it was a continuation of the currency wars. Investors saw more devaluations coming and more damage to U.S. corporate earnings.

For now, China is defending the new peg with more intervention. You should expect further devaluations. You should also expect more market shocks in the near future as China stumbles its way to a freely traded yuan.

China has also improved the transparency of its reserve reporting, especially with regard to gold. From 2009 to 2015, China reported no increases in its gold reserves. Yet the evidence (from mining statistics and Hong Kong imports) was conclusive that China was, in fact, acquiring thousands of tons of gold.

In mid-2015, China suddenly announced that its gold reserves had increased by 604 tons. The total rose from 1,054 tons to 1,658 tons. Since then, China has updated its gold reserve position monthly (in keeping with IMF criteria).

All of these figures are misleading because China keeps several thousand tons of gold "off the books" in a separate entity called the State Administration for Foreign Exchange. Small amounts are transferred from SAFE to PBOC monthly, and that becomes the basis for the official reserve reports.

China's case for admission into the SDR club was a mixed bag. The yuan met the use criteria and is close on the reserve criteria. China did not meet the criteria for an open capital account and transparent reporting. Still, they were moving in the right direction.

In fact, none of this mattered. The decision to include the yuan in the SDR was a political decision, not an economic one. The green light to proceed has already been given by the IMF's Executive Board, and it was announced on November 30, 2015, that the yuan would be included.

As I said, the new SDR basket will take effect on October 1, 2016.

The 11-month gap between the announcement date and the effective date creates a highly interesting and potentially profitable opportunity for you.

■ For the Fifth Time in 40 Years...

Why was there political urgency to include the yuan in the SDR if China does not meet the usual requirements? The answer is that a new global financial panic comes closer by the day.

These panics happen every five to eight years almost like clockwork. Look at the financial panics in Mexico (1994), Russia/LTCM (1998) and Lehman/AIG (2008) and you get the idea. Another panic in 2018, if not sooner, is a near certainty.

The next panic will be bigger than the central banks' ability to put out the fire. The only source of bailout cash will be the SDR. But a massive issuance of SDRs will require cooperation by China.

This is not because of IMF voting (China's vote is not that large). It's because SDRs are useful only if they can be swapped for other reserve currencies to prop up banks and liquidate panicked sellers of stocks. (The IMF runs a secret trading desk where these SDR swaps are conducted.)

When your neighbors are in full panic mode, they won't want SDRs from Citibank; they'll want dollars. But who will swap dollars for the SDRs printed by the IMF?

The answer is China. The PBOC and SAFE would love to dump dollar assets in exchange for SDRs. But there's a catch. China will only engage in SDR/dollar swaps if the yuan is included in the SDR. China does not want to pay club dues unless it's a member of the club.

The rush to include China in the SDR was the global monetary elites getting their ducks in a row before the next panic comes to destroy your portfolio.

In the 1960s, hippies had an expression to describe membership in a small group. They said, "You're either on the bus or off the bus."

Well, the IMF wanted China on the bus before the next panic hits.

When trillions of SDRs are issued in the next panic, China

will dump its dollars for SDRs (with the yuan inside).

As I said, the U.S. dollar will be reduced to the status of a local currency.

The dollar will still be used for local transactions inside the United States (the same way the Mexican peso is used inside Mexico), but it will no longer be the benchmark for sound reserve management.

The impact on the dollar from the issuance of SDRs will be highly inflationary. After more than 10 years of trying and failing, the Federal Reserve will finally have the inflation it wants.

But it will rue the day. Instead of the 2 percent annual inflation the Fed is targeting (really slow-motion theft), inflation of 10 percent or more can be expected. From there, it will spin even further out of control.

With trillions in SDRs and thousands of tons of gold, China will call the shots the same way the United States called the shots at Bretton Woods in 1944. The slow death of the dollar, which began in 2009 with the issuance of over $250 billion in SDRs, will be complete.

How can you hedge your exposure to a dollar collapse and also profit from the rise of the SDR? There's that old saying: if you can't beat 'em, join 'em! The solution to the fall of the dollar and rise of SDRs is to invest in SDRs.

That's a neat solution, but not as easy as it sounds. SDRs are for countries only; they are not walking-around money for you and me. There are almost no bonds denominated in SDRs, and no stocks at all.

The IMF has borrowed billions of SDRs from its members to fund its lending operations, but those SDR notes are held in reserve positions and not freely traded.

Eventually, a deep, liquid pool of SDR-denominated assets will be created, but we're not there yet. In January 2010, the IMF released a paper with a long-term plan to support the rise of the SDR.

It included specific instructions for the issuance of SDR notes by multinational corporations such as IBM and Siemens of Germany.

The paper also outlined the purchase of those notes by multilateral institutions such as the Asian Development Bank. It also suggested the formation of a dealer network led by Goldman Sachs and the creation of clearance and settlement procedures (the so-called "plumbing" of a bond market). All this will take years to develop.

Meanwhile, the largest, most sophisticated investors in the world (such as the $1 trillion sovereign wealth funds of Norway and Abu Dhabi) have found a way to synthesize SDRs. They are building portfolios denominated in currencies that match the official SDR weights.

For example, if you select fundamentally strong European companies in your portfolio, but the euro crashes against the dollar, you will suffer dollar-denominated losses even if your stock picks were strong.

Likewise, a portfolio of U.S. stocks may be strong on fundamentals. But if the dollar suffers a 1970s-style inflationary episode, your purchasing power is eroded relative to European and Asian investors.

This phenomenon of exchange rates dominating fundamental analysis is especially true during currency wars.

The way to prevent this and preserve wealth is to construct a portfolio that tracks the SDR. That way, dollar weakness is offset by euro strength, yen weakness is offset by sterling strength and so on. This "synthetic SDR portfolio" pushes the currency wars to the sidelines and lets you profit from fundamentally sound stock and bond picks.

A synthetic SDR strategy helps you not only avoid currency-war losses, but also profit from trends in the SDR itself.

The reason the IMF has created an 11-month delay between the announcement date and the effective date of the new SDR basket is to give the big guys like Norway time to "rebalance" their portfolios toward the new SDR basket.

When you have $1 trillion to rebalance, you can't do things overnight without an adverse market impact that hurts your own position.

An 11-month window lets you move daily in small increments so that you hit the target date without too much disruption.

This rebalancing will give a lift to the yuan as megainvestors reach to acquire high-quality yuan-denominated assets to conform to the new SDR basket weights.

It will also put downward pressure on sterling and yen, since their allocations in the SDR basket will be reduced to make room for the yuan. (The total basket always adds up to 100 percent, so when a new currency is introduced, some of the other currencies must be reduced in size.)

With the November 30, 2015, announcement, we know the composition of the new SDR basket. You can start creating that basket today, before the big players jump in. That's where I can help.

The composition of the new SDR basket, effective on October 1, 2016, looks like this:

U.S. dollar—42 percent
Euro—31 percent
Sterling—8 percent
Yen—8 percent
Yuan—11 percent

A securities portfolio allocated in these percentages by currency will insulate you from the currency wars to a great extent. (The dollar and euro are about equally weighted. Much of the volatility in the dollar is accounted for by the EUR/USD cross rate. In this portfolio, dollar weakness is offset by euro strength and vice versa.)

This is not the first time you could have gained from an

SDR rebalancing. When the euro was introduced in 1999, its value relative to the dollar was $1.16.

After an initial dip in 2000, the euro soared as high as $1.60 in subsequent years, producing 40 percent gains for the dollar-based investor.

And don't forget about gold. We still recommend an allocation of 10 percent of investible assets to gold as the best form of portfolio insurance. Gold is the leading challenger to SDRs as the new world money. You definitely want some gold in your portfolio. For the nongold allocation, a synthetic SDR strategy is a valuable approach.

What's the best way to invest in synthetic SDRs?

How can you get ahead of the sovereign wealth funds in this global monetary rebalancing?

We have discovered the perfect way to "create your own basket" using a new platform called Motif Investing. Here's what you need to know.

Motif allows you to create customized stock funds, called motifs. With a single transaction, you can use a pool of investment cash to buy specific amounts of several different stocks as a single unit. I'll explain exactly how it works in a second.

▪ The New World Money Motif

We've created a motif that mirrors the SDR, it's called the New World Money motif.

It's mostly made up of CurrencyShares, ETFs backed by bank deposits. They're denominated in a specific currency. Each CurrencyShares product pays the short-term bank-deposit interest rate that's being paid in each country.

For the U.S. dollar component of the SDR, we chose BIL, which is an ETF of U.S. Treasury bills with maturities ranging from one to three months. Treasury bills are the safest, most liquid U.S. dollar-denominated securities in the world.

The New World Money

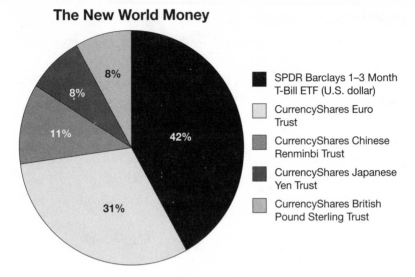

BIL is a good match for the dollar component of the New World Money motif because it's an ETF that closely resembles holding a bank deposit denominated in U.S. dollars.

Here is what we expect from the New World Money motif: it should rise in value as the U.S. dollar falls against the currencies (like the Chinese yuan) that will gain weight in the SDR in 2016.

Because our SDR motif is made up of bank deposits and Treasury bills, it will benefit from the deflationary environment we're currently experiencing.

Since there have not been many changes in the SDR basket, it has been remarkably stable since the early decades.

As we said earlier, the SDR was equal to 1/35th of an ounce of gold from 1969 to 1973. In 1974, it was set up as a 16-currency basket. In 1978, two currencies were added (interestingly these were Saudi riyals and Iranian rials). Then in 1981, all of the currencies were dropped except dollars, German marks, sterling, yen and French francs.

There were no changes from 1981 to 1999. Then, the marks and francs were dropped and the euro was added (this was really a substitution since marks and francs were being replaced by the euro).

This is good news and bad news. The bad news is that we don't have a lot of examples to point to for making gains. The good news is that this is a rare, once-in-a-decade opportunity.

There have only been four basket changes in 40 years. That's why this is such a big deal at the IMF and in Washington and Beijing.

Normally the five-year updates are boring, ho-hum events where nothing much happens and the basket is rubber-stamped. But this was not the case on November 30, 2015, when it was announced that the yuan would be included in the SDR basket.

Admitting a new member is such a big deal, which is why this is getting so much attention. It also means that most people have no idea how it will play out.

But now you do, which is why *Strategic Intelligence* gives you an edge. You get unique insights and the dynamic systems analysis behind what's happening.

There is an opportunity here. I told you that in 1999, the IMF replaced the German mark and the French franc with the euro. At the effective date of the change, the exchange rate was 1 euro = $1.16. The euro initially traded down to $0.8547, but by July 2008 had reached $1.5774.

It was an 85 percent gain from the low and a 36 percent gain from the opening price. In other words, investors who stuck with the dollar lost out, whereas investors who rebalanced with the SDR made double-digit gains on the euro component. These gains are real, not hypothetical or backtested.

The Federal Reserve itself recognized the power of SDR investing to improve risk-adjusted returns and reduce portfolio volatility 35 years ago in a landmark study called "The SDR in Private International Finance" (**www.agorafinancial.info/ht319**).

This is all to say we're not making this up! The IMF and Fed themselves are admitting what they are doing in writing; it's just that very few take the time to read this stuff and even fewer are willing to share the implications with everyday Americans. That's what sets us apart.

I expect even more dramatic gains with the yuan over time than there were in 1999. That's because the mark and franc to euro conversion was a substitution, whereas the Chinese yuan is an *entirely new member that will necessitate major portfolio shifts around the world.*

And remember, right now SDRs are for IMF members only (i.e., sovereign countries). This makes our motif idea even more attractive. Motif investing in our SDR basket is not one way to play, it's the only way to play for the time being and a good way to get ahead of the power curve.

At creation, the ETF allocations in our New World Money motif perfectly matched SDR's currency composition that will go in effect on Oct. 1. But as currency values have shifted, their weight in the SDR have shifted, too. Don't worry too much about that — the net effect is that you'll still be set for profits as the currency wars continue.

Just remember to stick with *Strategic Intelligence* for our thoughts on each individual component of the motif.

And that's not the only way we're putting Motif's unique capabilities to use.

"Jim Rickards' Exclusive Stock Fund" Motif

The global elites have planned a massive inflationary response to fight global deflation. They'll use SDRs issued by the IMF.

As SDRs take more of a reserve-currency role, at the expense of reserve currencies like the U.S. dollar, you'll want to own some stocks and ETFs that benefit from a more inflationary environment.

So we've created a second motif we're naming "Jim Rickards' Exclusive Stock Fund." It includes a few of the ETFs we've recommended in my monthly newsletter, *Strategic Intelligence*. And it includes a few new names to broaden our exposure to the inflationary global environment we're expecting over the long run.

Jim Rickards' Exclusive Stock Fund

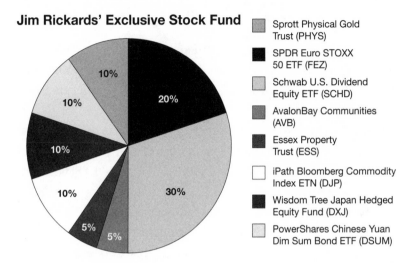

- Sprott Physical Gold Trust (PHYS)
- SPDR Euro STOXX 50 ETF (FEZ)
- Schwab U.S. Dividend Equity ETF (SCHD)
- AvalonBay Communities (AVB)
- Essex Property Trust (ESS)
- iPath Bloomberg Commodity Index ETN (DJP)
- Wisdom Tree Japan Hedged Equity Fund (DXJ)
- PowerShares Chinese Yuan Dim Sum Bond ETF (DSUM)

The Sprott Physical Gold Trust (PHYS) is our pick for exposure to gold. It's the best way to own allocated, vaulted physical gold bullion in a brokerage account.

For exposure to Europe, we recommend an ETF of high-quality companies, including Sanofi, Bayer, Banco Santander, Allianz, and Siemens. We chose the SPDR Euro Stoxx 50 ETF (FEZ), which offers exposure to 50 large-cap stocks, diversified across 12 countries within the euro zone. FEZ is the lowest-cost ETF that exclusively targets Eurozone stocks.

Our largest weighting is to own high-quality United States–based companies through the Schwab U.S. Dividend Equity ETF (SCHD).

When the SDR grows in prominence as a reserve asset, the U.S. dollar will weaken. Investors around the world, fearing a sustained period of high inflation, will look to exchange paper currencies for top-quality U.S. stocks.

Most listed companies are backed by real, physical assets.

Most have pricing power in an inflationary environment. SCHD, which charges a tiny management fee of just seven basis points, is a great way to own such companies. All the stocks held in SCHD must have sustained at least 10 consecutive years of dividend payments.

Next, in a sustained inflationary environment, following a global, SDR-driven reflation, U.S. real estate would hold its value. Real estate investment trusts, or "REITs," offer one way to buy into the sector.

REITs are dividend-oriented securities that own and collect rents on office buildings, hotels, and many other types of rental property. But instead of choosing a REIT ETF, we want to be more focused.

Under the REIT umbrella, many types (including office and retail REITs) are too expensive and economically sensitive. So we chose two REITs that are in the best-positioned area of rental real estate: apartments.

AvalonBay Communities (AVB) and Essex Property Trust (ESS) are well-managed REITs; they have great apartment portfolios located in areas with high barriers to new apartment supply; and both REITs are concentrated in areas where it's much cheaper to rent an apartment than it is to buy a house.

In addition, a broad mix of agricultural and industrial commodities would also rise in an inflationary environment.

The iPath Bloomberg Commodity Index ETN (DJP) offers broad exposure to commodities. This exchange-traded note ("ETN") is an unsecured obligation of Barclays, a huge British bank. In an SDR reflation scenario, global banks like Barclays will remain solvent and creditworthy. DJP is diversified across commodities including oil, natural gas, copper, wheat, soybeans and more.

Besides the U.S. dollar, the Japanese yen is another currency we expect to lose weight in the new SDR basket. The desire to hold yen as a reserve currency will fall, resulting in downward pressure on the yen versus most other currencies.

That trend is good for the export-oriented Japanese companies held by the WisdomTree Japan Hedged Equity Fund (DXJ). By excluding companies that get most of their revenue inside Japan, DXJ is tilted toward companies that benefit from a weak yen. DXJ is the ideal ETF to play the eroding influence of the Japanese yen as a reserve currency.

Finally, the last component of "Jim Rickards' Exclusive Stock Fund" motif benefits from the rising prominence of the Chinese yuan. Large investors and central banks will both seek to own more yuan-denominated assets. And because unsophisticated retail investors still dominate the Chinese stock market, international investors will first look to buy yuan-denominated bonds.

The PowerShares Chinese Yuan Dim Sum Bond ETF (DSUM) is our favorite vehicle to play both the rising yuan and global demand for Chinese bonds. It holds high-quality yuan-denominated bonds, including Chinese government bonds.

Again, you'll need to stick with Strategic Investment for my latest thoughts on these individual recommendations. But let me tell you exactly how Motif Investment takes the hassle of buying each of these stocks in the amount I recommend.

■ The Basics of Motif Investing

As I said, Motif Investing offers customizable bundles of stocks called "motifs." These are essentially "private" stock funds—offering you a chance to buy up to 30 stocks with a single transaction. Like an ETF, the motif can hold different amounts of stocks—for instance, more shares of a blue chip stock and fewer shares of a small-cap stock.

But there are some key differences. First, unlike with an exchange-traded fund, investors are free to customize what goes into a motif. If you buy an exchange-traded fund from a typical broker, you have no say what stocks the fund holds or how much of each stock it owns. The management is completely out of your hands.

Not only do motifs let you precisely control how each stock is weighted, you can also choose to exclude or add stocks as you see fit. In fact, once you buy a motif, you're free to add more stocks to it or sell individual stocks out of it.

That's because a motif doesn't represent a portion of a basket of stocks, like shares in an exchange-traded fund do. A motif is a basket of stocks. You actually own the shares of the stock in the motif.

You can choose exactly how much to invest in the motif (a minimum of $250) and Motif will automatically split your cash into the motif's holdings.

The company considers buying and selling a motif a single transaction. In other words, if you buy a motif that consists of 30 stocks, you'll pay a single commission of $9.95—even though you are actually buying shares in 30 separate companies.

The only catch is that you need to join Motif in order to take advantage of our "private" motifs. So while we don't have a business relationship with Motif, we strongly recommend checking them out. (Just keep in mind that you must be an American citizen or a legal U.S. resident to use Motif's services.)

■ Take a Risk-Free Test Drive

Motif makes it easy to open an account. In fact, you're free to explore the site without risking a single cent. Just go to **auth.motifinvesting.com/signup** and enter an e-mail address and password.

You'll next be prompted to open and fund an investment account—but you don't have to. To skip it, just click on the words "Motif Investing" at the top of the screen.

You'll be prompted to enter your first and last name—but

that's all the information you'll need to give to start exploring the site. (Motif will also send you an e-mail requesting you to verify your e-mail address. Just click on the link they send to be verified.)

Feel free to check out the rest of the site, including instructions for building your own motifs. But remember, you can't do anything like that until you actually open an investment account.

When you're ready to do that, click "Complete Account Application" at the top of the screen.

You'll be asked to enter basic information—name, address and so on. (Again, you need to be a U.S. citizen or a legal U.S. resident to open an account.)

The site will also ask about your financial goals and experience. Then it's time for regulatory information, including your Social Security number.

And you have to agree to the terms and conditions of being eligible to receive Nasdaq real-time stock quotes.

Finally, agree to Motif's terms and conditions, and your application is complete.

It could take one to two business days to process and approve your account. But while you wait, you can start the process of funding your account.

Or explore the site some more. When you're ready to put money in, so you can start trading, look for "Fund Account" under "My Investments."

■ Get Ready to Trade Motifs

You have several different options to fund your account.

You can have your bank link to your Motif account. The company has connections to several banks already—if your bank is one of them, simply click on its name to start linking your accounts. (You'll need the username and password you use to log into your bank's website.)

If you don't see your bank listed, just click "I have a different bank."

You'll need to enter your bank account number and routing number, which you can find on your bank's website or on your personal checks.

You can also choose to transfer money and stocks from an existing brokerage or IRA account by filling out an ACAT transfer form.

You'll find complete instructions on the form. Just follow the directions and mail, e-mail or fax the form back to Motif.

There's also an option to use a wire transfer, and you can even just mail Motif a check—though that is the slowest method for funding your account.

You'll need to deposit at least $250 to start trading motifs, and at least $2,000 if you want to trade on margin. And if you're opening an IRA or Roth IRA, you're subject to IRS contribution limits. But once your account is open and funded, you can start buying motifs.

◼ The Only Way to Own "The New World Money" and "Rickards' Exclusive Stock Fund"

We've decided to make our "New World Money" and "Jim Rickards' Exclusive Stock Fund" motifs "private."

That means the public won't be able to find them in Motif's database—only people like you who we direct to it. To buy it, you'll need the special link to their motif page. (Please make sure you're logged into the site before clicking these links.)

For the "New World Money" Motif, visit **www.agora financial.info/ht317** after creating an account

For the "Rickards' Exclusive Stock Fund" Motif, visit **www. agorafinancial.info/ht320** after creating an account

If you're logged into Motif, clicking the link will bring you to the motif's home page.

At the top of the page, you'll find the motif's name, its creator (unless the creator wishes to be anonymous) and the date it was created.

Next you'll see a box listing how the motif has performed, as well as measures of its volatility and valuation.

Below that are three tabs that tell you different information about the motif. The first is "Overview."

The first thing you'll see under that tab is the description, where you'll see an explanation of the motif's focus and goals.

To the right of the description, you'll find a chart comparing the motif's performance against the S&P 500.

Next you'll also see a table of every investment the motif holds. It breaks down each stock's weight in the portfolio as well as its current price, market cap and return.

Click on the "Performance" tab for a customizable chart of the motif. See how it did during certain time periods, and you can also compare it to other stocks and motifs.

Finally, click on "What Others Think" to see users' opinions on the motif. When you're satisfied the motif is worth buying, click "Buy Motif."

You'll be taken to an order page. Remember, you're not actually buying shares in a fund. Instead, you'll have to specify how much total money you wish to invest in the motif.

The minimum you can invest is $250.

The amount is completely up to you—we cannot tell you how much money you should risk on the investment.

So enter any amount of money you wish, as long as it doesn't exceed your total buying power, conveniently listed to the left of the ordering window.

When you enter the amount of money you wish to invest, the site will automatically calculate how that money will be divided into each stock in the motif based on how it's weighted.

The table at the bottom of the order screen will show you exactly how many shares of each stock in the motif you're buying and how much money you'll spend on each component.

Don't worry if it says you'll be buying fractions of a stock—Motif lets you buy fractions of a stock.

If for some reason you'd like to weight the stocks a little differently, you can choose "Customize Motif." (We do not suggest customizing motifs, but you are free to do so if you wish.)

After you've entered how much money you wish to invest in the motif, click the "Preview Order" button.

Verify that all the information is correct, and then place the order. No matter how much you choose to invest or how many stocks are in the motif, you'll pay just a $9.95 commission for the trade.

After that, it's just a matter of monitoring your positions.

■ Monitoring the "New World Money" and "Rickards' Exclusive Stock Fund" Motifs

When you log into your Motif account, the first thing you'll see is your Investment Summary—a breakdown of how much your portfolio is worth, how much money you have invested and how much cash you have in your account.

If you bought or are watching our motifs, you'll also see how they are doing.

The site shows you the current value of your positions and how much they are up or down for the day. You can get more information by clicking on the motif's name, just like you did when you bought it.

Motif will also let you know if we have rebalanced the motif, either by adding or deleting stocks or changing the weight of stocks in the motif.

Click on "See Available Updates" to see what has changed, and if you like, click on "Rebalance Positions" to buy and sell the stocks necessary to match the motif. (You'll pay a flat $9.95 commission to rebalance your motif, regardless of how many stocks are bought or sold.)

Remember, you have complete control over what's in the motif.

You can choose to buy more of any stock in the motif or sell stocks in it you no longer wish to own. To do that, just click the "Trade" button next to the stock's name on the motif's information page. Here's an example of how the page looks:

You'll be taken to an order page where you can choose to buy or sell that particular stock in the motif.

You will be charged a $4.95 commission for each individual company you trade in a motif.

You can also choose to close a motif entirely by clicking the "Trade Motif" button. Again, this is an example of how the site will look:

You'll need to decide if you wish to sell part of your motif or cash out completely. If you want to close the entire position, select "Sell All" under "Action."

If you only wish to sell part of the position, select "Sell." (You can sell part of your motif only if it is worth $250 or more. If it is worth less than $250, your only option is "Sell All.")

Below "Action" is a box where you can specify how much money you wish to extract from your motif. (If you choose "Sell All," this box will automatically fill in the total amount of your position.)

The box at the bottom of the page breaks down exactly how Motif will handle your sell order—the number of shares it will sell in your name and the amount of cash you can expect to receive from the sale.

Again, don't worry about fractional shares—Motif can sell fractional shares.

If you are ready to sell, click "Preview Order."

Review the details, and if everything looks good, click "Place Order." Motif will sell your allotted shares and deposit the proceeds into your cash account, minus a $9.95 commission. (Remember, Motif charges $9.95 per motif, so the total commission for selling one is $9.95, no matter how many stocks are involved.)

Assuming everything has gone well, you'll rack up some nice profits. You're free to take that cash off the table whenever you wish.

■ Claim Your Cash!

When you're ready to withdraw funds from your account, you have a few options.

If you funded your account electronically by linking Motif

to an outside bank account, just click on "Transfer Money" under "My Investments."

You'll be taken to the online transfer page. Then click on the "Withdraw Funds" tab.

If you've linked your Motif account to more than one outside bank account, you'll need to select where you'd like the money to go.

Then enter in the amount of money you wish to extract and click "Transfer." Motif will take care of the rest!

You can also choose to have Motif wire your money to your bank. Click on "Wire Transfer" on the Transfer Money page and then click on the Outgoing Wire Transfer form.

You can fill it out online, print it, sign it and then fax it back to Motif for processing. Motif charges $25 to wire money.

Finally, you can choose to have Motif send you a check. You'll need to call their customer service team at 1 (855) 586–6843.

▧ Time to Get Trading

To my knowledge, Motif Investing gives you the *only* way to invest in the new Special Drawing Right.

All you need is a Motif account, a minimum of $250 and the exclusive link above to our "private" "New World Money" and "Jim Rickards' Exclusive Stock Fund" motifs. Be sure to continue reading *Strategic Intelligence* issues and alerts to see analysis on anything that may change in both.

And remember, we don't have a business relationship with Motif. While we worked with them to create the Motif for you to invest in, we're not being compensated to tell you how to open an account.

We truly believe they offer the tools you need to get the most out of hot investments at an affordable price.

Please visit their website at **www.motifinvesting.com** if you have any lingering questions, and consider opening a risk-free account to check them out.

CHAPTER 13

Protection and Wealth-Building Strategies

Today's stock market is a bubble that's being propped up by zero interest rates.

There's nothing Wall Street doesn't like about free money. That's why leverage on the New York Stock Exchange is at an all-time high. This is about the worst possible time for the everyday investor to get into the market without proper guidance.

People like to say, "Oh, well, the stock market has more than tripled since the low in March 2009." But, that was then and this is now. We're seven years closer to the next collapse. Is this the time to be jumping in, or is it time to get out, at least on a selective basis? Besides, it has more than tripled with easy money, enormous leverage and very little participation. How long can that last? Volumes are low, so you have a steeply rising stock market on very low volume with massive leverage. That is almost the definition of a bubble, and that bubble will burst.

This is really the worst possible time to jump in. The everyday investor has to be very, very careful about stocks in here.

▧ Use a "Barbell Strategy"

Not a day goes by without some pretty significant developments in the markets. You should not react or overreact in a knee-jerk fashion to each piece of data that comes out. You'll just end up getting whipped around.

What you need to do—what analysts and investors need to do—is have a thesis to guide them. Don't pick one at random, but have a well-thought-out thesis. Then use the data to test that thesis. There's a name for this: it's called "inverse probability." You use subsequent data to test your original idea.

That method is different from a lot of science, where you actually get a bunch of data and then you come up with an idea. Here, however, you have an idea and you come up with data to test it. There is no better way of approaching the markets because nobody has a crystal ball.

Our thesis has a number of elements. One of them is that there is a tug-of-war going on between inflation and deflation, which I've written about in these pages before (in the short term, I believe deflation has the upper hand).

That confuses a lot of people because they understand one or the other, but it's challenging for them to keep both things in mind at the same time.

For your investment portfolio, that means taking a "barbell approach," which means having some protection at both ends. Have your deflation protection, your inflation protection and some cash in the middle all at the same time because that's the best you can do with this kind of uncertainty.

The uncertainty is caused by central bank policy. We are in unprecedented times. And that's not just my opinion. If you listen to Janet Yellen or members of the FOMC or members of the Board of Governors of the Federal Reserve, or leading economists and policy makers, they all say the same thing. They say these are completely unprecedented times.

In 2014, I had occasion to spend two hours one-on-one with one of the ultimate Fed insiders. Sometimes, when you do these things, you agree not to mention names, so I won't mention any names here. But this was a guy who was in the room for every FOMC vote for the past four-and-a-half years. Nobody's closer to Bernanke and Yellen than this individual I spoke to.

He's a Ph.D. economist and a very well-regarded scholar but not a very well-known name because he's not actually on the FOMC. Yet he's been invited into the room to help them figure these things out. And what he said was that we're not really going to know if the Fed's policies worked as intended for another 50 years. He said 50 years from now, there will be another young scholar like Ben Bernanke was in the 1980s who comes along and figures all this stuff out.

In other words, they're admitting that they don't know what they're doing. They're admitting this is kind of a big science experiment. What does that mean for us as investors, portfolio managers and people trying to make smart decisions?

It means that we have to be nimble, and we have to watch the data. We can't put a stake in the ground around one particular outcome because the chance of getting blindsided by something coming up from behind is pretty high.

In early 2014, monthly jobs creation had ticked up a bit, with upward revisions for prior months. Even more jobs were created in November and December of 2014 than we knew at the time.

Importantly, real wages went up a little bit. Not a lot, but the fact that that time series even had a pulse is interesting. I've said before that that's one of the things Janet Yellen watches most closely because the Fed has this crazy dual mandate of creating jobs and maintaining price stability at the same time.

They're not really consistent goals; sometimes they run together, but sometimes they pull in opposite directions. Yellen's been putting the emphasis on job creation, but she wants some early warning about inflation. Seeing real wages going up is one indicator where the two wings of the plane, if you will, work together.

Because if real wages were going up, that's a sign that slack was being reduced in the labor market. If labor can get a raise that might be an early indicator of inflation and that might mean we're getting closer to the point where she needs to raise interest rates.

I looked at data out so far in 2015, and I looked at my thesis, which is that deflation has the upper hand. There's a tug-of-war, as we've described, but in a tug-of-war one team seems to get the upper hand on the other from time to time, and right now it does look like deflation's got the upper hand.

Look at the oil patch, for evidence. The U.S. rig count is down, layoffs are going up, capital-expenditure plans are being cut; you can see all those things happening.

But they don't happen overnight. It takes a while to work through the supply chain and all of the places where oil is an input. It shows up at the gas pump pretty quickly, and it shows up in airfares pretty quickly. But for some industrial processes, it takes a while to filter through.

Those trends are still working their way through the economy—especially layoffs. They tend to come in waves. Companies start with some layoffs, and then do more the next month and more the month after that. They wait and see if things turn around, which I don't expect they will.

Compounding those problems is the big 800-pound gorilla in the deflation scenario—the currency wars. They're getting more and more intense. Between January 2015 and March 2015 we saw four rate cuts: from Denmark alone, and other cuts from Canada and Australia. Go around the world and you'll see they're popping up everywhere. And I think more are on the way.

I would expect another rate cut from Canada, and I think we'll see this continue as the currency wars rage on. And you can expect an even bigger announcement out of China. China hasn't cut rates since last November 2014.

They've only adjusted what they call their reserve-requirement ratio. That's how much in reserves they have to hold against their loan portfolio. They reduced it, meaning they can expand lending with the same amount of reserves. It was meant as a form of easing.

China's growth is still coming in below our expectations, so I would look for a rate cut there. You still have these phenomena where every country in the world, including the European Central Bank, is easing—using quantitative easing, cutting rates, working around the edges to cheapen their currencies. All of that weight of adjustment is falling on the dollar, which continues to get strong, or at least maintains its strength at a very high level, which is, as we've said before, deflationary.

You should be nimble and prepare for both inflation and deflation. Your initial portfolio should have gold, fine art, raw land, cash, bonds, select stocks and some alternatives in strategies like global macro hedge funds and venture capital. Not all of those strategies will pay off in every scenario, but some will do well enough to outperform others and preserve your wealth in the overall portfolio.

◼ "Indications and Warnings"

There are investment techniques that I've learned working for the national-security and intelligence communities that you can apply to understand the capital markets.

When you have a problem in the intelligence world, invariably, it's what mathematicians call "underdetermined." That's just a fancy way of saying you don't have enough information.

If you had enough information to solve the problem, a high school kid could do it. The reason it's a very hard problem to solve is because you don't have enough information.

What do you do when you don't have enough information? Well, you can throw up your hands—that's not a good approach.

You can guess—also not a good approach. Or you can start to fill in the blanks and connect the dots.

You're still not sure how it's going to turn out, but you can come up with three or four different scenarios. In all probability, the problem is going to come out one of several ways. Maybe those ways are deflation, inflation or a market crash like we've discussed. Maybe there's a good outcome too.

A lot of analysts don't get that far. They put a stake in the ground and say, "This is what's going to happen."

The truth is, however, that there are several things that could happen. There could be three or four outcomes. But even people who get that far start tagging probabilities on those outcomes. They say, "There's a 30 percent chance of deflation, 40 percent chance of inflation and so on."

I don't recommend doing that either. The way I think about these problems is that there's a 100 percent chance of one outcome happening and a 0 percent chance of the rest. It's just that you don't know in advance which one it's going to be.

What are you supposed to do? In the intelligence community, we come up with what we call "indications and warnings," or I&W. Indications and warnings are the signposts or the milestones on the path to one of these outcomes. Say we have four outcomes—four paths—and you start down the path. You don't know which path you're on, and you don't know what the outcome is. But you can come up with the indications and warnings—the signposts. When you see the signposts, then you can begin to know which way you're going.

Here's how I explain it to investors. I spend a lot of time in the New York area, and it just so happens that if you drive to Boston, all the roadside restaurants are McDonald's. And if you drive to Philadelphia, all the roadside restaurants are Burger King. So if you blindfold me, put me in a car and don't tell me which way I'm going but you tell me there's a Burger King, I know I'm not going to Boston.

In other words, Burger King and McDonald's are my signposts.

The art of applying this technique to your investments requires, first of all, getting the possible outcomes correct. Then, instead of just assigning arbitrary probabilities to them, figure out the helpful indications and warnings. Then watch the data, watch geopolitical developments, watch strategic developments and when you see a particular signpost you know you're on your way.

It's an intelligence-community technique that I've brought over to capital markets. Believe me, it works. I have years of experience using it. Now you can use it too.

▓ Preserve Your Wealth in the Face of Financial War

During the Cold War, the United States had enough nuclear missiles to destroy Russia and its economy, and Russia had enough missiles to do the same to the United States.

Neither adversary used those missiles, and the leaders were quite careful to avoid escalations that might lead in that direction. Proxy wars were fought in places like Vietnam, the Congo and Afghanistan, but direct confrontation between the United States and Russia was never allowed to come to a head.

The reason was that no matter how devastating a nuclear "first strike" might be, the country under attack would have enough surviving missiles to launch a massive "second strike" that would destroy the attacker. This is what was meant by "mutual assured destruction," or the balance of terror. Neither side could win, and both sides would be destroyed; therefore they went to great lengths to avoid confrontation and escalation in the first place.

In financial warfare between the United States and Russia, a similar balance of terror exists. It is true that the United States has powerful financial weapons it can use against Russia. The United States can freeze the assets of Russian leaders and oligarchs that can be found both in U.S. banks and foreign banks that do business in dollars.

The United States can deny Russian access to the dollar payments system and work with allies to deny Russian access to the SWIFT system in Belgium that processes payments in all currencies, not just dollars. Many of these tactics have, in fact, been used against Iran and Syria in the financial war that has been going on in the Middle East and Persian Gulf since 2012.

But Russia is not without financial weapons of its own. Russians could refuse to pay dollar-denominated debts to U.S. and multilateral lenders. Russia could dump the billions of dollars of U.S. Treasury notes they own, thus driving up U.S. interest rates and hurting the U.S. stock and bond markets.

Most ominously, Russia could unleash its hackers, among the best in the world, to crash U.S. stock exchanges. On August 22, 2013, the Nasdaq stock market crashed for half a trading day, and no credible explanation has yet been offered for the crash. Hacking by Syrian, Iranian or Russian cyberwarriors cannot be ruled out. This may have been a warning to the United States about enemy capabilities.

In short, the United States has no interest in intervening in Ukraine militarily, and even its economic response will be muted because of new fears of mutual assured financial destruction emanating from Russia and elsewhere. Putin has thought all of this through and has taken Crimea as his prize.

Russia's victory in Crimea may embolden China to assert territorial claims to certain islands in the South China Sea, which could increase tensions with Japan, Korea, Taiwan and the United States.

There is also always the possibility of a financial attack being launched by mistake or miscalculation, which could cause events to spin out of control in unintended ways.

Investors may not be able to change this dangerous state of the world, but they are not helpless when it comes to preserving wealth. A modest allocation of investable assets to physical gold will help to preserve wealth in the face of financial war or unexpected catastrophic outcomes.

Gold is not digital, cannot be wiped out by hackers and is immune to crashing stock markets and bank failures. Russia has increased its gold reserves 70 percent in the past seven years. China has increased its gold reserves over 200 percent in the same time period. Do they know something you don't?

An REIT to Protect Against 21st-Century Financial Wars

On January 12, 2015, I traveled to Washington, D.C., to meet with an elite group of intelligence, counterterrorism and national-security experts. It was the launch of a new think tank called the Center on Sanctions and Illicit Finance, CSIF.

After checking in at the Ritz-Carlton in the West End, my home away from home in D.C., I journeyed a few miles to a side street in Georgetown where our group gathered in a private dining room for our first joint session.

Included were several former officials of the White House National Security Council and advisers to the U.S. Treasury and U.S. Special Operations Command. It was an intriguing mix of seasoned professionals with roots in the military, intelligence and finance. It was exactly the kind of team needed to fight 21st-century financial wars.

Financial threats come in many forms. Some relate to criminal activities including money laundering related to drug smuggling and arms sales and hackers who steal credit card and other personal financial information. Other threats include efforts to end run economic sanctions. These threats involve countries such as North Korea and organizations such as Hamas that are the targets of U.S. and allied imposed sanctions.

The most serious threats, however, are strategic in nature. These involve rival states such as Iran, Russia and China that engage in clandestine financial warfare using everything from front companies in tax-haven jurisdictions to cyberattacks that threaten to shut down stock exchanges and banks. All of these financial actors—from criminal gangs to strategic rivals—are within the scope of our group's efforts to help the United States understand and defeat their threats.

Since the 1980s, the key to military planning and war fighting has been the concept of "jointness." Prior to the 1980s, the Army, Navy, Marines and Air Force were not only separate branches of the military, but they utilized their own communications channels, equipment requirements and war-fighting doctrine, among other attributes. The result was a lack of coordination and effectiveness.

These deficiencies came to a head in the darkly comical blunders surrounding "Operation Urgent Fury." That was the invasion of the tiny Caribbean island nation of Grenada in 1983. This was the first major combat operation conducted by the United States since the end of the Vietnam War, in 1975.

Intelligence was highly deficient to the point that invading forces were handed tourist maps of the island without military grid lines. U.S. Navy forces fired on and killed U.S. ground forces by mistake. Some invasion-force members received maps on which the landing zone had to be drawn in by hand. Communications between the military branches broke down.

As a result, Congress passed the Goldwater-Nichols Act in 1986, which enshrined the concept of joint operations and joint command. Today, it is not unusual to find an Army major general reporting to a Navy admiral who happens to be a combatant commander in one of the major commands such as Centcom. These reforms have made the U.S. military a far more effective and lethal force than it was in the 1980s.

A similar method is being used today in financial warfare. Major-threat finance initiatives typically involve participants from the Pentagon, CIA, U.S. Treasury and Federal Reserve and private-sector experts from Wall Street, major banks and the hedge fund community, all working together. Our CSIF team is using exactly such an approach to confront future financial threats.

Even as the United States and its allies are refining their ability to counteract financial threats, the bad guys and rival state actors are not standing still.

New technologies such as crypto-currencies, Bitcoin being the best known, are being used by the Islamic State and other enemies to buy weapons and pay troops without interdiction by global bank regulators.

Large Russian and Chinese cyberbrigades have been mustered to put those countries on the leading edge of financial cyberwarfare. Wealth can also be moved around the world undetected using accounting games such as inflated transfer prices in the sale of mundane goods and services. Forensic expertise in law, accounting and taxation is needed to counter those threats.

Ironically, the most ancient financial techniques can be just as effective at avoiding sanctions as the most modern. Classic stores of wealth such as gold, silver, jewels, fine art and land are effective ways to transfer and hide wealth without moving assets through modern digital-payments systems. Gold is scarce and valuable at about $1,300 per ounce.

But a Picasso painting, carefully rolled up and stashed in the lining of a suitcase, can be worth $500,000 per ounce. Better yet, a painting does not set off metal detectors in airports. Paintings are the best way to move wealth without detection.

In fact, enemies of the United States are using both the newest cybertechniques and the oldest wealth-transfer techniques—such as gold and art—to bypass the major banking channels and payments systems. Meanwhile, conventional financial channels, such as stock exchanges and banks, are completely vulnerable to cyberattack, which can close venues and wipe out account balances with a few keystrokes. These types of cyberattacks are one of the 30 snowflakes that could cause the next financial avalanche.

My takeaway from the meeting with the CSIF financial-threat team was that it is critical for you to keep at least part of your wealth in nondigital form. This can mean physical cash, physical gold, fine art or land. These are the assets than cannot be wiped out by digital warfare or attacks on the power grid.

When it comes to stocks, it is also useful to identify companies that have physical assets behind them. Even if banks and exchanges come under cyberattack, these stocks will retain value because they have tangible income-producing properties.

Real estate investment trusts are ideal for this purpose. They have tangible property assets behind them, which are a good inflation hedge, and they pay attractive yields, which is a good deflation hedge. That's because tax law allows them to avoid corporate income tax as long as they distribute 90 percent of their earnings as dividends.

■ One Gold Stock That's Outperformed Bullion by 200% Since 2007

There's one gold stock that's up over 200 percent since it starting trading in December 2007.

It's not an ETF or a gold miner. In fact, compared to bullion, a gold ETF or a gold miner, this play is a superior way to get exposure to gold.

As a rule of thumb, it's better to limit your portfolio to gold stocks with low financial risk. Many gold-mining companies, for example, are poorly managed and expanded too aggressively in 2010–11. After sinking billions of dollars into exploration and mine development, most deliver disappointing returns.

That's why it's better to look for low-risk gold-stock plays. Royalty companies tend to have the lowest financial risk. That's because they don't have the high costs that mine operators have.

A royalty company spends shareholders' money to finance gold miners' operations. In return, the royalty company gets a percentage, or "royalty," from the mine's revenue.

Franco-Nevada (FNV: NYSE) is an example of an expertly managed gold royalty company. Chairman Pierre Lassonde and CEO David Harquail lead FNV's executive team. They've delivered exceptional results for shareholders.

As you can see, compared with bullion or a gold ETF, Franco-Nevada is a vastly superior vehicle to get exposure to gold. Franco-Nevada's business model benefits from rising commodity prices and new mining discoveries. At the same time, it limits your exposure to gold miners' large capital and operating costs.

FNV has lots of cash, no debt and rising cash flow. That means it has lots of dry powder to add to its long track record of smart business deals.

Since its 2007 initial public offering, Franco-Nevada has generated almost $1 billion in revenue. Over the same period, FNV also expanded its proven and probable gold reserves by more than 102 percent. Unlike a regular miner, which must spend heavily to replace revenue with new mines, FNV only has to acquire new royalties.

In terms of revenues and number of gold assets, Franco-Nevada is the largest royalty company. Its 380 royalty interests include some of the largest gold development and exploration projects in the world. FNV's royalty portfolio is diversified geographically, with most exposure in safe mining districts: the United States, Canada and Mexico.

The company also holds high-return interests in oil fields. In November 2012, it acquired an 11.7 percent net royalty interest in the Weyburn Oil Unit in Saskatchewan for C$400 million in cash, or just C$16.53 per proven and probable barrel of oil. Weyburn has performed well for shareholders.

By owning a business with such high profit margins and a high return on invested capital, you can enjoy a large, growing stream of future free cash flow. The higher gold, platinum and oil prices rise, the faster FNV's free cash flow will grow.

Capital is scarce in the gold mining business, right now. That puts FNV in a great position. Management has $1.8 billion to invest—putting them in the position to create lots of value for you, the shareholder. At current prices, I believe FNV offers an excellent way to boost your portfolio's exposure to gold.

▨ One Safe Haven Where the Elites Hide Their Money

When elites and institutional investors see a catastrophe coming, the first things they look to buy are U.S. Treasury notes and bonds. Making money in the Treasury market is relatively straightforward because there is minimal credit risk.

Imagine a seesaw. Bond prices are on one side of the seesaw, and bond yields are on the other side. Treasury bond prices rise when yields fall; prices fall when yields rise. The longer the maturity of the bond, the more its price will rise or fall in response to changes in interest rates.

During the last crisis, in 2008, U.S. Treasuries soared. From Lehman Brothers' bankruptcy filing in September 2008 to the end of the year, the 30-year U.S. Treasury Bond Index rose 15 percent. Over the same period, the S&P 500 stock index crashed 28 percent. Treasuries would likely strengthen again if we faced another crash. Investors' demand for liquid, safe

instruments would overwhelm the supply of Treasuries, pushing up prices.

Conditions can change very rapidly in the bond market,
however. That's why I believe an actively managed mutual
fund is the best way for you to invest in Treasury bonds. Fund
managers can adjust the mix of bond holdings in response to
changing conditions.

Treasury Bonds Paid Off in the 2008 Crash

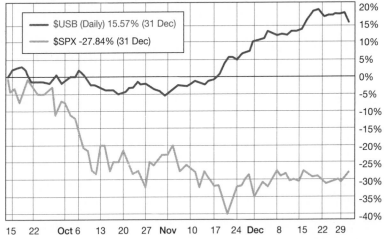

Van Hoisington at Hoisington Investment Management has
one of the best long-term track records managing a Treasury-
only mutual fund. He has managed the Wasatch Hoisington
U.S. Treasury Fund (WHOSX) since 1996, delivering an impressive 8.1 percent compound annual return over the past
decade.

Hoisington limits the risk of default by investing primarily
in U.S. Treasuries. All Treasury bonds are direct obligations of
the U.S. government and vary only in maturity and coupon.
Hoisington wouldn't hesitate to concentrate assets into 30-
year Treasury bonds—because the collapse would send their
prices soaring.

Going back to our seesaw analogy, the longest-maturity

Treasuries are at the far end of the seesaw. In response to falling rates, long-term Treasuries would rally much more than short-term Treasuries. In past deflation scares, Hoisington has positioned its investors to profit from sharp rallies in long-term Treasuries. WHOSX is an excellent deflation hedge for your portfolio.

It's a no-load fund with a $2,000 investment minimum and charges 0.71 percent per year in management fees. You can buy WHOSX through most discount-brokerage platforms.

■ The Ultimate Form of "Cash" in Financial Markets

Aside from emergency cash held someplace safe, there are safe options for the cash portion of your portfolio. If you want to avoid interest rate risk and want intraday liquidity, the iShares 1–3 Year Treasury Bond ETF (SHY: NYSE) is a good alternative to money market funds. Money market funds invest in commercial paper, which became illiquid in the 2008 crisis.

Treasuries approaching maturity are generally liquid and in demand—even during crises. They're the closest thing to cash in the financial markets. SHY seeks to track the investment results of an index composed of U.S. Treasury securities with remaining maturities between one and three years. SHY won't offer any measurable return as long as the Fed keeps rates at zero, but it won't lose money, either.

How is this any different than the Wasatch-Hoisington U.S. Treasury Fund (WHOSX)?

The key difference is that WHOSX has more risk and more potential reward. It has interest rate risk. Interest rate risk simply refers to how much a bond price moves in reaction to changes in interest rates. Think of a seesaw; as bond yields go down, bond prices go up.

Once the deflation fear has passed, though, and interest

rates rise, WHOSX is at risk of falling in value.

SHY, on the other hand is flat. It doesn't move and doesn't pay any measurable amount of yield. But that doesn't mean it's a frivolous recommendation. On the contrary, SHY is one of the safest places to park cash that you may want to use for buying stocks or bonds or real estate after the deflation panic has passed.

SHY is like the ultimate form of cash in your brokerage account.

■ Why You Should Consider Owning Both WHOSX and SHY

It's good to own both because WHOSX is more of a deflation "trade," with risk and reward, while SHY is more like a cash vault. Essentially, SHY is akin to "cash sitting in a safe" inside your brokerage account, ready at the click of a mouse to buy assets that others are panicking to sell.

If we continue to have mild inflation, soaring stocks and the Fed holding rates at zero, the risk is that you might hold back the potential performance of your portfolio. SHY will yield little (until the Fed starts raising interest rates).

Also, SHY steadily loses real value if inflation persists. But the other parts of your portfolio —inflation hedges like Franco-Nevada (NYSE: FNV)—should keep you ahead of inflation.

If the Fed surprises investors in 2015 and raises rates, both SHY and WHOSX will do well.

The biggest risk is the resumption of an inflationary environment. Interest rates would rise, which would depress the value of long-term Treasuries. The value of WHOSX would start falling too.

In the early stages of an inflationary sea change, SHY would gain. It would not fall in value, while it would start reinvesting in Treasuries with short remaining maturities paying higher yields.

WHOSX will perform better during a deflation scare that is driving investors into long-term Treasuries. If this continues—and it should until the Fed cries uncle and starts printing again—WHOSX should continue outperforming.

Both SHY and WHOSX would perform badly if there were a repeat of the spring 2013 "taper tantrum." Back then, long-term bonds sold off violently for roughly a month after Ben Bernanke implied that the Fed would taper at some point in the future. At the same time, SHY just held its value, and held the promise that it wouldn't pay interest for as long as the Fed held rates at zero. But that episode was unusual and is unlikely to repeat anytime soon.

And if the Fed surprises us this year and raises rates, as it's indicated it will, both SHY and WHOSX will do well. As the Fed raises rates, the interest rate on SHY's newly purchased Treasuries with short maturities will rise, and the stock market could crash in response to the rate hike, thereby spreading a deflation panic into long-term Treasuries.

With SHY as a cash component in your portfolio, you can afford to wait. If deflation prevails, your cash will be worth more in real terms and you'll be positioned to pick up bargains when other investments start to crash.

If inflation takes off, you should pivot away from cash and catch the coming inflationary wave with your other investments. This tug-of-war between inflation and deflation is not close to being over and will be the prevailing investment paradigm for some time.

In the short run, deflation is more likely. In the long run, inflation is more likely. And the reason is that the government has to get to inflation. It's not working. They're trying to get inflation, and they're not getting it. We're getting deflation in the short run. But they're not going to quit trying.

So in the short run, bonds are going to rally on deflation. That said, I still like gold and hard assets for a slice—not the whole thing, but for a slice, because in the longer run, they'll do well when inflation comes in.

You may be surprised to learn that even in deflationary times, gold can perform well. From 1930 to 1933, for example, cumulative deflation was 26 percent. The United States became desperate for inflation. It could not cheapen its currency, because other countries were cheapening their currencies even faster in the "beggar thy neighbor" currency wars of the time.

Finally, the United States decided to devalue the dollar against gold. In 1933, the price of gold in dollars was increased from $20 to $35 per ounce, a 75 percent increase at a time when all other prices were decreasing.

This shock therapy for the dollar worked, and by 1934, inflation was back at 3.1 percent, a massive turnaround from the 5.1 percent deflation of 1933. In short, when all other methods fail to defeat deflation, devaluing the dollar against gold works without fail because gold can't fight back.

So don't think that because our portfolio is prepared for either inflation or deflation that you're bound to lose a portion of your investments.

That said, I recognize that volatility and price drops may be nerve-wracking. That's why I've found a new precious-metals play I'd like to share with you.

▨ Introducing the PMC Ounce: The Best of Precious Metals With Less Volatility

In a better world, central bankers would aim for true price stability that wouldn't involve inflation or deflation.

But whether you like it or not, central banks favor inflation over deflation. Inflation promotes the goals of the policy elite: It boosts tax collections, cuts the burden of government debt and gooses consumption. It also punishes both savers and cautious investors.

The elites' fondness for inflation isn't going to change. That's why I recommend owning a sleeve of physical gold — in addition to stocks, bonds, cash, land and fine art.

Even still, investors ask me: "What other precious metal inflation hedge can I buy? Does platinum or palladium have a place in an investor's portfolio?"

I'd like to introduce you to a little-known investment that helps you fight back against inflation's corrosive impact: the PMC Ounce. It's offered by precious metals dealer Neptune Global.

The PMC Ounce is a dynamic physical precious metals investment asset. It tracks the "PMC Index".

What is the PMC Index?

It's a fixed-weight index of the four primary precious metals expressed as a single ounce. It basically diversifies you across precious metals. Gold makes up roughly half of the PMC Ounce. The rest is split between silver, palladium and platinum.

The PMC Ounce is liquid and trades in real-time. Yet it also allows you to capture each metal's proven characteristics as a store of wealth, inflation hedge, currency hedge and industrial input.

Keep in mind that a PMC Ounce is not just a claim on physical metal; it's physical bullion stored in an insured, non-bank vault in Delaware. It's 100% bullion, it's not a fund, not a derivative and not "paper gold."

When you buy the PMC Ounce, there are no financial instruments between you and the bullion, thereby eliminating the counterparty risk associated with Wall Street-created financial instruments.

The metals are allocated in your name at a nonbank bullion depository and verified to you by them. With one day's notice, either the bullion or the bullion's cash equivalent can be delivered to you on demand. (The tax status for the PMC

Ounce is the same as that for physical bullion.)

I like the PMC Ounce because it's a way to own four precious metals in a more diversified, stable manner.

For example, if gold is getting smashed, one of the other three metals may be rising. As the global monetary system experiences convulsions, the volatility of metals will spike. Most of the volatility will be to the upside, but there will be jarring corrections, too.

Over time, the PMC Ounce should yield a higher, smoother return than the return from each metal on its own.

Individual Bullion Metals vs. PMC Ounce

Price Change: Base 100—Price Data London Fix

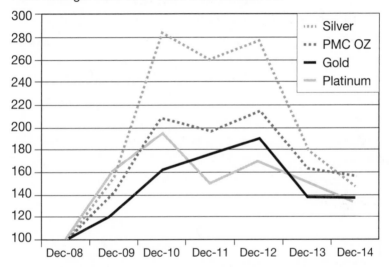

How would the PMC Ounce perform in a deflationary environment? We experienced a mild deflation stress test from late 2014 to the present. And the results were good.

Oil prices and stocks were weak and investors bid up Treasury bonds. Yet these four precious metals held their value. On several occasions throughout this deflation stress test, these metals rose, making them great instruments to diversify your investment portfolio. As investors keep searching for hedges against both deflation and inflation will find their way to precious metals.

You don't need to worry about management fees, since the PMC Ounce is not a fund. There is a modest premium over the spot price, as with any bullion purchase. You can find the realtime PMC Ounce spot price easily through the PMC Index on Neptune Global's site.

You can also own the PMC ounce within or outside your IRA. For more information, visit **www.neptuneglobal.com/pmc-ounce/**, or call Neptune Global at (302) 256-5080. Be sure to mention that you're a *Jim Rickards' Strategic Intelligence* reader.

What I like best about this is that the index actually outperforms three of the four index components with less volatility. That means a much higher Sharpe ratio—a measure of risk-adjusted performance—than either gold or silver.

The reason is that when gold is getting smashed, silver is not, and vice versa. The blended product dodges these bullets and reduces volatility, for a higher total return.

Of course, this product was been beaten down in 2015, like the precious metals themselves, but with metals prices recovering, this could be your last chance to get in at such an attractive entry point.

■ Gold Coins

I recommend you have a 10 percent allocation to physical gold if you don't already. Here I recommend American Gold Eagle or American Buffalo gold coins from the U.S. Mint.

The American Eagle is 22-karat gold, and the American Buffalo is 24-carat gold. The Eagle is more durable than the Buffalo because it has some alloy, but both have one ounce of gold.

You should not buy so-called "collectible" gold coins or

older coins, because dealers charge a premium that is not worth it in terms of numismatic value. Stick with new or relatively uncirculated Eagles or Buffalos.

Prices are usually at the daily market price for one ounce of gold plus a premium, which can range from 4 to 8 percent, depending on the dealer. Storage should be with a reliable, insured, nonbank vault near your home or in a home safe. The best security is not to let anyone know you have the coins in the first place.

▧ Monster Box

If you haven't already, I recommend buying a "Monster Box" issued by the U.S. Mint. You can buy one through reputable precious-metals dealers. A Monster Box is a sealed container of 500 one-ounce pure-silver American Silver Eagle coins. The box is colored "Treasury green."

You should not break the seal on the box unless you actually need the coins for transactions. The price varies with the market, but one box would be about $8,000 plus a small commission based on the current price of silver.

This is not only a good store of wealth, but the coins will prove useful for shopping and smaller transactions in the event the power grid and banking systems break down in a future financial crisis or natural disaster. You can store the Monster Box in a reputable nonbank vault or in a home safe—just don't let anyone know you have it.

▧ Emerging Markets

Some investors wonder if they should put their money into emerging markets.

Go back to the spring of 2013 when Bernanke first mentioned the "T word"—tapering. He implied that the Federal

Reserve would reduce its long-term asset purchases and perhaps get on a path to taking the program all the way to zero. What happened to emerging markets? They collapsed immediately.

Why is that? It's because of the "carry trade." That's when interest rates are at zero, and investors say, "Okay, I'll borrow dollars at almost no cost, convert them into another currency, and buy local stocks and bonds in places like South Africa, India, Brazil, Indonesia, Thailand and other emerging markets that have much higher yields."

Investors do this on a leveraged basis. That means they have a low cost of funds, a high returning asset, probably an appreciating currency—all of which could lead to 30 percent returns on equity.

What's wrong with that trade? Well, the risk is that U.S. interest rates go up and the whole thing falls apart. The minute that Ben Bernanke started talking about tapering in 2013, people reversed the carry trade.

They dumped emerging-market stocks and currencies, went back to dollars, paid off their debts and reduced their balance sheets and went to the sidelines. It's a good example of why emerging markets are not necessarily a safe haven. Think about the linkages we've discussed so far. If you're going to invest in emerging markets, put in the due diligence beforehand and don't go all in.

■ The Risks of Owning Bitcoin

In late 2014, I met with senior officers of the U.S. Special Operations Command (USSOCOM) in a secure location near their headquarters at MacDill Air Force Base.

USSOCOM includes the Navy SEALS, DELTA Force, Green Berets, and other highly trained and specialized units operating under joint military command to carry out the most difficult combat and intelligence missions. They conduct these missions both alone and in conjunction with CIA paramilitary units depending on the theatre of operations.

The particular unit of USSOCOM that sponsored our meeting was "J36," the Transnational Threats Division. J36 is commanded by U.S. Army Lt. Col. Joshua J. Potter, and is assigned the task of detecting, disrupting and defeating threat networks that transcend geographic and regional boundaries. Such networks are both criminal and terrorist in nature, and may be involved in narco-terrorism and terrorist finance among other activities.

Our meeting was attended not only by USSOCOM operators but also by members of other combat commands including CENTCOM and AFRICOM, and other government agencies including the U.S. Treasury, the CIA and the Federal Reserve. Our purpose was to consider ways to disrupt financial support for the Islamic State and other transnational actors.

In particular, the Islamic State and associated terrorist groups have the ability to use crypto-digital currencies such as Bitcoin to transfer funds from wealthy Saudi Wahhabi supporters to arms dealers and other suppliers of provisions and services. We had assembled financial and computer experts to work with the USSOCOM operators to disrupt the use of Bitcoin by terrorists.

The particular counterthreat techniques we discussed cannot be disclosed because it would give an advantage to enemies of the United States. But the session was an excellent opportunity to consider just how far the crypto-currency community has come in a relatively brief period.

So-called crypto-currencies such as Bitcoin have two main features in common. The first is that they are not issued or regulated by any central bank or single regulatory authority. They are created in accordance with certain computer algorithms and are issued and transferred through a distributed processing network using open source code.

Any particular computer server hosting a crypto-currency ledger or register could be destroyed, but the existence of the currency would continue to reside on other servers all over the world and could quickly be replicated. It is impossible to destroy a crypto-currency by attacking any single node or group of nodes.

The second feature in common is encryption, which gives rise to the "crypto" part of the name. It is possible to observe transactions taking place in the so-called block chain, which is a master register of all currency units and transactions. But, the identity of the transacting parties is hidden behind what is believed to be an unbreakable code. Only the transacting parties have the keys needed to decode the information in the block chain in such a way as to obtain use and possession of the currency.

This does not mean that crypto-currencies are fail-safe. Large amounts of crypto-currency units have been lost by those who entrusted them to certain unregulated Bitcoin "banks" and "exchanges." Others have been lost to old-fashioned fraud. Some units have been lost because personal hardware holding encryption keys or "digital wallets" has been destroyed. But on the whole, the system works reasonably well and is growing rapidly for both legitimate and illegitimate transactions.

It's worth pointing out that the U.S. dollar is also a digital crypto-currency for all intents and purposes. While we may keep a few paper dollars in our wallets from time to time, the vast majority of dollar-denominated transactions, whether in currency or securities form, are conducted digitally. We pay bills online, pay for purchases via credit card and receive direct deposits to our bank accounts all digitally.

These transactions are all encrypted using the same coding techniques as Bitcoin. The difference is that ownership of our digital dollars is known to certain trusted counterparties such as our banks, brokers and credit card companies, whereas ownership of Bitcoin is known only to the user and is hidden behind the block chain code. Another difference is that dollars are issued by a central bank, the Federal Reserve, while Bitcoin is issued privately.

The future of Bitcoin and other crypto-currencies is uncertain. One problem is that the value of a Bitcoin is not constant in terms of U.S. dollars. In fact, that value has been quite volatile, fluctuating between $100 and $1100 over the past two years.

This gives rise to tax problems. For example, if you acquire a Bitcoin for $200 and later exchange it for $1,000 of goods or services, you have an $800 gain on the purchase and sale of the Bitcoin itself. From the perspective of the IRS, this gain is no different than if you had purchased a share of stock for $200 and later sold it for $1,000. You have to report the $800 as a capital gain.

It seems unlikely that most Bitcoin users are reporting these gains. Those who do not may be involved in tax evasion. The IRS has broad powers to investigate evasion, and may require counterparties to reveal information, including computer keys, which can lead to discovery of the transacting parties.

Given the fact that the IRS has engaged in selective enforcement against Tea Party activists and other political opponents in recent years, this is a serious potential problem for libertarian users of Bitcoin.

Another problem is that Bitcoin and the other crypto-currencies have not survived a complete business and credit cycle yet. Bitcoin, the first crypto-currency, was invented in 2009. The global economy has been in a weak expansion since then, but has not experienced a financial panic or technical recession.

Investors have some experience with how stocks, bonds, gold and other asset classes might perform in a downturn, but we have no experience with Bitcoin. Will liquidity dry up and prices plunge? Or will investors consider it a safe harbor, which will lead to price increases? We don't know the answer.

In the end, it may be the case that Bitcoin will fade as a currency, but survive as a technology. The encrypted block chain technology is useful for a variety of asset transfers beside currency. It can be used to transfer title to land, securities, and other assets in secure, inexpensive ways.

It is this technology potential, more than the currency itself, that has attracted the interest of investors such as the Winklevoss twins and Marc Andreesen. While start-up companies in Bitcoin may be highly speculative for the time being, there may be attractive investment opportunities in this arena in the years ahead.

My day with the operators, as the Special Forces are called, was a fascinating blend of technologists, commandos, and economists working together to counter a threat to U.S. national security from the use by terrorists of crypto-currencies to finance terror. I have participated in such collaborations before, and it's always heartening to encounter the brilliance of our military leaders and elite forces.

Many of the colonels and generals whom I meet have graduate degrees in demanding technical fields, speak multiple languages and have deployed in diverse civilizations and cultures on every continent. The United States has the finest military in the world, capable of defeating any threat including new threats arising from the blend of technology and finance.

In addition to being a threat, Bitcoin and its crypto-cousins also represent an opportunity. It is still too early for investors to hold Bitcoin in their portfolios due to excessive volatility and unresolved tax issues.

But the time may come, sooner rather than later, when some Bitcoin technology companies might warrant investor interest based on their possible role in the future of payments and in other forms of wealth transfer. Companies such as Western Union and PayPal dominate the private-payments systems space today. They may have company from crypto-currency start-ups soon.

CHAPTER 14

Recommended Reading

In addition to actionable investment opportunities, there are several books I recommend to my readers. Each will help investors understand our complex financial system...

◼ Money and Tough Love

The Washington, D.C., area is thick with secret agencies with "three-letter names," such as CIA, FBI, NSA and less well-known outfits such as the Defense Intelligence Agency (DIA) and the Director of National Intelligence (DNI).

One of the most powerful, and also most secretive, of these agencies is an institution that is not even part of the U.S. government. It's an autonomous part of an emerging scheme of global governance accountable only to a small elite of central bankers, finance ministers and heads of state. That institution is the International Monetary Fund, or the IMF.

Everything about the IMF is designed to deceive you—beginning with the name. The IMF is not really a "fund" in the sense of an endowment or mutual fund; it functions as the central bank of the world, taking deposits, called "borrowings," from countries around the world and making loans to its members.

It prints money like most central banks, but this world money has the opaque name of special drawing right, or

SDR. It has a convoluted governance structure in which the highest decision-making body, the Board of Governors, has little power because the votes are weighted in favor of the largest economies, such as the U.S. Actual power rests with the blandly named International Monetary and Financial Committee, the IMFC.

Everything about the IMF is designed to make it difficult for outsiders like you to have any idea what is going on. The insiders like that arrangement just fine.

Given this culture and history, it was surprising to see the recent publication of a book by Liaquat Ahamed, *Money and Tough Love—On Tour With the IMF.* The book is the most detailed account yet from behind the scenes at IMF headquarters.

The author also reports on an IMF annual meeting in Tokyo and goes on the road with IMF "missions" as they monitor large and small governments around the world. These missions are the key to forcing governments to conform to the "rules of the game" as established by the global monetary elites.

Ahamed had difficulty getting the cooperation of the IMF and access to IMF meetings and missions he needed to write the book. In the opening section, he writes, he soon discovers that gaining access to the world behind its doors will not be easy. The fund is the repository of many secrets, which it guards ferociously. It does its work behind the scenes, out of the public eye, and has a history of being wary of the press... The fund benefits from a certain mystique that could be lost by too much openness.

In the end, Ahamed was granted access by IMF Managing Director Christine Lagarde. What follows is a revealing account that is part history, part economics and part James Bond as Ahamed travels from Washington to Tokyo; Dublin; and Maputo, Mozambique. He describes IMF interactions with other members of the global power elite as well as the IMF's member countries in both the developed world and among the poorest.

Importantly, the book is highly accessible. Ahamed avoids the arcane jargon that fills most accounts of the IMF as well as the IMF's official publications and reports. Anyone with the slightest interest in the workings of the international monetary system will find this book an excellent guide to how the IMF goes about its business on a day-to-day basis, and how the IMF has the power to make or break sovereign governments by deciding whether or not to make loans when those governments are in financial distress.

One of the book's main takeaways is the demonstration that the IMF is just as powerful as the military and CIA when it comes to forcing regime change in governments that do not follow U.S. orders. Of course, the IMF does this without firing a shot. They use money as a weapon just as effectively as the military uses special operations or the CIA uses drones.

Second, if Western nations lose votes in the IMF and those votes are given to communist China—as is currently planned—then the IMF money weapons may be aimed at the U.S. in the future.

In recent decades, the emerging markets and southern Europe have needed IMF bailouts. In the future, the U.S. may be the one that needs to be bailed out, and we may have to accept conditions imposed by China or the BRICS using the IMF as their monetary agent.

The book is also timely. While the IMF has always been opaque, its importance to global finance has waxed and waned over the decades. Now the IMF is about to enter its most powerful stage yet. Central banks bailed out the world in 2008. The next financial panic will be bigger than the ability of central banks to put out the fire. At that point, the only source of global liquidity will be the IMF itself.

The issuance of 5 trillion of SDRs, equal to $7.5 trillion, to paper over the next financial panic will be highly inflationary. The difference between this coming inflation and those in the past is that few investors will know where the inflation is coming from. Politically, it will not be easy to hold the U.S. Treasury or the Federal Reserve accountable, because they will just point a finger at the IMF.

This book will make you better acquainted than most with this hidden source of inflation. Ahamed's book is a good chance to meet the financial world's fire department before the next great fire.

▨ The Downfall of Money

Despite the widespread identification of "Weimar" with hyperinflation, few investors know the detailed history and political dynamics that led to Germany's catastrophic outcome. The facts that Germany had recently been defeated in the First World War and bore a heavy debt burden in the form of reparations to France, the U.K. and other victorious powers are necessary background.

You may also know that communists and proto-Nazis fought street battles, led regional rebellions and engaged in assassinations of high-profile political figures. But even this backdrop does not tell the whole story.

To understand exactly what happened, and why a repetition in the U.S. is a real possibility today, I highly recommend *The Downfall of Money: Germany's Hyperinflation and the Destruction of the Middle Class,* by Frederick Taylor. This is the best and most thorough account of the Weimar hyperinflation yet and is likely to remain the definitive history.

Most accounts of the Weimar hyperinflation focus on Rudolf Havenstein, the director of the Reichsbank, the central bank of Germany. Havenstein had control of the printing presses and was directly responsible for the physical production of the bank notes, eventually denominated in the trillions of marks.

At one point, the Reichsbank printed such huge volumes

of currency that they were physically constrained by paper shortages. They even resorted to printing on one side of the bank note in order to save ink, which was also in short supply. Havenstein is routinely portrayed as the villain in the story — the man whose money printing ruined the German currency and its economy.

Yet Taylor makes almost no mention of Havenstein, referring to him only a few times in this 400-page book. Instead, Taylor takes aim at the political leadership that refused to compromise on the structural reforms needed to restore growth to the German economy so it could begin to deal with its debt burden.

Politicians looked to the central bank to paper over their problems rather than fix the problem themselves. In this analysis, Havenstein is not an autonomous actor out to destroy the currency. He is simply the handmaiden of a weak, dysfunctional political class who refuse to make hard choices themselves.

This insight, which is well documented by Taylor and clearly described, is of the utmost importance as you try to assess the risks of hyperinflation in the U.S. today. Investors like to point fingers at Ben Bernanke and Janet Yellen for "printing" (actually digitally creating) trillions of U.S. dollars out of thin air.

But today's problems in the U.S. economy—too much debt and too little growth—are identical to the problems confronting Germany in 1921. Then, as now, the solutions were mainly structural. Then, as now, the politicians refused to compromise on solutions and looked to the central bank to paper over the problems. Then, as now, the central bank accommodated the politicians.

The name for this phenomenon is *fiscal dominance*, something described by former Federal Reserve Governor Frederic Mishkin in a classic academic paper in 2013. Mishkin says that central bank independence is largely a myth and only appears to be a reality during stable economic times.

But when the legislative and executive branches become dysfunctional, as they are today, and when debts and deficits spin out of control, as they appear to be, then central banks must bow to the politicians and monetize the debt by money printing. This is what happened in Germany in 1921–23. Something similar may be starting to happen in the U.S. today.

The U.S. is not yet at the point of no return that Germany reached in 1921. But it is moving in the same direction. It has a dysfunctional political class and accommodating central bankers. Taylor's book is must-read if you want to know about the warning signs of hyperinflation before its most virulent stage wipes out your savings and pensions.

Mark Twain is remarked to have said, "No occurrence is sole and solitary, but is merely a repetition of a thing which has happened before." Taylor's insightful and lucid account offers a historic guide to something that has happened before and that may repeat in the U.S. under remarkably similar conditions.

■ When Money Dies

Taylor's book is the second account of the Weimar hyperinflation published in recent years. An earlier book, *When Money Dies*, by Adam Fergusson, was republished in 2010 and received excellent reviews. I recommend it too, but it does not have the depth of Taylor's account.

Fergusson extensively chronicles events and includes moving anecdotes about food riots, starvation and suicide, showing the social impact of hyperinflation. Taylor's book does too, but dives deeper into the political dynamics that allowed the hyperinflation to begin and continue. In short, Fergusson gives you the *what* and *when* of Weimar, while Taylor gives you the *why*.

■ The Forgotten Man — A New History of the Great Depression

The Great Depression in the United States is conventionally dated from 1929–1940. It began with the stock market crash in October 1929 and only ended when the U.S. massively restructured its economy to produce war materiel, first for our allies, particularly the U.K., in 1940, and later for our own forces after the U.S. entered the Second World War, in December 1941.

Like any dating scheme, these dates are somewhat arbitrary. The U.S. Depression was part of a larger global depression that was visible in the U.K. in 1926 and in Germany in 1927 and that was not fully resolved until the new international monetary arrangements agreed upon at Bretton Woods in 1944 and implemented in the post-war years. But the core period, 1929–1940, covering President Hoover's single term and the first two terms of President Franklin Roosevelt, are the object of intensive interest by historians and scholars to this day.

The term *depression* is not well understood and is not in wide use today. Economists prefer terms like *recession*, which means two or more consecutive quarters of declining GDP with rising unemployment, and "expansion," which covers periods of rising GDP between recessions. Economists like the fact that *recession* is mathematically defined and measurable, whereas *depression* is subjectively defined and somewhat in the eye of the beholder. Policymakers avoid using words like *depression* for fear that the public may become depressed and stop spending—the opposite of what is desired. As a result, the word *depression* has been more or less swept under the rug of economic discourse today.

This is unfortunate, because the term *depression* is useful in economic analysis. *Depression* does not imply long periods of declining GDP. It is possible to have rising GDP, falling unemployment and rising stock prices in a depression. Indeed, this is exactly what happened from 1933–36, in the middle of the Great Depression.

What characterizes a depression is that growth does not return to long-term potential and total output, labor force participation and asset prices languish below prior peaks in some combination. This definition was first laid out by John Maynard Keynes in 1936 in his magnum opus, *The General Theory of Employment, Interest and Money.* It is not mathematically precise, but it is highly serviceable.

The importance of Keynes' definition is that depressions are not merely longer or more persistent versions of a recession. They are qualitatively different. A recession is a cyclical phenomenon amenable to liquidity and interest rate solutions applied by central banks, whereas depressions are structural and do not respond to central bank remedies.

Depressions are only cured by structural changes in areas such as fiscal policy, regulation and labor markets, which are not controlled by central banks, but rather by legislatures and the executive. Indeed, the U.S. is in a depression today, and its persistence is due to the fact that positive structural changes have not been implemented. Federal Reserve policy is futile in a depression.

Because depression has been dropped from the economist's tool kit, few are familiar with depression dynamics. Because the Great Depression was 80 years ago, there are few Americans alive today with living memories of it. This vacuum of analysis and experience lends urgency to the historical study of depressions, and there is no finer history of the Great Depression than Amity Shlaes' *The Forgotten Man.*

The conventional narrative of the Great Depression is known by rote. Herbert Hoover and the Federal Reserve are the typical villains who committed a series of policy blunders that first caused the Depression and then failed to alleviate it.

Franklin Roosevelt is portrayed as the hero who saved the day and led the country back to growth through activism, government programs and massive spending. This narrative has been the blueprint and justification for liberal government intervention and spending programs ever since.

What Shlaes shows is that this narrative is almost completely wrong. Her book is a kind of alternative history, but one much closer to the truth of what happened in the 1930s. She shows that there was a great deal of continuity between the Hoover and Roosevelt administrations. Both were activists and interventionists.

Both believed in public works and government spending. Major Depression-era projects such as the Hoover Dam were begun in the Hoover administration; Roosevelt merely continued such hydroelectric and flood control projects on a larger scale with his Tennessee Valley Authority and other projects.

Importantly, Roosevelt did not end the Depression in the 1930s; he merely managed it with mixed results until the exigencies of war production finally helped the U.S. escape it. Indeed, the U.S. had a severe relapse in 1937–38, the famous "recession within the Depression" that reversed some of the gains from Roosevelt's first term.

Shlaes also shines a light on the dark side of government policy in the Hoover-Roosevelt years. She exposes the admiration that many at the time had for dictators such as Mussolini and Stalin, who seemed to be achieving economic growth through top-down central planning.

She also describes the collectivist farming communities and labor concentration camps launched by the U.S. government in those years. The extent of socialist and communist leanings among major Roosevelt administration figures is well-known, and Shlaes covers that ground thoroughly.

The book is balanced in its approach. Shlaes is meticulous in describing the growth that was achieved and the jobs that were created by FDR's programs. She is also glowing in her praise for the artistic, literary and architectural achievements in those days coming from various government-sponsored programs for writers and artists and in public works.

The mystery of the Great Depression is not why it began

but why it lasted so long. The U.S. had been in a severe depression in 1921, but it lasted 18 months, not 12 years. The answer appears to be something economists call *regime uncertainty*.

The Hoover-Roosevelt programs seemed to come out of nowhere and disappear just as quickly, confusing business leaders. Programs were launched with great fanfare and then abandoned based either on Supreme Court decisions declaring them unconstitutional or because of their failures to produce results.

In response, private capital went to the sidelines and refused to invest. Instead of a labor strike, there was a capital strike. No amount of government intervention could make up for the lack of private capital investment caused by the policy uncertainty of those years.

Shlaes makes this clear both through quantitative research and through individual portraits of Andrew Mellon, Wendell Willkie and lesser-known figures such as Bill Wilson, the founder of Alcoholics Anonymous. These individuals kept private initiative alive during a decade in which government pretended to have all the answers.

Shlaes has done prodigious research and writes indelibly. Her book is worth reading for its literary and historical qualities alone. But the book carries important economic lessons for investors and policymakers today.

As the U.S. struggles through a new depression, regime uncertainty in policies such as Obamacare, environmental and Internet regulation and labor laws have once again caused capital to go on strike. The implication is that the current period of low growth in the U.S. will continue indefinitely until positive structural changes and greater clarity in public policy are achieved. This new depression may be a long one.

Shlaes' excellent book is a great work of history but an equally great guide to where we are today and where we may be heading. I recommend it to you.

CHAPTER 15
Fifty Frequently Asked Questions Answered

I often receive questions from my Strategic Intelligence subscribers. We try to get to as many of them as possible during our monthly intelligence briefings and in our monthly issues. I've noticed that many are the same. Here are thirty-five of the most frequently asked questions answered. I hope you find them useful as you invest...

1) What is one book that I can read on complexity theory?

There's a book called *Simply Complexity* by Neil Johnson. I recommend that as an introduction.

2) What, if anything, do you know about an Iraqi Dinar upward revaluation?

I have followed the Iraqi Dinar situation closely. Sadly, it appears to be a scam aimed at returning U.S. veterans of the war there and at other Americans. A story has been concocted that the Iraqi Dinar will be suddenly and radically revalued upward against the U.S. dollar. This would produce huge gains for holders of Iraqi Dinar. In fact, there is no evidence whatsoever to support this story. It's not clear how Iraqi Dinar holders would be able to convert their currency to U.S. dollars even if the revaluation did happen. Another variation of the story is that the IMF will declare the Dinar a "reserve currency." This is another fiction. There is no basis for the Dinar revaluation story and everyday investors should avoid purchases of Iraqi Dinar.

3) Would you recommend buying silver in addition to gold?

Silver has a place in investors' portfolios. I don't believe in a fixed silver/gold ratio. A lot of people put stock in that concept, but silver's harder to analyze because it's a precious metal and also an industrial input, so it moves on different vectors. That said, if gold's going to $7,000 per ounce, which I expect, silver's going to go to $100 or more. So silver's along for the ride, and I think silver has a place.

By the way, I do recommend the U.S. Mint's "Monster Box." It contains 500 1-ounce American Silver Eagles. That's good to have because if the time comes when they shut down the ATMs and you need precious metal for walking-around money to buy groceries for your family, you're not going to want to hand over a gold coin. A silver coin's probably enough. Having a monster box is a good insurance policy.

4) Do you think inflation or deflation is more likely?

I think they're both likely, and that's what makes it so challenging for investors. Again, I go back to our friend Warren Buffett. He owns hard assets as his inflation insurance. But he also has $55 billion in cash—the most cash that Berkshire Hathaway has ever had—as his deflation insurance. Buffett understands that both are possible.

I think we'll end up with inflation, but we could go through a deflationary episode first. That's why investors need a barbell approach so they're ready for both outcomes.

5) Is money safer in a small local bank or a big "mega-bank"?

Small local banks are good if they're highly rated. Some of them are solid and some are not. I don't want to get into the business of recommending banks because I don't know every investor's particular circumstances. But there are rating services out there. If it's a highly rated bank that's small and local, it may be a better option. I would also recommend just having some cash—for example, $5,000–10,000 in $100 bills—so when they shut down the ATMs you'll still have walking-around money.

6) Do you think that gold will be confiscated like it was in the 1930s?

I don't think it will be. The government might want to do that, but I think there would be pushback. In the 1930s, trust in government was much greater than it is today. People went along with it because they felt desperate. Today, they may feel desperate, but they don't trust the government. I think the government knows that.

7) Are credit unions safer than banks?

Generally, yes. Again, I don't want to be in the business of recommending specific names because I don't know everyone's circumstances. But I am familiar with the credit union business, and they're very solid. They have not been a source of any problems over the last 30 years.

8) What are the chances of gold and silver mining companies being nationalized during the crisis?

There's some possibility of that. But in countries like the United States and Canada, where there's the rule of law, they could only be nationalized on one of two bases. One is they'd have to change some laws, which you would see coming because the legislative process is so clunky. The second way is through the president's emergency dictatorial powers. When I say that, most people roll their eyes and respond, "What're you talking about? He's not a dictator." Well, in a way, he is—he's a dictator in a legal sense.

Few people know that the United States is operating under a state of emergency today. President Obama extended the state of emergency. Every September, it expires, and this past month, the president extended the state of emergency.

Using his emergency powers, the president could nationalize the mining companies. The government might do that in the extreme, but we're not at the extreme yet. I don't want to be binary and say what will happen or won't happen. What I would say is it's always a process. It's a dynamic. Some things might happen, but we'll see it coming. Again, that's the importance of being a *Strategic Intelligence* reader. You'll be the first to know.

9) Why do you recommend a 10% portfolio allocation to gold? Why not 20% or more?

I'm not giving personal portfolio advice. I want to be clear on that.

There's no smart way to give individual investors advice unless you know all their circumstances. I do have private investment clients. When you do something like that, you sit down with the individual and say, "Give me your whole portfolio. Give me your net worth. Give me your family situation. How old are you? What goals do you have?"

There's a lot of work you have to do. I'm not going to tell anyone, "You should have 10%" or "You should have 20%." Ten percent is just a general recommendation.

Gold is very volatile, so if you're liquid, have a reasonable-size net worth and you want to lean into the trade a little bit, there's nothing wrong with 20%.

10) Do you really believe gold could go to $7,000?

I'm very candid about the fact that I think gold is going to $7,000. But it could go to $800 on the way.

There could be some big jumps in between as this dynamic takes off. I think it's going to end up at $7,000, but I'm not going to say to anyone it couldn't go to $800, because it certainly could.

I think people spend too much time watching the ticker tape. Dollar by dollar, they get all excited when gold goes up a little bit and they get depressed when it goes down a little bit. I don't do that. I watch it. I analyze it. I have a view on where it's going, and I explain it in my books and in *Strategic Intelligence*.

11) What do you mean when you say store your precious metals in a "reputable nonbank vault"? Where can investors find one?

Most banks will give you a safe-deposit box, and bigger banks have vaults for large amounts of gold. Of course, the government tightly controls the banking system. At the time you want your gold, or if you really need your gold, there's a strong possibility that the banks will be closed, at least temporarily, and you won't be able to get it. That means you need to find a nonbank vault.

When I say reputable, I mean one that's been in business a long time and can give you good references and has insurance. You can find them online. They're all over the country. Just find one that suits your needs and has been around a long time. Make sure they have insurance.

12) Do you see the U.S. using bank bail-ins to recapitalize the banking system during the next crisis?

It's more than talk and more than a possibility. It's actually in one of the G-20's working documents. You can find the G-20 Finance Communiqué online, which says as much. It's just about five pages long, but there is one page of annexes and additional working papers. There were dozens of those. If you click on each one, you'll find thousands and thousands of pages. It's a bit of a geek-fest, but I did go through quite a bit of it, and the bail-in language is there.

In an extreme crisis, everybody wants his or her money back. Last time, they printed money to give people their money back. Next time, they're going to say you can't have it. Instead, they're going to close the banks and close the accounts, at least temporarily. I do see something like that happening.

13) Do platinum or palladium play a role in an investor's portfolio?

They can. I like just gold for portfolio purposes, but I think for some investors, there is a place for platinum or palladium. There's also an investment called the PMC Ounce offered by a firm called Neptune Global. That's physical metal. You actually have physical metal. It's not a derivative contract. You get all four of them.

It's better than having any one of the metals because it reduces your volatility. I think that's an attractive play.

14) Are Middle Eastern oil countries trying with concerted effort to drive down oil prices?

They certainly are, in the sense that the oil price is very much a product of output and they control the output. Saudi Arabia has reduced its output recently. The question is why. What's going on? Are they trying to put pressure on Iran? Are they trying to put pressure on Russia as part of the penalty for what they've done in Ukraine?

There are some geopolitical reasons going on behind the scenes. But I also think we have to recognize that this is part of a global slowdown. Geopolitics are always intriguing, so there could be some of that going on. It's also indicative of deflation and a global slowdown, which we're seeing around the world. I think that's going to catch up to the U.S. by early next year.

15) Do you recommend expatriation?

That's a personal decision. I'll just say that factually, expatriation is going up. There are more and more people dropping their U.S. passports. I'm a U.S. citizen. I'm proud to be a U.S. citizen. I still have my passport, and I have no plans to expatriate, personally. But it is a fact that expatriation is increasing.

16) Is there another country where a person could open a savings account that would be safe to hold funds?

I do like the Swiss banking system. The problem is you're not going to be off the radar screen. I don't, obviously, counsel any kind of tax evasion. But if you're a U.S. citizen and you have a foreign bank account, you have to check a box on your U.S. tax return, and that would certainly attract the interest of the U.S. tax authorities.

From a safety and soundness point of view, however, I like Switzerland because I think they have a well-run banking system and well-run economy. But don't think that that's going to get you off the radar screen.

17) In the coming bad period, is it good to be a lender, a borrower or neither? Should investors pay off their mortgages now, for instance?

That's really asking whether inflation or deflation is going to prevail. If inflation is going to prevail, you really don't want to pay off your debts—or at least, you don't want to accelerate the payments—because those debts could be worth a lot less in an inflationary world.

But right now, I see deflationary forces prevailing. My advice would be, if you have a legitimate reason to borrow, such as to finance a house or something like that, and you can afford it and you're not overleveraged, that's fine. I wouldn't necessarily run out to prepay a mortgage, though.

I would not be going out and borrowing a lot of money right now to lever up. That's a strategy that does work in inflation—but the inflation might not come right away. We might be facing prolonged deflation. My approach is to have a balance of hard assets and cash. The hard assets protect you in inflation. The cash protects you in deflation and reduces volatility. It's hard to know which one we're in for, so I like to prepare for both.

18) When you say "hold cash," do you mean bank notes? If so, what currency?"

When I say cash, I mean the highest-quality instruments you can get. For a U.S. investor, that would be U.S. Treasury bills or maybe some kind of one-year notes. There are foreign equivalents. Basically, find Treasury debt in your own currency. That's the lowest risk, I think. But I don't consider money market funds or bank CDs to be cash in this sense.

19) You recommend physical metals as well as long Treasury bond funds. Can both of these deliver at the same time?

The answer is no, they can't both deliver at the same time. That's exactly the point. I think people who say they know exactly what's going to happen don't really know what they're talking about. We could have inflation for a whole bunch of reasons. We could have deflation for a whole bunch of reasons. The smart investor has a little bit of protection in case of either. And by the way, the best example of that is Warren Buffett. Buffett is buying railroads, transportation assets, oil and natural gas, which are all hard assets. He also has $55 billion in cash. That way, if things do crash, you have the cash to scoop up the bargains.

20) Do you see the G-20 moving to 100% electronic currency so they can charge negative interest rates on deposits?

Yes, it's out there. Ken Rogoff and Larry Summers have mentioned it. The G-20 doesn't do anything quickly, but the move toward a cashless society, which basically means you're trapped in the banking system and they can impose negative rates, is just a way to steal your money.

That trend is pretty well underway. It's another reason to have physical gold—because it's nondigital.

21) The dialogue between Russia and the U.S. has broken down. Has the economy deteriorated so much that the U.S. will opt for war, as it has in past depressions?

That's a compound question. Putin is a noneconomic player. He's a power player.

I met with some top national security experts in Washington recently. We had CIA officials, U.S. ambassadors, think tankers, people from the Defense Department, people from the Treasury Department and people from the financial world. There were about 15 of us around the table, behind closed doors, and we talked this through.

Believe it or not, I laughed at them. I did it in a nice, respectful way, but I said, "This is the worst case of mirror imaging I've ever seen." Mirror imaging is an intelligence analytical flaw where you make the mistake of thinking the other guy thinks the way you do.

The mistake the U.S. is making is thinking that Putin thinks like us. The U.S. thinks that if we inflict enough economic pain on Putin, he'll change his behavior, because if he inflicted economic pain on us, it would change our behavior. But Putin is not like us, and we are not like him.

In other words, sanctions don't work on Putin. He has other goals, priorities and ways of thinking about it. So the short answer is no. But that doesn't mean that the U.S. won't persist in escalating the conflict because we are thinking about it the wrong way.

22) Is now a good time to consider the ruble and Russia's oil sector?

With the understanding that it is more of a speculation than investment—and only as a small slice of an investor's portfolio—I don't think it's too soon to look at Russia. The ruble has been down almost 60%. Russia's stock market is down, and their economy is in recession. That's a good time to buy, quite often. Russia's not going away. It's the eighth-largest economy in the world. It has a population of about 150 million people, is a nuclear state and heavily integrated with Europe. So Russia's not going to zero.

It might be a little early, but keep your eye on it. There will come a time soon to invest a little bit there. As always, my suggestion would be don't go all in. Have it be a slice, and do other things with your portfolio.

23) Is it possible for the U.S. government to raise interest rates? Wouldn't the cost of interest payments bankrupt the United States?

If you had normalized interest rates, meaning for this stage of recovery 3–5%, yes, that would blow a hole in the budget the size of the one that sank the Titanic. That's not what we're talking about today, however. Today, we're talking about 25 basis-point increases.

Maybe the Fed funds rate goes to 50 or 75 basis points. Maybe they try to get 10-year notes to 2.50%. I don't think any of that's going to happen, by the way, but the question is if it did happen, would it bankrupt the United States?

At higher, normalized levels, it could. But what the Fed's thinking about right now wouldn't—at least in the short run. I don't think they're going to do even those small rate increases, because I think the economy's too weak.

24) Who are the power elites that really call the shots in this country?

When I say "power elites," I'm not referring to the boogeyman or other conspiracy theories. I'm not talking about the Illuminati or anything like that, either. These are real people. We know who they are.

They are Treasury secretaries, CEOs of major banks, finance ministers, some other deputies, central bankers, Janet Yellen, Mario Draghi, etc. But also some academics and Ph.D. professors, like Larry Summers and Marty Feldstein, and some corporate CEOs of the largest corporations. It's not a huge group.

They all know each other and hang out—whether in Davos or on the sidelines of a G-20 summit or at an IMF annual meeting. They all go to the Clinton Global Initiative, and they like being in New York during the United Nations General Assembly.

I'm able to talk to a lot of them. What they tell me privately is not what they say publicly. And this is what I put in my books and in *Strategic Intelligence*. I don't always mention names, because sometimes I'm not at liberty to do so. But I do mention the conversations.

I've had conversations with central bankers, people who are on the FOMC and the Board of Governors. They tell me point-blank: We don't know what we're doing. We're making it up as we go along. Again, they will never say that publicly because it would freak people out.

Sometimes the power elite retire and new people come along. You have to watch for the newbies—guys like Michael Froman. He's not a household name, but he's one of Robert Rubin's protégés who's in very powerful positions.

The rules for the power elite club are never criticize another member and never say what you really think. The art of the exercise is to—even if you're not a full-fledged member—have at least enough access to them that you know what they are thinking.

25) What are SDRs?

As I explained in chapter 12, they're essentially world money. Now, when I say world money, it sounds kind of spooky or scary, but it actually has a funny name. It's called the special drawing right, or SDR. The global financial elites pick strange names for what they're doing so people don't understand what it is. The International Monetary Fund (IMF) can print these SDRs. They have in the past— there's nothing new about it. SDRs were created in 1969, and hundreds of billions of them have been issued over the years. But the IMF only issues them when there's a financial panic. They don't issue them every day or when times are good.

26) Will we be able to spend Special Drawing Rights (SDRs)?

You will not be able to use them, touch them or feel them. You will not be able to spend them. You will not have them.

In Philadelphia, we have something called walking-around money. SDRs are not going to be walking-around money. You'll still have dollars, but the dollars will be a local currency, not a global reserve currency. So for example, when I go to Turkey, I cash in some dollars and get some Turkish lira. I use the lira to pay for taxis in Turkey. Then when I leave, I cash them out again. That will be how the dollar is used.

You'll use the dollar when you come to the United States, but it'll be like Mexican pesos: something you use when you go there. The dollar won't be the important global reserve currency.

The SDR will be used for the settlement of the balance of payments between countries, the price of oil and perhaps the financial statements of the 100 largest global corporations.

The impact on everyday investors will be inflationary. The difference, however, is that, right now if we have inflation, everyone blames the Fed. In the future, however, you'll have inflation coming from SDRs. That means when people try to blame the Fed, the Fed will say it's not us; it's those guys over there on G Street in Northwest Washington. Go blame them. No one even knows where the IMF is. So the SDR is just a way to get inflation through the back door.

27) Can the U.S. ever recover from the economic situation it's in?

It is possible, but it's not likely. There are a set of policies that would encourage growth. The key is growth. The problem is we can't do it by printing money. We can do it by structural changes. But since the White House and the Congress aren't talking to each other, I don't see the structural changes coming.

28) If there is a "strong dollar," does that mean the dollar will not collapse?

The question confuses the cross-rate with the systemic risk. If the dollar is strong, it's strong versus euro or versus yen. The people base that on what's called the DXY, which is a dollar index. The dollar index is heavily weighted to the euro.

A strong dollar, however, doesn't mean that the whole system isn't nearing a point of collapse. Looking at the cross-rate is like you're on the Titanic while it's sinking and your chair is fine but the person's chair next to you is a little lower than yours. In other words, a strong dollar cross-rate is actually adding to the instability because it's very deflationary from a U.S. perspective.

Many people think I favor a strong dollar.

What I favor is a stable dollar. It could be stable at a strong level, but the point is when you go from 2011, when the dollar was collapsing, to 2015, when the dollar is king of the hill, there is enormous volatility, which is very destabilizing.

The death of the dollar or the collapse of the international monetary system means a loss of confidence in money as a store of value by markets, investors and people around the world.

You might get paid in dollars, but you don't want them. You take them and you turn them into something else: land, hard assets, gold, silver, fine art or whatever.

If that's happening to the dollar, it'll be happening to everything else at the same time. There's no way that confidence in the dollar is going to collapse without confidence in other countries' currencies collapsing also. You're not going to have a crisis of confidence in the dollar when everyone demands euros.

I would not judge the state of the dollar or international monetary system based on cross-rates. I would judge it based on the instability of the system as a whole.

29) Should investors consider buying Treasury inflation-protected securities (TIPS)?

They have a place. They're a kind of cash equivalent with an inflation insurance policy inside. They are also very liquid. They give you liquidity and safety, which is good in deflation, but they have an inflation protection built in too. In the short term, TIPS are actually one instrument that covers both sides of a barbell strategy.

In *Strategic Intelligence,* we've recommended 10-year notes, which are on the deflation side of the barbell, and some gold, which is the inflation side. But short-term TIPS are right there in the middle and might be worth considering.

30) What's the difference between Austrian economics and complexity theory?

They have a lot in common. Complexity theory is a branch of science that only emerged in the 1960s. It's a relatively new science. It's come a long way in 50 years, but as the history of science goes, complexity theory is relatively new and a lot of that has to do with computers. When you want to actually solve complexity problems, you need massive computing power, and that didn't exist prior to the 1960s.

The main Austrians, going back to Carl Menger, Ludwig von Mises and Friedrich Hayek, were doing their work in the late 19th and 20th centuries. That's why there's little overlap with them. What Hayek said, however, was exactly what complexity theory says. Essentially, central planning will always fail. This is what he said in *The Road to Serfdom,* and what he said in one of his very influential articles.

Hayek said that nobody is smart enough or has enough information to plan an economy, no matter how much power they have. At the time, he was thinking the Soviet Union.

That's exactly what a complexity theorist would say, too. They would say that economic phenomena are what are called "emerging properties." They seem to come out of nowhere. They come out of the decisions of tens of thousands, or millions or tens of millions or hundreds of millions of market participants all individually expressing a certain preference, but collectively producing results that no individual could possibly foresee.

I get into debates with hard shell Austrian economists all over the world. I am not anti-Austrian economics. I think Austrian economics has a lot to offer. The only thing I would say is that science moves on, and there are new tools that we can use to get an even better understanding of the world.

I like to use Austrian economics the same way Einstein used Newton. Einstein produced a special theory of relativity, which overthrew part of what Newton said about gravity. That doesn't mean Newton was a dope; it just means Newton took the science so far and Einstein built on it. Einstein would agree with that, and said as much.

Likewise, it doesn't mean Austrian economics is wrong, but that complexity theory can advance the state of the art. The way I shut down the debate is by saying that if von Mises were alive today, he would be a complexity theorist.

31) How is it that the "powers that be" still allow you access when you warn everyday investors about the things policymakers are doing to muck up the economy?

The short answer is that no one allows me to do anything. I do what I want.

This is a very loaded question. It suggests that I am a government puppet and that the government is a monolithic, unified force. All of that is wrong and untrue.

I do a lot of work for the U.S. government. I have been a government contractor. I've worked on government projects. I talk to government officials all the time. If you knew how messed up they are, you'd be a lot more relaxed about conspiracy theories.

There is no "government." There are many, many, many agencies, individuals, bureaus, departments and branches all over the country and the world—and certainly all over Washington, D.C., and northern Virginia.

I like to joke that we have two governments: the downtown government and the Virginia government. Downtown are the Treasury and the Fed, and in Virginia are the Pentagon and the intelligence community.

The simple fact is that the government is not monolithic. You can go around the different agencies of the government, as I do, and hear different views. People reach out to me, saying, "Jim, you won't believe what my boss is doing," or "I can't even believe what my agency is doing."

There are individuals who are dealing in good faith, are working hard and are patriotic, who don't like what they see inside the bigger nexus. My advice is not to assume the government's monolithic or uniform.

One thing I've heard my whole career, which is now tiptoeing up to the 40-year mark, is, "Jim, you never do what anybody tells you." There's some truth in that, and I think that's good, because it enables me to have some originality, which is what I try to bring to my *Strategic Intelligence* newsletter. People who know me well will understand this, too.

The notion that the insiders have wound me up like a clock or a little robot and turned me loose to warn the world is not true. I take it upon myself to do what I do. I always tell people my 84-year-old mother motivates me. She lives on a retirement check. Thank goodness she's fine, but there's nobody who's more vulnerable to inflation than my mother because she relies on that check to make her ends meet.

She's a good anchor for me. She helps me think of the tens or maybe scores of millions of Americans who are in the same place. They are why I do what I do. Those are the people who are victimized, who are most likely to be victimized again and have always been victimized throughout history by inflation. Meanwhile, it's always the insiders, the hedge fund types and the government officials who see it coming and are in the position to protect themselves. Candidly, there are probably people who I've spoken to who wouldn't be entirely happy if they knew what I wrote in *Strategic Intelligence*, but maybe they're not subscribers.

My point is that the picture's a lot more nuanced and complex. The government's a lot more diverse. There are people inside who don't like what they see, and any suggestion that I'm operating within a monolithic system isn't true.

32) What does your personal portfolio look like? What percentage of your money is in physical gold and/or silver, and do you own any stocks?

My personal portfolio is a blend of cash, fine art, gold, silver, land and private equity. I do not own any publicly traded stocks or bonds, partly due to restrictions under various regulatory requirements applicable to my role as a portfolio strategist and newsletter writer.

The mix in my portfolio changes from time to time based on valuations of the particular asset classes. My recommended mix is 10% precious metals, 10% fine art, 30% cash, 20% land and 30% alternatives such as hedge funds, private equity and venture capital.

Currently, my personal allocation is overweight land, fine art and private equity and underweight cash and precious metals. However, this will change, because the fine art fund is currently making profit distributions, which are being reallocated to gold at what I consider to be a good entry point, and to cash.

All investors should be able to purchase precious metals and land and hold cash without difficulty. Alternatives such as hedge funds, private equity and venture capital are not open to all investors, because they are frequently traded as private funds limited to accredited investors who can pay the high minimum subscription amounts.

If you are unable to purchase such private investments, there are still publicly traded equities such as high-quality bond funds and companies holding hard assets in energy, transportation, natural resources and agriculture that offer good protection from the dual dangers of inflation and deflation.

33) I read in the introduction of your book *Currency Wars* about the possibility of an 80–98% "windfall profits tax" on gold (if and when it goes up to $7,000-plus per ounce). If that happens, wouldn't that mitigate the benefits of holding gold?

My reference to a future windfall profits tax on gold in the introduction to *Currency Wars* was intended to form a contrast to the confiscation of gold in 1933. The point simply is that the government sometimes works to suppress the price of gold, but when gold goes up anyway, the government finds a way to steal the profits from private investors. A windfall profits tax is one way to do this, but not the only way. I mentioned it as an illustration of what could happen, not as a hard-and-fast prediction.

The possibility of such a tax is not a reason to avoid holding gold today. The surge in the dollar price of gold that I expect has barely begun. If the price does move up sharply, there should be time to sell the gold at a high level and reinvest in another asset class, such as land or fine art, that is less likely to be targeted for confiscatory taxation by the government.

Of course, deciding when the profits on gold are large enough to justify the pivot into other hard assets will not be an easy call, but that's one of the things I will be thinking about and pointing out to *Strategic Intelligence* readers in the months and years ahead.

34) Why do you think that there is a corporate debt problem? Aren't U.S. companies sitting on hoards of cash?

Debt comes in many forms, including high-quality U.S. Treasury debt, high-grade corporate debt and junk bonds. Debt is also issued by both U.S. companies and foreign companies. Some of the foreign corporate debt is issued in local currencies and some in dollars. In discussing debt defaults, it's necessary to keep all of these distinctions in mind.

The U.S. companies sitting on hoards of cash, such as Apple, IBM and Google, are not the ones I'm concerned about; they will be fine. The defaults will be coming from three other sources.

The first wave of defaults will be from junk bonds issued by energy exploration and drilling companies, especially frackers. These bonds were issued with expectations of continued high energy prices. With oil prices at $60 per barrel or below, many of these bonds will default.

The second wave will be from structured products and special-purpose vehicles used to finance auto loans. We are already seeing an increase in subprime auto loan defaults. That will get worse.

The third wave will come from foreign companies that issued U.S. dollar debt but cannot get easy access to U.S. dollars from their central banks or cannot afford the interest costs now that the U.S. dollar is much stronger than when the debt was issued.

The combined total of all three waves—energy junk bonds, auto loans and foreign corporations—is in excess of $10 trillion, more than 10 times larger than the subprime mortgages outstanding before the last crisis, in 2007.

Not all of these loans will default, but even a 10% default rate would result in over $1 trillion of losses for investors, not counting any derivative side bets on the same debt. This debt will not default right away and not all at once, but look for a tsunami of bad debts.

35) How do alternative investments (like land and art) fit into your inflation/deflation thesis? What do they help protect against?

Inflation is a general rise in price levels, so things like gold, fine art and land will almost certainly go up in price. The value of money goes down, and the value of these tangible assets, hard assets, goes up, so you're going to preserve wealth by investing in them. Sometimes they'll outperform because there's a slight quality. People start dumping money—literally dumping money, because they're not sure of money as a store of value—and rushing into art and gold. We're not there yet; we're far from it, but at that point, you'll have to put your bubble hat on and say, "When is gold a bubble? When is fine art a bubble?" In my view, they're both very far away from bubble status right now, so these are interesting entry points, and they'll do very well in inflation.

Deflation, of course, is a decline in the level of prices, and investors say, "Why would I want to buy something that's going to go down?" Yes, gold could go down in deflation. Art could go down in deflation. But I think we have to define going down. It's going down in nominal space. That is, the dollar price can go down, but what's really happening is that the value of the dollar's going up, and you have to ask yourself a couple questions. One, how am I doing relative to other asset classes? In other words, if the price level goes down 10% and the nominal value of your asset goes down 5%, you actually made 5% in real terms. It's very hard for people to understand. You're talking about subtracting, and maybe it's nonintuitive math, but if the price level dropped 10% and your asset only went down 5%, you outperformed—you actually made real money. So again, I think of it as a store of wealth.

Inflation and deflation are just two sides of the same coin, no pun intended. What they really mean is price instability, and both are very damaging. Inflation destroys the real value of capital, and deflation destroys capital in different ways because people can't pay their debts and they go bankrupt and have distress sales and all that. What you want, of course, is price stability. So I think of art, gold and land as doing well in both inflation and deflation, not because the nominal price is always going up, but because they're real stores of value at a time when the value of money is uncertain.

36) Is the U.S. fracking industry flexible enough to ramp production back up quickly when oil prices start to climb again?

The industry is flexible enough, but will the money be there? What I mean is this: Saudi Arabia wants to put the frackers out of business, and they are doing so, but it doesn't happen overnight. They're actually going to increase production in the short run. But let's say it's now late 2016, so we've had two years of low oil prices. And fields have been shut in. Guys have been laid off. Contracts have been canceled, rig counts down. The thing about fracking is it's a lot easier to find the oil, but the wells have a shorter life. So frackers have a higher probability of hitting oil, and they can pump like crazy, but the well has a shorter life. But then they just drill more wells. And the fracking industry is very different from the oil wildcat days. So the point is, the way you expand production in fracking is by constantly drilling new wells, and it's the new well that gets shut in, not the old ones.

So once the old ones are dry, and the new ones haven't been launched because the price isn't right. Now the fracking industry has dried up. So the question is can the frackers get back in business quickly? The answer is yes, but the question is will they get the money? If you've got to write off a trillion dollars of bad debt because you couldn't pay your bills from the last time, are the junk bond funds and the lenders and the banks going to be there to lend the money to expand production? That's the question. I don't know. On the one hand, people, no matter how many times they get whacked by a two-by-four, seem to be ready to write more checks. But to the extent that Wall Street has put this high-yield debt into funds and crammed it into 401(k)s, you know if you get these write-offs, will they even notice? It's hard to say.

But I think that my expectation would be that production would ramp up slowly. And there's another factor. Again, put this in dynamic space. So let's just say the price of oil goes back up to $80 in late 2016/early 2017. So fracking looks economic again. And let's just say that investors have short memories and Morgan Stanley's sitting there saying, "We'll underwrite some more junk bonds. We'll sell it to a bunch of people who don't know what they're buying." So we got the money, right. But then do you want to do it, because Saudi Arabia can just take the price down again. In other words, as long as Saudi Arabia is sitting there with a baseball bat ready to smack the fracking industry, how attractive is the fracking industry? The technology is there; the money may or may not be there remains to be seen. But the threat of Saudi Arabia is not going away.

And so until the nominal price goes up because of inflation, I don't think oil will go up. But I don't see inflation in the short run. It's not just the nimbleness of the frackers but the financing capacity and the ability of Saudi Arabia to do it again that could stand in the way of bad fracking coming online.

37) What could cause Saudi Arabia and others to stop using the petrodollar?

Well I think they're already tiptoeing up to that. These things don't happen overnight, but the United States stabbed Saudi Arabia in the back from a geopolitical national security point of view. Remember the petrodollar deal was a two-sided deal. Saudi's side of the deal was we'll price oil in dollars. Everybody needs oil. Therefore, everybody needs dollars. Therefore, the dollar will remain the dominant reserve currency, which is a good deal for the United States because we can print it and pay our bills. So that was Saudi Arabia's side of the deal, and it benefited us. So what was our side of the deal? What did the United States promise in exchange for that?

We promised to preserve the rule of the House of Saud and to preserve the national security of Saudi Arabia. Well we reneged on our side of the deal, and it wasn't a problem in the '70s because Saudi Arabia's didn't hate the Shah because the

Shah was not leading the Jihad against the rest of Islam. But Iran is. Iran is an exporter of terrorism, instability and Shia theology, and the Shah wasn't any of those three things. So maybe the Saudis can live with the Shah, but they can't live with the Iranians. I just see this instability continuing, and Saudi Arabia is going to look more and more away from the United States toward China.

With the inclusion of the yuan in the SDR basket, Saudi Arabia is going to deepen their relationship with China. China's become their biggest customer. It's not as if they're going to price oil in yuan tomorrow, although they could start doing that.

You might start to see oil/yuan trade deals. So Saudi Arabia will sell their oil for yuan. What do they do with the yuan? That's the problem. China will pay them in yuan, but what are they going to do with it? I mean how many Chinese exports do they need? Not that many. And so they end up having to swap the currency, and they know they're sort of stuck in dollars whether they like it or not. But at the margin, I'd include the yuan and the SDR. I think what I would expect is that you'll start to see oil priced in SDRs. Maybe in late 2016/2017, there will be a tendency to start pricing things in SDRs. China will be happy with that. China doesn't want the yuan as the world currency because that actually reduces their degrees of freedom. They want the SDR as the world currency, but they want one other thing first.

They want a bigger vote at IMF, which they don't have today. So watch for that. Watch for China to be given a bigger vote at the IMF. That's less certain maybe this year or next year. But that happens, the IMF can start to roll out the SDR as the world money. The implication of that for the United States is not that the dollar goes away. It's just that its role is diminished, and it's probably inflationary, but not yet. Again, you can see a trend two or three years out, but that doesn't mean that you wake up tomorrow and trade on it, because two years out is a long time. You can lose money being right. You can be right two years from now, but you can lose a lot of money in the meantime. So I'm not looking for inflation tomorrow; I am looking for it a couple years out.

38) Could the Asian Infrastructure Investment Bank (AIIB) compete with the IMF or the SDR?

It's kind of mixing apples and oranges. The AIIB is a bank like any other. Everyone puts in capital. They just closed a subscription period. Quite a few countries around the world—not the United States and Japan, but a lot of other important countries—signed up. They're all going to send in their subscriptions, almost like a private placement. You sign your subscription book, send in your money and you're in. It will be based in Beijing, and will lend money initially for Asian infrastructure projects. And there are plenty of those to build—natural gas pipelines, oil pipelines, railroads, highways, airports, etc.

But like any bank, they're going to leverage. Now here's where it gets interesting. So you've got I think the initial capital is $50 billion, which is a lot of money, but you have potentially hundreds of billions, even trillions of dollars of infrastructure projects, so how do you leverage that up? Well the way you do it is by borrowing money, so you got a capital base and then you issue bonds, and then you take the bond proceeds and you go make loans to do your projects. So the importance of it, the reason all these countries signed up is, I borrowed some money, I'm going to make a loan, I'm going to build an airport or a railroad. Who gets the contract, right? Do I call a Canadian company? Do I call a U.S. company, or do I call a German company? Who's getting those multibillion-dollar contracts to go build the stuff?

That's where the action is because that's where the profit is.

So the bank is really just an intermediary to make loans to build structures. The real question is what construction companies get the contracts? The reason England and the U.K. and Germany and all these countries signed up is they want the contracts for their construction companies. British Airways, British BEI and British Aeronautics Enterprises and so forth, they want those contracts. Then that begs another question, which is if the AIIB is going to borrow, what currency is it going to borrow in? Dollars? Maybe. But do you want a dollar balance sheet? My estimate is they're going to borrow in SDRs, because they don't want to do it in yuan. The yuan is an up-and-coming trade currency, but it hasn't really found its legs as a reserve currency. It's getting there, but that'll take time, and it has to do with bond markets. But this is sort of a two-for, because now if you build the AAIB balance sheet and you start borrowing in SDRs, you're creating SDR bonds. And then Goldman Sachs can start trading the bonds.

And all of a sudden you wake up and there's an SDR bond market out there. Well, the bigger the SDR bond market, the more useful the SDR is as a reserve currency. So this is all connected. Now the question is: Is China doing this to in effect pick a fight with the IMF? The answer is no. China's in the IMF, obviously; they want a larger voice in the IMF. They want more votes at the IMF. They have a wish list of things at the IMF. They don't really want to pick a fight with the IMF. But the U.S. Congress is refusing to pass legislation that would give China what it wants, and I'm not quite sure what the U.S. is thinking. We should want to be friends with China. But the U.S. is standing in China's way because we have some stuff that we want from China.

China needs a forcing strategy. It's like any negotiation. You come in, you need some chips on your side of the table. You can't be negotiating with the other guy with no chips. So China is building the BRICS bank, the AAIB. They're building this whole parallel structure to the Bretton Woods institution, not because they want to turn their backs on Bretton Woods, but because they want to be in Bretton Woods at a higher level. So I'm not saying this bank is not important. It's happening, and it's going to work to the disadvantage of the United States because U.S. companies are not going to get these contracts if the U.S. is not in this bank. The U.S. won't join the bank because they wanted to support the World Bank for the same thing, or the Asian Development Bank, which is kind of run by the U.S. in Japan. But China is using this to force Congress to give it what it wants so it can have a bigger role in the IMF.

39) Given the threat of losing digital assets, does it makes sense to request physical stock certificates to prove ownership?

No, because legally, under the uniform commercial code, your account statement is as good as a stock certificate. In other words, if you have an account statement from Merrill Lynch or Charles Schwab, that does legally mean something, and if you had your stock certificate, that would legally mean something. I guess the question is if you get your stock certificates and put them in a safe or safe-deposit box and then the market closes, what are you going to do? Go out on the street and try to sell it to somebody passing by. You're still effectively relying on the market for your liquidity. That's what markets are supposed to do. They're supposed to give you liquidity in addition to price, discovery and providing venue for IPOs. They're not supposed to be gambling casinos. And they're not supposed to be digital targets, but they are. My advice there would be to have some of your assets not in the stock market. So if you do have some assets in the stock market, I'm not sure getting your physical stock certificate puts you any further ahead. But because you should have your accounts, you do have some written evidence of your ownership. I'm not saying that goes away. I'm just saying that digitally, it can be attacked and you have to restore these records. That burden is really going to be on the broker. You would have to have a good legal claim based on your account statement. It would be the broker's problem to kind of re-establish the title to that stock if it were some kind of digital attack on the stock market.

So I don't think paper certificates are really the answer. I think the answer is to have some of your assets of things that are not paper or digital but are physical.

40) Everyone is saying to get your money out of the U.S. banking system, but no one is saying specifically how to do that. Do you have any recommendations, or is the only safe way to empty your bank accounts just buying things?

One way to hold cash not in the banking system is to buy Treasury notes—Treasury bills. You can buy them directly. The U.S. Treasury has a system called Treasury Direct that you can use to buy Treasury bills online. When you pay for them, you would electronically credit your bank account and then debit Treasury Direct, so your bank account would go down. Then, on Treasury Direct's system, you would show up as the owner of a Treasury bill. So there is a way to do that. But as far as getting cash out, I think it's too late for that. If people asked me how the war on cash is going, I would say it's over. The government won.

41) Do credit unions provide protection against bail-ins in the U.S.?

There's no absolute protection, but obviously credit unions are safer than banks. But again, I think the key is to look at the deposit insurance and make sure you don't have more than the insured deposit level, and if you do, spread it among multiple banks.

42) How do you feel about emerging-market fixed-income allocations? Are there any areas that should be avoided?

Well, the problem with fixed income is you've got opposite forces. On the one hand, any fixed income instrument could rally on cheaper interest rates, but on the other hand, you've got the currency exposure. So if it's currency-hedged, fixed-income emerging markets, that's interesting, But the problem is what you make on capital gains you could lose on the currency. So it's a little tricky that way.

Whenever I talk about fixed income, I immediately distinguish between sovereign debt and corporate debt. Sovereign debt might be fine—I think Malaysia's not going broke, but some of the corporate companies might, so I'm a lot more positive on some of the emerging-market sovereign debt than I am on the corporate debt. I would keep away from Brazil, though. Brazil looks like a mess right now.

43) There's overwhelming evidence that the gold market is being manipulated and the price is capped. What is to prevent this from going on indefinitely? And if it can go on indefinitely, why invest in gold if there's no hope for true price discovery?

With regard to manipulation, it absolutely goes on. There's very good evidence for it. I talk about this in my book, *The Death of Money*, in Chapter 9 and Chapter 11. My advice is to get over it. I mean, it's policy, right? So countries have interest rate policies, they have tax policies, they have foreign exchange policies and they have a policy on gold. They don't talk about it. Nobody talks about it publicly, but the governments have been in the gold market for 3,000 years, so you should expect that will continue to be the case.

First of all, I don't accept the fact that it's all about price sup-pression. The government actually wants the price to go up, but they want it to go up in an orderly way. They don't want it to go up in a disorderly way. That's a really important dis-tinction to bear in mind. What we saw in August 2011, when gold went to $1,900, that was getting disorderly because that run—it was chugging along, it was $1,200, $1,300, $1,400—but that run from about $1,600–1,900 going closer to $2,000 was a spike. I mean, I looked at that and thought, "This is like a mini-bubble inside a much longer trend." If it had hit $2,000, that would've changed the psychology, and maybe next stop would have been $3,000.

So governments definitely organize. They definitely crushed the price then, but it wasn't all about keeping the price low; it was about keeping it orderly. Governments want inflation. And they've said that. It's not secret. Janet Yellen says it every time she opens her mouth. Well, if you're going to have inflation, the price of gold is going to go up. So you can't say that they're suppressing the price of gold. What I would say is they want the increase to be orderly.

So why buy gold? Well, the answer is: These manipulations fail in the end. They don't fail in the short run, but they always fail in the long run. Look at the history. The London gold pull in 1968. The U.S. and the IMF dumping 1,400 tons in the late '70s. Gordon Brown dumping most of England's gold in 1999. They always fail in the end. But they do work in the short run.

So what I counsel investors is to have your 10% allocation and be patient.

44) Why does the U.S. government keep the old $42.00 per ounce gold price on its books instead of marking it to

market? Wouldn't raising the price make the Fed and the Treasury's finances look a whole lot better?

It's an accounting convention. Generally accepted accounting principle says you keep most things at a historic cost unless they're tradable or investable assets. If you're a bank or a financial institution and you've got things that you might trade before maturity or you're a hedge fund, for example, you do have to mark things to market, but most things, if you have a building and you paid $1 million for it and it's worth $5 million, you'll carry it on your books at $1 million. So it's really just an accounting convention. Everyone knows what the price of gold is and everyone knows how much gold we have, so it's eighth-grade math. I don't think it's that big a deal.

45) Will the crash look like high volatility or one great steep plunge?

Both. It's kind of like small earthquakes before a big one. I would expect to see volatility pick up. In fact, we're seeing it already. Look what happened at the end of August and October 2015. But there will be something that is a lot more dramatic. By the way, it doesn't happen in a day. This is a big system. What happens is the stock market goes down 2%, which is a 360 point day and everybody goes, "Oh, it was a bad day," but then people on CNBC and Wall Street say, "Well, buy the dips." And then it goes down 2% the next day, another 360 points, and people start selling. And then it goes up, and they go, "Oh, man, that was so stupid, I'm going to buy again." And it goes down again.

You get this really jagged pattern. And you have to stay focused on the trend. Don't get too hung up on the day to day, because there'll be good days and bad days. That's what volatility is. But what happens is that it's down 2000 points before you know it. You're looking at the good days and trying to buy the dips and be nimble, but it just keeps going down and down and down, and then it will rally back and then go down again. It's not easy; it's nerve-wracking. But it could go down 30% in a matter of a few months. It's not going to be one day. If it started to do that, they would shut the markets. Don't rule that out either. That's a reason to have cash and gold. But it will go down a lot in a fairly short period of time. A short period of time is two months, but that's really fast for the market to go down 30%. So don't be surprised if that happens.

46) If the critical countries continue to devalue in a coordinated manner, what prevents this fiasco, the monetary system, from continuing, say, another 10 years?

Well, the monetary system can continue for 10 years, but the question is, what about inflation? In other words, if the solution to everything we're talking about is SDRs or more money printing, you'll get the inflation. To be candid, the Fed printed $4 trillion in the last six years and we did not get inflation. That's because printing money alone is not enough to cause inflation. I've said before, it's a ham and cheese sandwich. Printing money is the ham, but you need the cheese. You can't make a ham and cheese sandwich with just ham. Well, what's the cheese? The cheese is philosophy; the cheese is psychological. You've got all this money out there — I've never seen so much money — but people don't want to spend it. They don't want to borrow it. Banks don't want to lend it. So unless you get the lending-and-spending machine going, you're not going to get the inflation.

So how do you change that? It's psychological. And I don't see anything in the short run changing the psychology, and it won't change unless there's a shock. The problem with a shock is that it could change all at once. In other words, instead of kind of gradual inflation, which is what the Fed wants, it could go from zero to two to three to nine in a heartbeat if people suddenly wake up and say, "You know what, now I'm on the other side of the trade. I'm dumping these dollars as fast as I can."

So that's how it works, and that's why I like a portfolio that's positioned for both.

47) You have talked about that buying physical gold, buying American Eagles, and American Buffaloes. What is the use of gold bars, though? If I buy gold bars as insurance, I can't use them in exchange in crisis time like I would, maybe a silver coin or a gold coin, if I was exchanging for groceries or something a little bit larger. What are gold bars good for?

It depends how much money you have. If you have $10 million, that's a lot of coins. So if I was investing $10 million dollars in gold, I'd have maybe $9 million in bars. I'd have 1 kilo for my bars and take $1 million in coins.

By the way, I just want to make it clear, I do not foresee, and I have never said I foresee, the end of the world. Apocalypse, end of the world—those worlds get put in my mouth a lot by other people, but I've never said them, nor do I see that happening. However, could you see a breakdown of critical infrastructure, power grid out for a power of time, exchanges close, banks closed, people reverting to a slightly more agrarian kind of society, sure, I think all those things are possible, maybe even likely.

There may come a time, by the way, this is not that real. I lived without power for eight days during hurricane Sandy. I lived in Connecticut. We lost power for eight days. Some people had generators, some didn't, but gas stations were closed, ATM's were closed. Some of the stores had generators, but you get by. In a more extreme scenario, I'd recommend a monster box.

A monster box is 500 1-ounce American Silver Eagles. You have 500 silver coins. At the market, they're about $15 apiece, maybe they'll be worth more in extreme circumstances. Maybe if it's just deflation, the purchasing power will go up, and if you want to go out on your bicycle and get groceries, or farm fresh produce for your family in a disruptive situation, I'd rather have a silver coin than a gold coin. Because a gold coin is probably a year's worth of groceries, the silver coin might be a week's worth of groceries or a couple days' worth of groceries.

I wouldn't picture myself sitting there with a file and a knife, shaving little chips off a gold coin to buy groceries. I would just pull out a silver dollar. For that kind of walking around money, get a monster box. It's about $9,000 at the market, but get one of those. Put it in a safe place. That's your walking around money. To preserve wealth, I recommend 10% gold. I think American Gold Eagles are what I recommend. The Buffaloes are out there also, but as far as bars are concerned, it all depends on how much you have.

If you're putting $100,000 in, if you have $1 million in liquid assets, I recommend 10%, so that's $100,000 in gold. That would be 80 1-ounce coins, and you can hold them in one hand. It's kind of heavy, but it's not too much to carry around. If you're investing $20 million or $30 million, then you're not going to spend it all. No one is going to spend $30,000,000. If you do want to preserve $30 million in wealth, that's where the bars would come in handy. The idea is you're not to spend a bar but to keep it and give it to your children.

48) What do you think the impact of helicopter money will be?

Helicopter money will get you the inflation that they've been looking for, for eight years. A lot of people say "Gee, you've had rates at zero for seven years, from 2008–2015. You've raised them minuscule amounts, 25 basis points now. Where's the inflation? Oh, and you printed $4 trillion."

The answer to that is money printing alone does not cause inflation. Causing inflation by printing money is like making a ham and cheese sandwich with ham. You need the cheese. The cheese is philosophy, which is the turnover of money. All the money printing in the world won't get you inflation unless people borrow it and spend it, and they're not right now. The banks don't want to lend. People don't want to borrow, and they don't want to spend.

If people get money through the gasoline price cut, they'll pay off debt or save it before they'll go out and spend it. We're not seeing the inflation from monetary policy. The central banks want inflation. The governments want inflation, there's no question about it. The way you get it is with helicopter money, which is where you combine fiscal and monetary policy.

The sequence is: get larger deficits, spend more money, have the Treasury cover the deficit by issuing more debt and then have the Fed monetize the debt by buying the bonds and printing money. It's like QE. Whenever the Fed buys bonds, that is QE. Instead of doing the kind of QE where you give the money to the banks and the banks give it back to the Fed in the form of excess reserves, you buy bonds that are used to cover deficits to cover government spending. The government spends the money. They'll spend the money, believe me, somebody will get that money.

Whether it's for liberal social programs, or conservatives want to spend on defense, that's a political choice. One way or another, they'll spend the money, or get it out there. That's what helicopter money is. Will it cause inflation? If you do enough of it, it will. That's also six months away.

A problem that I think a lot of market participants have is that some of these things move slowly. I'm talking about negative rates in the middle of 2017. I'm talking about helicopter money in the middle of 2017 in a new administration. You can see these things coming, but people are like "Gee, I think helicopter money is coming tomorrow. I think negative rates are coming tomorrow."

You say "No, they're not." And then they forget about it. Unfortunately, we live in this age of a two-second attention span, and I like to make the point that you can definitely see both of these things coming. You can see helicopter money coming. You can see negative rates coming, but they're probably a year away. Maybe a little bit longer. That's a long time for people to stay focused on it, but of course, that's what we do.

At *Strategic Intelligence,* we stay focused on it. We update continually. If there are changes, we'll be the first ones to shout them out, but this thing is moving at the pace of a glacier. It's not moving at the pace of a roller coaster. You still have to pay attention, because a glacier can move a mountain, but it takes time.

49) When you talk about "official gold," what is official gold?

Official gold is gold held by central banks, and finance industries in sovereign wealth funds. Since the gold owned by countries is distinct by the gold owned by private individuals. You may have some gold in a private vault, you may have some rings or watches or necklaces or earrings or jewelry or whatever that's gold, but that gold is not supporting the money supply. That's your gold. That's your wealth. Indian brides wear gold around their necks. It looks pretty, but that's actually wearable wealth. That's their bank account. That's their 401(k).

All that private gold is wealth to individuals, but it's not available to split the money supply. It could be, if central banks want to go out and buy it. Print money and buy gold necklaces from Indian brides or gold bars from some of the listeners on the call. That's fine. That's no different than buying bonds. The Fed prints money and buys bonds today. Well, the Fed could print money and buy gold if they wanted to. You can increase this supply of official gold, but at any given point, your money supply is not being supported by private gold; it's being supported by official gold, the gold that's held by central banks.

That's about 35,000 tonnes, which is a relatively small part of all the gold. All the gold in the world is about 180,000 tonnes.

50) If banks aren't a safe place for cash because of risks of bail-ins or negative interest rates, how safe is keeping cash in a brokerage account?

It's worse. When you keep cash in a brokerage account using a money market fund—and the FCC just changed the rules last year—that money market funds can suspend redemptions, which was not true before. In 2008, money market funds did not have the ability to suspend redemptions. Americans were pulling tens of billions of dollars out of the money market funds. That was what gave Bernanke a heart attack. That's when Bernanke went over to Paulson in the White House and said if you don't do something in the next day or two, the whole system is going to collapse.

They changed the rules that money market funds can suspend redemptions. Now, a bank can close, and the money market fund can close, but it's a lot easier for the money market funds to close, than it is for the banks. I'm not a big fan of lots of cash in the bank, but it's safer than money market funds.

Conclusion

Money is transitory, and wealth is permanent. A lot of people confuse money and think, Well, I have a lot of money, so I'm wealthy.

In the short run, that may be true, but in the longer run, the money can go away. Wealth, on the other hand, is something that prevails. The value of money may collapse, but there are things you can do and strategies you can pursue to create and preserve wealth that will survive a monetary collapse.

When everyone else is getting wiped out, just surviving is coming out ahead. That said, I think it's possible for you to outperform most other asset classes and actually increase your net worth in real terms in the process.

You always have to think about things in real terms. It's not enough to talk about things in nominal terms. The stock market could go to 40,000. If the dollar loses 95% of its purchasing power, what good is Dow 40,000 if the dollar is only worth a nickel?

That's why it's imperative you prepare now. You can't wait until the crisis strikes. A lot of things could cause the next crisis. It could be a failure to deliver physical gold because gold's getting scarce. It could be a Lehman type of collapse of a financial firm or another MF Global. It could be a prominent suicide. It could be a natural disaster. It could be defaults in the junk bond market. It could be a lot of things, but my point is it doesn't matter. It will be something.

What matters today is that the system is so unstable. The blunders have already been made. The risk is already there, embedded in the system. We're just waiting for that catalyst to trigger the collapse. It will happen sooner, rather than later. This is not necessarily something that's going to happen tomorrow—although it could—but it's not a 10-year forecast, either, because we're not going make it that far.

The dynamics—what are called the scaling metrics or the size of the system—are an exponential function. What that means is that when you triple the size of the system, you don't triple the risk. You increase risk by 10 or *100 times*. That's what we've done today.

So I would say two things. First, the crisis could happen very suddenly, and likely you won't see it coming. Investors always say to me, "Jim, call me up at 3:30 the day before it happens and I'll sell my stocks and buy some gold."

But it doesn't work that way, for the reasons I just explained. And even if it did, you might not be able to get the gold. That's very important to understand.

When a buying panic breaks out and the price of gold starts gapping up not by $10 or $20 per ounce per day but by $100 and then $200 per ounce and then, all of sudden, it's up $1,000 per ounce, people will say, "I have to get some gold." At that point, you won't be able to get it.

The big players will get it: The sovereign wealth funds, the central banks, the billionaires and the multibillion-dollar hedge funds—they'll be able to get it. But everyday investors won't be able to get it.

You'll find that the Mint stops shipping it and your local dealer has run out of supply. You'll be able to watch the price on television, but you won't actually be able to get the gold. It'll be too late. That's why the time for action is now.

I like to say that every individual has a Ph.D. when it comes to managing his or her own money. You may not know a lot about economics, but you can and should focus on your own net worth.

You are not helpless. You don't have to feel like a cork on the ocean or like a victim of whatever policy the central bankers are putting out there.

You can take your net worth and take your retirement and take your portfolio into your own hands.

There are families in the United States, like the Rockefellers, that have had money for, say, 100 years. That's the old money.

When you go to Europe, however, you find families that have had wealth for 300, 400 and even 500 years. That's the really old money.

In early 2015, I was at the magnificent Palazzo Colonna, in the heart of Rome. The Colonna family's had their wealth since the 13th century. For 800 years, they've been wealthy and never lost it.

They not only survived 2008, but they survived the Thirty Years' War, Napoleon, Louis XIV, World War I, World War II, the Holocaust and more.

If you ask them how they did it, they'll look at you and say, "A third, a third and a third"—one-third land, one-third gold, one-third fine art.

Let's say you're living in Bavaria and it's 1620. The enemy is five miles away and they're burning down everything in sight. What do you do? You put your gold coins in a sack, you cut your painting off the wall and roll it up and put it in your backpack, you get on your horse and you ride away.

Then a few years later when the dust settles, you come back and you should be able to reestablish title to the land, put your gold back on the table, put your art back on the wall. You're wealthy and your neighbors have all been wiped out.

My point is there are survival strategies you can use. You

are not helpless. You can protect yourself. You can definitely see the crisis coming using the warning signs present today.

The idea is to take the story forward, see the collapse, see what comes next and then go back to square one and do what you can today to survive the collapse and survive into the new system and preserve wealth.

It can be done, and as a *Strategic Intelligence* reader, you're in a better position than most Americans to make it happen.

About the Author

James Rickards is the editor of the monthly financial newsletter *Strategic Intelligence*. He's also the author of the national best-sellers *Currency Wars, The Death of Money* and *The New Case for Gold*. He is a portfolio manager at West Shore Group and an adviser on international economics and financial threats to the Department of Defense and the U.S. Intelligence Community. He served as facilitator of the first-ever financial war games conducted by the Pentagon.

Follow @JamesGRickards

Index